NO PLAN B

DISCOVERING GOD'S BLUEPRINT FOR YOUR LIFE

NO PLAN B

Discovering God's Blueprint for Your Life

WITH A FOREWORD BY JAMES L. RUBART

NELSON HANNAH

NO PLAN B: DISCOVERING GOD'S BLUEPRINT FOR YOUR LIFE

Copyright © 2014, Nelson Hannah

All rights reserved. Reproduction in part or in whole is strictly forbidden without the express written consent of the publisher.

Unless otherwise noted, Scripture are taken from the NEW AMERICAN STANDARD Bible copyright symbol 1960, 1962, 1963, 1971, 1972, 1973, 1975, 9177, by the Lockman Foundation. Used by permission.

Scripture quotations marked (NLT) are taken from the Holy Bible, New Living Translation, copyright (symbol) 1996. Use by permission of Tyndale House Publishers, Inc. Wheaton, Illinois, 60189. All rights reserved.

WhiteFire Publishing
13607 Bedford Rd NE
Cumberland, MD 21502

ISBNS: 978-1-939023-34-6 (print)
         978-1-939023-35- (digital)

*To my little red-haired, blue-eyed granddaughter,
Audrey Elizabeth.
There is no greater calling than to be "your" Papa.
Your smile captures my heart.
Your imagination unlocks my creativity.
Your carefree abandon spurs me to take chances.
Your hugs and kisses melt me.
And your unconditional love humbles me.
Playing with you gives me incomprehensible joy.
May all those blessings spoken over you
unlock the door to your destiny in Christ
and equip you to experience the joy
of God's Plan A for your life.*

Foreword

Most of us are aware of the identity crisis happening in our physical world. Social Security numbers hijacked. Credit cards being stolen online. E-mail accounts being hacked. But there is an identity crisis happening in the spiritual realm many of us are not fully aware of. And the consequences of this kind of ignorance are far more severe.

We have been blinded. Our spiritual identities stolen. We don't know who we are anymore. The enemy of our souls has placed us inside a bottle and, as I'm fond of saying, it's impossible to read the label when you're standing inside the bottle.

No Plan B by my good friend Nelson Hannah will show you how to get outside the bottle. It will show you how to reclaim your true identity in the King of Kings, Jesus Christ our Lord, see who you truly are, and discover the original glory-filled plan God designed for us to live in from the beginning.

I know what you're saying. You've been trying all your life to make things work. And they just aren't. You've been wondering why God isn't coming through. Or why you seem to blow it so often. You can't understand why your plan isn't working, and the only thing you can see on the horizon is failure. But that's the key, isn't it? Your plan. My plan. Not God's.

Nelson has titled his book, *No Plan B*, but that's not true. There *is* a plan B. But it's been designed by the enemy of your soul who is focused on three things: Kill. Steal. Destroy.

The good news: God has a plan too. Plan A. And it's possible to live plan A right now. More than possible. It's your Spirit-infused destiny—if you choose to step into it. Plan A will bring you intimacy with God. Purpose. And such freedom!

You need this book.

I need this book.

Why? Because when we step into each day knowing who we are... truly knowing who we are, we can't help but alter every life we come in contact with. When we step into our day with eyes wide open, living HIS perfect, divinely crafted plan, every life we meet will be imparted the Life they desperately need.

Soak *No Plan B* in. Then read it again and soak more of its life-changing message into your soul, because that's where this book needs to take root. Not in your mind, but in your heart.

James L. Rubart ~ April 2014

Section 1
God's Plan Revealed

God, in his infinite wisdom, conceived and designed a plan long before he spoke creation into existence. This plan is perfect in its conception, design, purpose, and destiny. It was a relational plan that would allow him to share his unconditional love and boundless grace with creatures formed and fashioned in his own image and likeness. It was God's A Plan—his only plan!

Chapter 1
Choosing the Right Plan

Define yourself radically as one beloved of God.
This is the true self. Every other identity is an illusion.
~ Brennan Manning

The light was brilliant. It was so bright in those brief moments that anyone peeking through the bushes would have been forced to shield his eyes or the result would have been instant blindness. The air was saturated and dripped with the glory of that glow, like the white-hot arc of a welder. The intensity seemed to withdraw after a few moments as though something or someone had stepped back. Once again the brightness of the noonday sun ruled the sky, but noticeably dimmer in comparison to what had transpired only seconds before.

There beside the river an exquisite creature, by all accounts, lay motionless in a small crater surrounded by reddish dust. It had not fallen from the sky, but rather it seemed to have been scooped from the very soil it now rested in. Well-proportioned and muscular like a Greek statue chiseled out of ruddy marble, the figure lay on its back facing the heavens—still and silent.

The gentle breeze blowing from east to west suddenly changed and began swirling downward. The wind began to pick up and in an instant became a howling vortex. Suddenly this violent rushing wind descended from the heavens and engulfed the motionless, mounded figure. The upper half of the body lurched upward, as the wind filled it like a hand in a glove. A glorious shadow passed over in that moment, and power surged like an invisible switch had been flipped. Then the figure relaxed and its chest began to rise and fall in a rhythmic motion. *Adamah*, the lifeless red dust of creation, had now become *Adam*, a living soul.

The Creator leaned back and gazed at his creation and proclaimed, "This is very good!"

But—another set of eyes witnessed the miracle of the dust that day. Hidden in the lush undergrowth near the river's edge, a creature known as *Nahash*, the serpent, plotted his next move. Filled with jealousy and disgust, he coiled to stay hidden, muffling the roar that now arose from within the depths of his dark soul. He strained to hear the conversation, as those first intimate words were spoken between Father and son. With contempt, he watched as that same Father introduced his son to the safety of a specially prepared garden—and *Nahash* waited, remembering his own marvelous creation and his subsequent fall from grace, kicked out of a garden with the same familiar name. In time, he too would visit this special garden, this exquisite environment, and see what could be done to confuse the creature and thwart the Creator's carefully designed plan. *Nahash* would have his revenge, and God would be forced to come up with another plan. Yes, that's it—mess up Plan A, and then God will be forced to come up with Plan B.

And so "the plan" unfolds. But…which plan are we following?

Design by the Divine

God designed the man and woman to live life from the garden. Eden was divinely designed and carefully constructed to educate the first couple in all the nuances of what identity meant—to discover who and what they were as they discovered who God is. Without that discovery and exploration of God, there could be no real discovery of themselves. This discovery would form a relationship, and trust would evolve. This trust would then produce love, and the relationship would come full circle.

The garden was the meeting place where God and humanity would intersect and interact. It was the place like this—a place of wonder and discovery—a place of choice and decision. It was Adam and Eve's address, not God's. It was the place God had fashioned so that the first couple could step into the destiny he had personally designed for them. From the garden they would learn to live out Plan A—God's perfect plan.

Everything they needed to discover the abundance of God's love and grace were present in the garden. God had thought of everything. Food and water were in abundance. The weather was perfect—not too hot or cold. No need to build a house—the whole of the garden was their mansion. Rain, snow, sleet, and hail were not yet a part of their environment. The sun warmed them by day, and the moon and stars served as a nightlight to guide them through the dark hours. They were immersed in the vast goodness of God's gifts, through which they would soon discover the intimacy of his heart. It was a special gift—his heart—he longed to share without holding anything back. It was truly an opportunity *of* a lifetime and an opportunity *for* a lifetime with no expiration date stamped on the label. The opportunity was open-ended—eternal. Did I say "was"? I'm sorry; I meant to say "is" open-ended—eternal.

At this point you may be thinking, "Hey, what do you mean 'is'? That's not the quality of life I'm currently experiencing. In fact, that seems a bit bizarre. My life is just the opposite of that. That sounds like a fairy tale—too good to be true!"

It sounds too good to be true because we have settled for a bogus plan. We have accepted less than what God intends. We have embraced Plan B although God never initiated anything but Plan A. Somewhere along the way, we have been deceived. Plan B has robbed us of our relationship, our identity, and our purpose.

The Quest for Identity

What the devil fears, he seeks to confuse. Where confusion reigns, chaos results. When chaos exists, ignorance runs rampant. And as ignorance picks up speed and shifts into high gear, all kind of bad things happen. Fear, uncertainty, insecurity, and weakness soon become the trademark threads that weave the fabric of an identity. Fear begets fear, and the result is that we are robbed of the very thing God intended to be a source of encouragement and strength—our identity as his child—his son or daughter.

Nothing intrudes on this archdemon's territory more than a person who knows who they are in Christ. Some say superior knowledge or physical strength is power, but a settled identity produces a confident internal unity that is impregnable to the forces of darkness. If Satan cannot get a foothold, he is powerless. If he cannot gain a partner, he is impotent. If he cannot confuse us, uncertainty, insecurity, and weakness are rendered null and void and cannot be used against us.

Satan (that crafty serpent *Nahash*) fears the implications of Plan A. Plan A gives us a relationship with God, an identity from God, and a purpose in God. The scope of that plan is endless, but unless we understand who we are because of *whose* we are, it is likely we will never enjoy the riches of this relationship.

This is not a book about a cunning serpent—a devil in disguise. This is God's schematic masterpiece for the ages—his only plan for all of humanity. This is the tale of who we already are—the real us—the person God sees and says we are. This is a tool to help us reclaim every smidgen of our full identity in Christ. But for this to be a reality, we must recognize the lie and jettison the idea that God has ever entertained a Plan B. That's not even possible. He has one plan, and it is perfect. This is the unfolding of our true identity.

This Entity Known as Identity

Two very common questions that often arise in a counseling session are: (1) who am I; and (2) why am I here? They are profound questions of identity and purpose that must be discovered and answered by each of us. Tragically, many don't seem to know where to look or how to find the real answers to these life-altering dilemmas. Unless a person recognizes who they are and realizes what their purpose is, they are doomed to wonder endlessly as they wander aimlessly through life, tossed to and fro on the cruel waves of what may come next in the crashing surf of life's situations and circumstances.

Identity is the key, but it is a tough concept to define if we depend solely on the philosophers, psychologists, or anthropologists to come to our aid. There are numerous studies and theories, but no simple definition. Add to that the proliferation of the Internet with social media like Facebook, Twitter, and countless online communities where we can anonymously be anyone we choose to be as long as we don't get caught. Identity seems to be a relative term that can mean any number of things to different people. Therefore, it is essential that we construct a general definition of identity so that we are all on the same page, if we eventually hope to arrive at the same destination together.

You and I are unique. Every human being is. We may be similar with much in common, and yet we are not exact. There are no absolute or faithful and accurate copies walking around that perfectly mirror you. That's the case even if you are a monozygotic (identical) twin, meaning you and your sibling developed from one zygote that split and formed two embryos. In spite of this, you possess quite a few unique qualities or characteristics that are extraordinarily different from your brother or sister. No one has your fingerprints or the iris pattern of your eyes. Your tongue has both geometric shapes and physiological texture that make it exclusive to you. No other dental records perfectly match the X-rays taken of that mouth full of incisors, canines, premolars, and molars that are embedded in your jaws. Even your DNA, although very similar in many ways to various other creatures, makes you distinctively you.

Yes, as human beings we all have similar characteristics, but no two of us are alike, and the reason rests within the heart of our Divine Designer. He was the architect of creation and with his voice spoke everything visible and invisible into existence, everything except us. We are made in his image and in his likeness (Genesis 1:26-27). God formed the man from the *adamah*—the dust of the earth (Genesis 2:7) and fashioned the woman from a fistful of tissue, blood, muscle, and bone he took from the man's side (Genesis 2:22). Each was unique in his or her own creation, yet similar. Consider this for a moment: God is so complex, infinite, and so beyond anything our finite minds can fully comprehend, that perhaps out of his love for diversity—in the creation of us as human beings—he put a pinch of his infinite self in the mix to make each of us a tiny bit different. There is no cosmic human cookie cutter that God uses to stamp out this diverse tribe we call the human race. As Homo sapiens, we are surprisingly and gratifyingly different. This distinctiveness is the structure on which our identity hangs.

An identity defines you as a person. Your personal identity is singularly you. It is who you really are and one of your most treasured possessions. It is composed of your own individual comprehension of yourself (meaning you realize that you are alive and exist—which is what Adam learned in the garden), those physiological traits that are exclusively yours, and certain information amassed over time that can be used to identify, contact, or locate you from among the other 6.5 billion human residents of this community we call Earth. That identity is a vital element of Plan A.

Documents that Identify

Adam never asked, "Who's my daddy?" His first glance was up into the eyes of God, and the answer was obvious. Some might want to argue that this was simply a symbolic or spiritual familial illustration, but the words of Scripture document the paternity of Adam by divine creation and supernatural decree. According to the genealogy of Jesus found in Luke 3, the last four words of verse 38 seem to indicate far more than merely the use of symbolism or a metaphor to communicate a spiritual truth. It designates in simple, straightforward terms that Adam was *the* son of God, not just *a* son of God. The verse is unique in all of Scripture, because it is the only place where anyone other than Jesus Christ is called *the* son of God.

In the spring of 1956, a baby was born to a young couple at Carraway Hospital in Birmingham, Alabama, in the wee hours of the morning. As an anxious husband and dad paced about in the waiting room (this was long before birthing suites and direct daddy participation), a doctor named Boulaware made a final check of both mother and infant, scribbled a few notes to confirm sex, weight, length, date and time of birth, and headed out the doors of the delivery room to give a waiting father the good news. I was that infant, and those notes the doctor made quickly found their way into my initial record—the paper trail that identifies me. The hospital issued a birth certificate stating my name, date of birth, my father and mother's names, the city and state of birth, and the attending physician, along with other pertinent information that became a part of my identity even before I had any sense of my own existence (other than the occasional dirty diaper and the incessant and ravenous desire for milk). This official credential certified and verified that I was now a bona fide citizen of the United States, entitled to certain inalienable rights under the Constitution. A copy was mailed to my parents, and another was filed at the Jefferson

County Department of Health.

Over the course of my life, my birth certificate proved to be the indispensable means of confirming I am who I claim to be. It was the required identification along with a certificate of immunization that ensured I was accepted into the world of public education. Later, that same identifying document was required to obtain a Social Security card, play high school football, and get a driver's license. My Social Security card came with a number that verified my identity and allowed me to open a bank account, get a job, pay my taxes, obtain a passport, and vote. My driver's license doubles as a picture ID and can be used when my identity is questioned, or I want to purchase an airline ticket, rent a car, or verify my ownership of a charge card. I also have a passport that allows me to travel to other countries and validates my American citizenship. Each of these documents is an essential verification of my identity.

Like Adam, I too have clear proof that I am who I claim to be. I have an identity that can be proven by documentation.

A Crippling Dilemma

You probably have all or at least some of these same documents. Each one is a treasured benefit of living in this country—a part of what it means to be a United States citizen. Each of these documented details confirms our personal identities as citizens of this country and gives us access to specific benefits and liberties. This access enhances and protects our ability to conduct business and take care of our families. It allows us the privilege of writing and cashing checks, as well has having a savings account or a credit or debit card. It enables us to pay only the debts we incur and allows the proper amount of taxes to be withheld from our earnings.

It is essential that we have access to these documents and understand their value and worth. It is our responsibility to know how and when to use them. We must take the initiative to guard and protect them. It is mind-boggling to think about where I would be right now or the things I would have missed if I had never accessed each one of them. It would have been absurd not to have properly obtained each one and preposterous to have received them but never to have opened the envelope they came in. Any of these actions would have seriously crippled my ability to enjoy the quality of life and the freedoms living in this country affords.

Sadly, when it comes to one's spiritual identity—who we are in Christ, which is God's original intent—this is the crippling dilemma that the vast majority of Christians find themselves in at this very moment. I'm not talking about misplacing one's driver's license or Social Security card. Nor am I referring to the loss of one's passport or voter's card. Thank God we are not required to have a spiritual set of those. I am talking about your spiritual birth certificate. Spiritually speaking, do you really comprehend its value? Are you intimately familiar with the rights and privileges it affords you? Do you really understand who you are in Christ? Do you know who you are, whose you are, and why you're here?

I am not questioning if you know Christ. Only you and the Holy Spirit can answer that. I am asking if you know who you are in Christ, and if you are living out of the benefits and privileges of that identity on a daily basis. Far too many believers are living light years below the spiritual poverty line. They are scratching out a meager existence, scrounging through the leftover crumbs of another person's experience with God, instead of having their own. They are frustrated, hungry, and ready to give up. They are picking through the scraps of some empty theology that has been perpetrated in a pulpit but not substantiated from the Bible. Or worse, the enemy has lured them into his own garbage dumpster and convinced them that what they are choking down is the best that God can provide—camouflaged with a devilish forgery the serpent has designated as God's Plan B.

Instead of living in the victory of the cross and enjoying a life-giving relationship with Jesus, many of us have gulped down a belly full of religious Kool-Aid, which promised everything but delivered little, and now we suffer the pangs of poisoning. Many have chosen to be victims of circumstance and happenstance—gorged on helplessness and despair, existing but not really living—rather than partners with God, having access to all the riches in the heavenly realms in Christ. This is not about "health and wealth" or "name it and claim it." This is about opening the rest of the gift you received when you were born again by the grace of God. That precious gift of salvation contains far more than a celestial fire insurance policy that provides you with one free get-out-of-hell card and entrance into some narcissistic retirement community with the guaranteed satisfaction of your every whim. It's time to spread the plan on the table and take a closer look at the blueprints. It's time to open your gift box from God and find that the devil has deceived you into accepting far less than what God has provided. The time has come to examine and claim the rights and privileges contained in the same Plan A God offered to Adam.

An Invitation

Before you read further, please consider the following statement made by Jesus to his disciples on the night before his crucifixion and to us as well: "I tell you the truth, anyone who believes in me will do the same works I have done, and even greater works, because I am going to be with the Father" (John 14:12 NLT). Faith in Jesus is the only prerequisite mentioned in this verse. Faith in Jesus is required for salvation. Therefore, if we are saved, we should be doing the works Jesus did and even greater ones. That's what Jesus said, and that's what he meant. That's a part of God's Plan A.

Simple question: Are you doing the works Jesus did and even greater ones?

Before you answer, I know most of the excuses because at one time or another I've used them. You know the ones—God no longer does that…or that…or that. The only problem with that is it won't stand up under the scrutiny of the Scripture. He is the same yesterday, today, and forever (Hebrews 13:8). Forever reaches back past the creation of Adam, before time began, and into the far horizon of eternity. He is the same God who scooped the clay, formed it into a shape, and jump-started it with a breath of his Spirit. He has not changed, nor can he change. To do so would forever alter and destroy his immutable character. There cannot be one plan for Adam and another for you or me. The same plan—Plan A—is still in effect. What was possible for Adam has already been assured for us in Christ.

Our problem is unbelief, and this unbelief has its roots in our ignorance of who the resurrected Jesus really is and what he has done for and in us. We have believed the same lie—that God has another plan—and we have swallowed it hook, line, and sinker.

Here's the invitation: If you love Jesus and you hunger to know him in a deeper way, so that you might become all he says you are and be able to achieve all he says you can do, consider pondering prayerfully the following chapters. If your world is marked by confusion or chaos, and the fists of fear, insecurity, or uncertainty pummel you unmercifully into the dust, this may be the cool sip of water and mind-clearing moment of biblical truth that will help you regain your balance and swing back. If you sense there's something missing, this may help you find what you're looking for.

But if you're satisfied with who and what you are right now, content with the person you have become, put this book down. It's probably not for you. If you have become secure in yourself, there will be little interest in who Jesus says you are anyway. Receive this sincere warning in love: satisfaction with yourself and the enemy's tool of confusion are virtually indistinguishable.

Chapter 2
God's Original Intent

> I saw the angel in the marble and carved until I set him free.
> ~ Michelangelo

The shipment had finally arrived. Right on time! The workmen strained to slide the bulky block of freshly quarried stone into the center of the workshop. Finally, the job was finished and they patted one another on the back with a sense of accomplishment, gathered their ropes and rollers, and went out the door. As the workshop fell silent once again, a man slipped quietly through the rear door, his piercing eyes looking into the rough slab of Carrera marble as though it were transparent. As he slowly circled the stone, he began to rough out the form of something on his sketch pad. "Yes! Yes! I see it, I see it," he muttered occasionally under his breath. Each time he would stop and draw a little more or make a note on the page. Hours passed, yet this circular dance of man and stone continued in an almost rhythmic motion. Suddenly he paused, frozen. For the longest time he remained transfixed, staring as though seeing something or someone for the first time.

After a time, he smiled and placed the drawing pad on the table and picked up a hammer and a chisel. Carefully he positioned the point of the chisel on the face of the stone and struck it with the hammer. Chips of white stone flew off. Again and again the sound of the hammer striking the head of the chisel echoed through workshop. For weeks, the neighbors listened, tried to catch a peek, and wondered what the young sculptor named Michelangelo Buonarroti was working on this time.

Michelangelo is perhaps the greatest sculptor who ever lived. He was an ardent student of human anatomy, and his artistic style is distinctive—muscular precision and reality merging to create poetic beauty. At twenty-five, he carved the magnificent *Pieta* while in Rome. Over six feet wide and sculpted out of a single slab of Carrera marble, it portrays Mary holding the crucified, lifeless body of her son Jesus across her lap. Later, in the city of Florence, he took a seventeen-foot high piece of marble and transformed it into the dominating figure of *David*—the young shepherd, psalmist, and future king of Israel.

Michelangelo, after carving an angel, was asked how he could sculpt such serene beauty out of cold, lifeless stone. His reply: "I saw the angel in the marble and carved until I set him free." He believed the sculpture lived within the stone already perfect and complete. His job was to simply chip away the stone to reveal the masterpiece within. Through the eye of his imagination, he could see the finished work before he ever picked up his hammer and chisel. Before he struck the first blow, the artist's plan and purpose was set—his original intent fixed, though weeks and months would pass before the stone would surrender its inward treasure.

Daydreaming or Destiny

The imagination of a child is a theater of splendor and wonder. In the spotlights of that make-believe stage, reality becomes irrelevant as a kid is transformed into whatever his genius can conceive and act out. The creativity of that young mind is practically limitless, especially one who has not yet tasted the poison fruit of skepticism, pragmatism, or materialism of the adult world. Perhaps the daydreams of our childhood were more than just fantasy. Perhaps they are keys to our destiny.

Every person has dreamed of being more than their environment, family, belief systems, or finances would seem to allow. Most of us have dreamed of being royalty at one time or another. It may have been a childhood fantasy with a cardboard crown covered in aluminum foil, or a refrigerator box that became a magnificent castle, or a medieval drama whose stars were Barbie and Ken.

This particular daydream is not just confined to children. Adults engage in it all the time. This voyeurism and fascination for Prince William and Kate (heirs to the throne of Great Britain) is off the charts right now. Every move they make is scrutinized and imitated. Kate's trendy fashion statements are reproduced worldwide the next day after a princess sighting. We are captivated by their "royal" appeal, but not because they appeal to us as real people. We long to be what they are (royal people), rather than who they are (real people). We dream of trading places and living that life of privilege.

Perhaps somewhere back in your family tree you are somehow connected to royalty, but nothing remains of that heritage except a family name or the snippets of a fanciful tale passed down through the family like the remnant of a page ripped from a now-lost chronicle of ancient lore. Perhaps fantasy and reality have merged over the years, and truth is hard to separate. Or perhaps you just wish it were so. The memories of antiquity, the daydream of "what if," and the games of childhood all resonate deep without our spirits, but in reality life is what it is—or is it?

Like a great treasure lost and buried beneath the debris of time, this idea—this yearning for an identity not ours—persists and will not die for some reason. Perhaps in it resides a bit of truth rather than just the folly of a childhood fancy. Perhaps the longing is far more than a hunger for power or money or fame. Perhaps that hunger is our spirit crying out for the reality of an identity that was once given but not fully experienced—the memory of a single spiritual shred of DNA crying out for the freedom resting dormant deep within the genetic composition of who we are. Perhaps what we imagine we hear really is deep crying out to deep—Spirit crying out to spirit.

I believe that hunger exists not because it is a fleeting dream, but rather because it is our true identity. Once a person experiences a life-changing encounter with God's grace through Jesus Christ, this longing eventually bubbles to the surface. It is distinct, real, and haunting, but hard to verbalize. It's so hard to put your finger on—to discern what it is. We know something is missing, so we seek answers from others who have either not found the solution to the longing or who deny the longing ever existed. Due to our religious traditions, the solution is usually an attempt to do more. In other words, get busy for God! Serve Jesus! If you will get busy serving, God will bless you! Busyness has the same effect on a person searching for answers as telling a child with a vivid imagination to grow up. Over time it kills the sense of wonder, excitement, and discovery, but not the hunger. The hunger recedes and continues to gnaw, so the devil refocuses those teeth of ravenous desire into the tender meaty areas of our self-confidence and self-worth, and we consume ourselves over time. We are always longing but never measuring up, busy doing but never able to do enough. Hunger unquenched!

God is not interested in the doing—yours or mine. He is consumed with being—that capability of enjoying being who we truly are, who we were born again to be. That hunger, that desire—whatever we may choose to call it—is the longing to walk in both our identity and our inheritance, which are bound up together. In biblical times identity and inheritance were not determined by what you could do. It was determined by the family you were born into. Perhaps it is time we all check our spiritual birth certificate and see whose name is listed on the line marked *Father*.

The Bible is very clear when it declares that we are the sons and daughters of God. He is our Father and we are his kids. He is also the King, which makes us royalty—children of nobility and destiny. That deep craving is a desire God put there so that we would seek out our inheritance (what we get), but more importantly so that we might discover our identity (who we are). Inheritance without identity results in eventual poverty. Identity always determines whether the inheritance is cherished or wasted. The prodigal son of Luke 15 never grasped who he was until his money was gone. His identity had become confused with his inheritance because that's what the world told him was important. Hunger brought him back to his senses so that his father's love could re-establish his identity.

Our identity ensures our inheritance. Sadly, most of God's children, offspring of the King—royal sons and daughters—live out lives of silent mediocrity, scrounging for scraps in the garbage cans of theological amnesia, totally blank about their true identity. This book will help guide you in discovering it, but it will be your responsibility to embrace it and walk in it.

Creation, according to Romans 8:19, longs for the revelation—the unveiling—of the sons and the daughters of God. But before that happens, we must strip off the wretched rags of unbelief and vile robes of religious duty we have dressed ourselves in and step into who God says we already are. Perhaps the time has come to strip ourselves bare once again and discover the details of God's original intent—God's Plan A. Perhaps if we come to understand this, the expanse between daydreaming and destiny—restless longing and real-life—will disappear. Perhaps the magnificent creature God envisioned in the dust will once more emerge like the angel freed from the stone by Michelangelo.

Pay Attention to the Instructions—Please!

Before I became a pastor, I had a *real* job (a little sarcasm for those who think pastoring is a not a *real* job) as a plumbing contractor. I worked for over twenty-five years in the plumbing trade, starting out as an apprentice and eventually becoming a master plumber operating my own business. One of the most important things a plumber can do when he arrives at a construction site is to get a copy of the blueprints and study every page.

The blueprints are the essential element of construction, whether you're building a storage building, a house, or a skyscraper. If you want to know and understand what the owner wants, the architect envisions, and the governing officials who enforce the building code require, look at the blueprints. They give a step-by-step plan to follow so that the contractor can achieve his purpose and turn a profit. The blueprint is the key to the original intent—the real purpose—for the investment of time, effort, and money in the construction of a building. The blueprints reveal all the details needed to complete a building that will eventually fulfill what the owner desires.

If someone chooses not to study the blueprints and goes about their work like they think it should be done, there is always a problem. The only question is how big the problem will be and when it will be discovered. That person may work harder and faster than anyone else on the job, but their work is wasted, and what they do or don't do usually interferes with everyone else's part of the work. Essential elements of the building are put in the wrong locations, vital measurements are missed, and critical pieces get left out. Walls are framed in the wrong places, windows and doors won't fit, commodes end up in bedrooms, or the elevator shaft is ½ inch too small for the elevator, just to name a few. You have one big, expensive mess to repair. And it could have all been avoided if the blueprints had been consulted and followed.

Blueprints are called by various names, such as a recipe or an instruction sheet. We follow a recipe so we can wow our family at the annual Thanksgiving feast with the exact coconut cake we saw Martha Stewart create in her kitchen. Or we (at least some—maybe a handful) always read (eventually) the step-by-step instruction sheets for those toys we are frantically trying to complete before the first rays of Christmas morning reveal our total ineptness, or we end up with a few (well, maybe more than a few) extra pieces that are obviously critical because the talking doll refuses to speak, no matter how hard and how often we bang it on the floor. Without following the instructions, the original intent of the item is not accomplished, and the purpose is lost. When we follow the instructions to the letter, good things usually happen. When we follow the instructions, we usually reap the fullest benefits for our investment. When we heed the steps, things work like they were designed, stress evaporates, and the kids think we hung the moon. And if we don't follow the instructions—well, you know what always happens.

God has a blueprint as well. He has a plan—or as I choose to call it, *an original intent*—for creating us. There is a purpose. It is not some Indiana Jones mystery locked away and loaded with hidden clues that only a seminary-trained PhD. fluent in the ancient languages of Hebrew, Greek, and Aramaic can decipher. A blueprint does exist and is readily available right now and readable on your laptop, cell phone, iPad, Kindle, or right out of that leather-bound book sitting just inches from your elbow on the end table. That's right, God's original intent—his Plan A—is found in the pages of the Bible.

In the Beginning

To understand any story you must start at the beginning. Every good story has clues to the plot and the eventual outcome interwoven in those first few paragraphs and pages. The better the novelist, the more difficult it is to spot the obvious. But the Bible is not a mystery novel. It is an instruction manual, a love letter, a historic and credible account of God's dealings with humanity all rolled into one. This revelation is the unfolding of God's plan. It had a beginning and all of it is there for us to discover. The Holy Spirit did not endeavor to hide the plot. He sought to make it clear so that every human being could follow the instructions and end up at the same destination.

God was so intent on each of us making the trip that he spelled out his plan in the very first chapter of Genesis. In the beginning…God put his plan in action. There were no behind-the-scene, back-room deals. Everything was placed out in the open and put there for public scrutiny. He did not want us to miss it. Instead he made it so obvious that we would trip over it, and when we did, we would be forced to roll over on our backs and look him squarely in the face.

His will for your life and mine is not a secret that requires special knowledge that can only be gained by years and years of memorization and secret handshakes. His will does not require a super-duper decoder ring to unravel a series of clues. No, his will is rather obvious but rarely read. If we ever hope to understand who we are and why we are here, we must go back and consult the blueprints from which humanity was created. We must grasp God's original intent to understand his plan—his only plan.

Under Construction

Perhaps if we travel back to that original construction site and look closely, we might find the instruction sheet rolled up and tucked under Adam's arm.

> *Then God said, "Let us make man in Our image, according to Our likeness; and let them rule over the fish of the sea and over the birds of the sky and over the cattle and over all the earth, and over every creeping thing that creeps on the earth." And God created man in His own image, in the image of God He created him; male and female He created them. And God blessed them: and God said to them, "Be fruitful and multiply, and fill the earth, and subdue it; and rule over the fish of the sea and over the birds of the sky, and over every*

living thing that moves on the earth" (Genesis 1:26-28).

This amazing feat is carefully detailed, step-by-step, beginning in Genesis 2:7. God formed the man from the dust of the ground and breathed into his nostrils the breath (or Spirit—the Hebrew word is *ruach* and is the same word used for both) of life; and man became a living being (or soul). The wording of this verse compares man's formation to that of a clay pot made by a potter. Later that same day, God fashioned the woman from a handful of tissue, blood, and bone he took from the man's side. The Lord God fashioned (or built) a woman from the rib which he had taken from the man and he brought her to the man. The wording of this verse is graphic as it paints a picture of God as a craftsman toiling over a masterpiece as he fashioned the fistful of life he had taken from the man's side into the woman.

The first man and woman were created in the image and likeness of God. Oh, wow! Let that grab hold of your heart and your brain for a moment. We are made in the image of God. We were created to be like God. We were made according to his image. His portrait is the blueprint for us. That simple phrase is pregnant with tremendous meaning, and theological libraries are filled with dusty tomes debating the magnitude of that meaning. I have no desire to debate anyone or get too deep here. But in simple terms, created in the image and likeness of God means our abilities mirror God's abilities. The creation mirrors the Creator. We are like him.

Don't miss this. We correspond to God in our abilities to reason, to experience emotions, to make choices, and to commune spirit to Spirit. God created us to look and to act like him. We are not him. We are not God and never will be.

God created us with relationship in mind, so he made us like himself. He desired to share the depths of his love with his children. God was not lonely, nor did he need relationship. In the tri-unity of the Godhead—the Father, Son, and Holy Spirit—there was perfect relationship. God did not need, God wanted—God desired—relationship, and that is a huge difference. God chose in his grace to create a race of creatures he could fully reveal his heart to in relationship because he chose to do so. Therefore, he created the man and the woman.

This is a key in our discovery. God created a familial connection (a family) by making them in his image according to his likeness. They were supposed to look and act like their Creator—like their Father. His original intent was for us to be his kids and he was to be our Father. Do your kids resemble you (image)? Do they act like you (likeness)? Do you see the connection?

I discovered a simple phrase a few years ago while reading one of those long genealogies that the Bible is famous for. The genealogies tell us the concept of family was vital to the Hebrew people. If you knew the record of your ancestors, you understood your origins—where you came from. It was critical in understanding your identity. Today most people skip them while reading Scripture, but I found the key to God's original intent and purpose for my life in Luke 3—the family tree of the Lord Jesus. The last entry in verse 38 should end with Adam, who is the fountainhead of the human race, but it takes one step culminating with an incredible declaration: *the son of Enosh, the son of Seth, the son of Adam, the son of God* (NASB).

Don't miss the phrase that follows Adam's name—*the son of God*. Like I said before, this indicates far more than merely the use of symbolism or a metaphor to communicate a spiritual truth. That phrase—*the son of God*—appears 45 times in the Bible, and it always refers to Jesus Christ. It's not a typo or a scribal error either. This is the handwriting of the Holy Spirit. It is here for a reason.

Adam is called *the* son of God, not *a* son of God. Adam—our forefather, the first man—was God's boy. God was establishing that family connection. This relationship with the man and the woman was not master-servant; it was parent-child. God would be their Father, providing everything they needed so that they could enjoy a happy and healthy existence. This family relationship was a vital part of his original intent.

Now think back for a moment to Genesis 2:7, to that picture of God breathing his breath, or Spirit, into that lifeless lump of clay formed into the shape of a man. The same imagery is found in Ezekiel 37 where the prophet is commanded by God to speak to the dry bones scattered in the valley. As Ezekiel obeys, the bones begin joining together, sinew and skin covers them, but as of yet there is no life in them. Finally, in verse 9 God says to prophesy (speak what you have heard me say) to the *ruach* (wind, breath, spirit), and tell it to come. Ezekiel does so, and the lifeless bodies are energized and come to life. It's the same picture in Genesis with Adam. Later in Ezekiel 37:14, God says, "And I will put my Spirit within you, and you will come to life."

Perhaps that's exactly what happened at Creation. God breathed the Holy Spirit—the same Spirit who raised Jesus from the dead (breathed resurrection life into a dead, crucified body)—into Adam, his son. Perhaps at that moment, God implanted his spiritual DNA into the cellular structure of his son Adam and within that indwelling the man became a living soul. This sounds hauntingly familiar when we come to the New Testament and see that without the indwelling of God's Spirit we are dead in our trespasses and sins—we are not saved (made alive in Jesus Christ). Amazing imagery, or is it God's original intent?

The Original Intent—Plan A

It seems clear that God's Plan A, his original intent, was to create a son and daughter with whom he might share his love in relationship. He created male and female in his image and in his likeness and filled them with the life of His Spirit so that they might respond in the fullness of all that God is. In the details of Genesis 1:26-28, we find this couple was designed to represent God. When we look into a mirror, we see a credible image and likeness of who we are. The man and the woman were mirrored reflections of God. The invisible now made visible. In everything they did, they were to mirror (or reflect) the invisible attributes of God by their actions, their attitudes, and their relationship. They were to reflect the glory of God for all of creation to see, especially the fallen angels. For all eternity this couple was to be a visual aid of the glorious splendor those dark angels had once existed in and the vast distance they had fallen.

This would be accomplished with the aid of the blessing God spoke over them. Perhaps that blessing was the wrappings of God's glory. Perhaps the man and the woman were enveloped in the righteousness and holiness of God, and this manifested itself in a covering of light. This would certainly explain the serpent's envy since in his former position he was known as the "shining one" (Isaiah 14:12). Perhaps their shiny covering evoked his jealousy and hate.

God's original intent expands in Genesis 1:28: "Be fruitful, multiply, and fill the earth." The man and the woman were to do more than reflect; they were to reproduce accurate (true) representations of their Father, the King. The man was to mirror the glory of God and with the help of the woman reproduce that image and likeness of God in their children. They were endowed with the ability to create like God.

Their mission was to replicate themselves in their children as God had replicated his image and likeness in them and fill the earth with mini-mirrors. Let your imagination run wild for a moment. Nothing is more beautiful to me than a Christmas tree filled with mirrored ornaments and lights. As a kid, I would slip into the living room after dark, while no one was looking (entrance to the living room at my house was strictly forbidden and corporally enforced except on Thanksgiving day and Christmas day). I would lie on my back with my hands folded behind my head and stare in wonder at the twinkling mass of reflection as it shimmered in the darkness. For a kid, it was like looking at the city lights of planet Earth from outer space. God's intent was to fill this planet, every nook and cranny, every mountain and valley, with reflective outposts who would declare his glory to the universe. This planet was designed to be set ablaze with light, and the light of the stars would have dimmed by comparison.

There was more. The prince and the princess were given a parcel of the King's domain to rule and reign in. The garden was their responsibility—their domain—with options on more real estate readily available. God told them to subdue the earth and rule over all the creatures in it (Genesis 1:28). God's original intent was for the man and woman to rule as his stewards or regents over the earthly realm of their Father the King.

God's plan was to gradually introduce them to rulership by giving them responsibility for the care and oversight of a small garden kingdom called Eden. It would be their castle and throne room to learn the responsibilities and fulfill the expectations of royalty. Here they would enter the apprenticeship program of kingdom rule and learn day-by-day the true definition of subdue and rule under the tutelage of the King of kings and Lord of lords.

We have a warped view of what it means to rule. For most of us, the ruler is the person who gives the orders—who gets served. That's why there's so much conflict in the world today. Everybody wants to be in charge. That is not the principle God planned on teaching the first couple. They would rule by serving creation—by stewarding it. They would care for the garden by tilling or cultivating it. Cultivate simply means "to serve." As they served the garden, as they plowed, planted, pruned, and irrigated, that paradise would become even more fruitful and beautiful. Their rule would release fruitfulness, which God's rule does every time his kingdom touches earth.

To rule means to represent the heart of God to those whom he puts in our sphere of influence. That's what Jesus did when he came. He put it in these words: "The Son of Man did not come to be served, but to serve, and to give His life a ransom for many" (Matthew 20:28). He represented God's heart and fleshed out the lesson the man and woman were scheduled to learn in the garden of Eden's Leadership Academy.

Ultimately, the culmination of God's original intent was the gift of relationship. The man and the woman would experience what it means to know God without limit or restriction. The opportunity to have their deepest need fulfilled stood before them, willing to disclose himself to them. This is a passionate love story, make no mistake about it. God passionately loved the man and the woman, and his desire was for them to learn to love him.

What must it have been like to walk with the manifest presence of God—to bask in the shadow of his Shekina glory in the cool of the day? My mind can't comprehend that, but my heart hungers for it with ravenous desire. There in those shared moments, the three of them talked, whispered, sang, giggled, and laughed out loud at each new discovery. The fire of a passionate love was lit. God shared his secrets and gave detailed instructions for the care of the garden. He shared his plan with them and there was no fear, no apprehension, no insecurity, no frustration, no shame, because there was no sin.

Here in the safety of the garden, God refreshed them with whispers of his love for who they were. He coached them as they learned to care for and cherish one another. He cheered their abilities, encouraged their capabilities, taught them to dream, and validated their identity and legitimacy. In essence, they found fulfillment in his presence.

What must it have been like to hear the presence of the Bridegroom moving through the garden, as he came to be with his bride? Could they contain it, or did they shout out in spite of themselves? What was the excitement like when God burst through the bushes and they unashamedly leaped into his arms, entering his glorious heart of intimacy?

That was God's original intent—the genesis and genius of Plan A.
Relationship.
Rulership.
Reproduction.
Reflection.
And it still is…

Section 2
God's Plan Relinquished

This marvelous plan of relational intimacy, identity, and inheritance was not stolen or lost, contrary to what has been often taught. It was bestowed by God's divine choice; and by a personal choice, Adam freely gave it away. Tragically, God's Plan A was relinquished for an empty promise the caretakers of Eden's garden already possessed.

Chapter 3
Hiding in Paradise

My children...where are you?
~ Abba God

We live in a crazy, hectic world. Rush, rush here. Run over there. Return a call. Send an e-mail. Shoot a text. Finish the list. Run by the bank, the grocery store, and make sure you pick up the kids. At the end of the day, one thing is for sure: this ain't paradise...or is it?

Recently, I got away. Retreated! Why? Because I was worn out and utterly exhausted. And early in the morning I got up and went to sit on the pier. Where is not really important. It's on a river so far back in the woods, if you hold your breath you can faintly hear the banjo music.

The sun is slowly rising over the brilliant red, gold, and burnt orange autumn foliage still draping the trees, as a shadowy mist hovers just a few inches above the surface of the river. I close my eyes, let my imagination run wild, and wonder if this might be what Eden was like. In a quiet place (which most of us rarely visit) sounds become sharper, more distinct. Acorns and hickory nuts are falling, and whenever one hits a boathouse roof along this sluice, it sounds like a rifle shot. Behind me on the steep hillside, a wood hen calls, and for a brief moment the sound reminds me of a Tarzan movie.

A gentle breeze swirls, and the falling leaves serve a gentle notice of a crash landing. Squirrels scurry after one another in a joyous game of tag. The surface of the river, smooth as glass, is broken occasionally by the splash of a fish dining on breakfast. I simply can't take it all in. I can't drink in enough of the sounds or feast on the banquet of sights my eyes are gorging themselves on. Ahh...is this what paradise was like?

And then all of a sudden the silence is broken by loud, intrusive crows. Big coal-black ones, with crass, arrogant caws that trumpet their arrival like a tornado siren. With hundreds of miles of shoreline to land on, they decide to invade my tiny parcel of paradise. My idyllic little moment in the garden is gone just like that. For what seems like an eternity, those ebony devils strut back and forth on the roof of the boathouse across from what was once my solace of solitude.

I hate crows. I have a personal conviction that crows are nothing more than demons with feathers. They're loud, obnoxious, mean, and they live off the dead carcasses of other unfortunate creatures. There is a belief in ancient lore that they are the eyes of the devil, sent to and fro throughout the world to report back the events of the day. This morning I'll second that motion with a hearty amen! This little hit squad seems to be calling in my co-ordinates with zeal. It seems the devil has found me, intruded on my once-pristine paradise, and now he's stolen my little inch of Eden.

Or has he? Perhaps, but…perhaps not. Technically, one can't steal something that has been given up freely without a fight.

Naked and Not Ashamed

Have you ever wondered how much time passed between Genesis 2:25 and 3:1? I often do. Was it a few hours, several days, a couple of weeks, or perhaps even years? God is silent on that, but perhaps we can take a moment and do a little "sanctified" daydreaming of what must have gone on.

For the man and the woman, exploring Eden must have been like a child's first peek at the brightly wrapped gifts hidden under the tree on Christmas morning. Everything was a fresh new discovery. Life was filled with carefree exploration, continual examination, and consummate experience. The sight, the sound, the smell, the feel of new—of pristine—must have been overwhelming for their senses. What must it be like to smell the fragrance of a flower for the first time? To hear the inaugural trumpet of a bull elephant or the roar of a lion. To feel the sensation of hot and cold and learn the difference. To reach down and scoop up a rich handful of soil and savor the damp aroma of your origin. To experience the utter delight of tasting the sweetness of a grape or the richness of a banana. To savor love without restriction—without any limits—unconditionally. That's what the garden was like. Two children, clad in the bodies of maturity, free to run, to swim, to laugh, to shout, to ponder and explore one another's wonder, to unwrap the gift of just being. Not doing—being. Here in this paradise they were fully content in who they were—the identity God had bestowed on them.

Perhaps we can't remember what that's like because it is locked away in the recesses of our imagination. Most of those first times happen to us as infants and children, a stage of innocence that passes far too quickly. I find God's verbal description of those first moments of discovery fascinating: *"naked and not ashamed"* (Genesis 2:25). Narratively, the words are refreshingly candid, yet utterly innocent.

There was nothing hidden and no reason to hide. Transparency reigned. There were no smudges on the glass. The couple was free to experience life and to feel—that's right—to feel, caress, stroke, touch, handle that life and its bounty of gifts to the fullest. They were naked in far more ways than what has been made obvious by our crude depictions of this man and woman strategically covered by bush and branch. They were totally exposed for who they were—the man and the woman. The ones God formed and fashioned. Personally for himself—for relationship. There was nothing (no thing hidden) between them and God. No higher purpose can or will ever exist. They were robed in the light of his glory. And to ever experience it again fully, we too must be stripped of the garment of guilt woven intricately with the lethal threads of shame. But that garment has proven far harder for us to take off than it was originally for them to put on.

What's Love Got to Do with It?

Love is the highest virtue a human being can attain. It is the ultimate experience we can immerse ourselves in. We were created by God to be loved and to respond by loving. Love can be received, but to be given there must be a response. But every response requires a choice. Therefore, we as human beings cannot experience true love without making the right choices. Choices require freedom and opportunity.

If paradise were simply having everything we wanted or needed at our beck and call, Eden would have been the place. Everything essential for a person's joy, fulfillment, and life was present, and then some. It was not overkill; it was instead a lavish gift without equal. Often the degree of one's love is evident in the details or simplicity of their gift. There could be no doubt from the gift that surrounded the man and his wife that they were the beloved of God. That particular detail has not changed either.

And to put frosting on the cake, God came for a visit each day. Each evening, as the cool winds began to blow from east to west, they would walk together, and God would teach the intricacies of relationship. It was vital that they understood the heart of God—the "who I am" rather than "what you can do for me." These were lessons of relationship, not the rituals of servitude. God was no monarch demanding entertainment; he was a lover longing for intimacy. He had no interest in any performances designed to please him, only in conveying the simple rudiments of enjoying presence—his of them and theirs of him. These lessons were unforced, as simple as breathing. The plan was so natural…so easy…so fulfilling.

The choice was straightforward and amazingly simple. No complex forms to fill out in triplicate. No raising your right hand with the solemn repetition of an oath or the recitation of a precise vow. No cross your heart and hope to die promises. There were none of those things. Instead, God imposed one limitation in an otherwise unlimited realm of potential: "From any tree of the garden you may eat freely; but from the tree of the knowledge of good and evil you shall not eat, for in the day that you eat from it you shall surely die" (Genesis 2:16-17).

In the center of the garden, God planted two trees: the tree of life and the tree of the knowledge of good and evil. The fruit of one would freely grant life without end and the other knowledge, but at a high price. Divine permission was conferred to eat from the tree of life but forbidden from the tree of knowledge of good and evil.

The choice rested in the permission God offered, not in the prohibition he instituted. For some reason, most tend to see it only as prohibitive, almost as though God had a flashing billboard with a message board blinking POSTED—KEEP OUT! NO EATING! HUMANS NOT WELCOME HERE! And he stuck it in the ground at the base of the tree of knowledge. But on the contrary, God's command was filled with almost unlimited freedom. So much more was possible—not less.

A part of being created in the image and likeness of God is the privilege of exercising our will, that ability to make choices that provides the capability of determining what we will do and who we will become. A choice automatically implies at least two options from which one must make a selection. So with the capacity of a will comes the responsibility to use it wisely. That wisdom can't be gained instantly by eating forbidden fruit. It can only be achieved by listening to the voice of the Holy Spirit who would guide them. This was and still is a vital part of God's Plan A. God would provide the knowledge on a need-to-know basis. When they needed to know, God would give insight. The couple would trust God for answers, and he would trust them with the answers. Revelation, not information, would bestow all the knowledge they needed, plus the wisdom to use that knowledge, but this would only come through their daily appointments with God, as their relationship grew.

In the process, trust would be established and provide the fertile soil from which real love would spring forth. Love is an act of the will. It is something one chooses. It cannot be forced; it must be given. Love is a response. The two trees at the center of the garden provided a contrast, a choice demanding a response, but the choice was really about love rather than fruit. The couple's obedience to the prohibition would ultimately demonstrate what they truly believed. Our true beliefs are always manifested in our actions. Jesus put it this way, "If you love me, obey my commandments" (John 14:15 NLT). In other words, do what I say. Talk is cheap! Show me! That single prohibition was the golden opportunity for the man and the woman to respond—to hear God's voice and to choose accordingly—in love with love because of love. That's what love has to do with it.

The Anatomy of Temptation

Temptation is a cheap promise to gain something illegally or illegitimately that God has given or will eventually give us in his grace. If the gifts of God were not so good, the enemy would not attempt to duplicate them with cut-rate imitations. Temptation works only if we refuse to choose the goodness of God.

Temptation is successful only if it can awaken, create, or fuel an unfulfilled desire. It must arouse an intense passion for the bait, or it will not be effective. Temptation is ultimately a heart thing. It causes us to set our heart (feelings/emotions/longings) on something it was never designed to crave. That craving turns into lust, which is the desire to possess something that is not legitimately ours to possess.

James, the half brother of Jesus, put it this way: "But each one is tempted when he is carried away and enticed by his own lust. Then when lust has conceived, it gives birth to sin; and when sin is accomplished, it brings forth death" (James 1:14-15). Let me illustrate what James is saying. While I was relaxing at the river, I went fishing. When you boil the art of fishing down to its basics, it is intellectually very simple, but practically a bit tougher. It is nothing more than temptation visualized. If I plan to be a successful fisherman, I must lure the fish out from the safety of its watery domain and entice it to bite a blob of bait impaled with a sharp, barbed metal hook. Sounds simple, but it's not. As long as that fish stays under that sunken log, it's safe and nothing happens.

My plan was to take some live red wigglers (earthworms) and an ultra-light rod and reel and have a few hours of fun catching bream. I hoped to sit in a comfortable chair, bait the hook, and let nature take its course. I waited…and waited…and waited. Nothing. Not a nibble. I waited a few more minutes, retrieved my bait, and cast it over to another area. This same scenario played out for over two hours, and nothing. The fish were unwilling to leave the safety of the submerged brush tops and nibble on the wiggler delight I was serving up. Finally, I changed baits and put a tiny artificial minnow on the ultra-light and began to cast and retrieve it ever so slowly.

Contact! The tip of the rod dipped, and it was fish on. The first bait did not work, but the second was more than the bream could stand. In less than a minute, two nice, hand-sized bluegills left the shady safety of the sunken logs and were enticed to grab my little fake minnow. That tiny, artificial shad-shaped piece of plastic swimming so close to their domain was more than their taste buds could stand. It doesn't get any better than this—as long as you are not the fish.

And so it is with us. A successful temptation is all about luring us out from the safety of God's bountiful boundaries and enticing us to bite counterfeit bait that resembles the real thing. Remember, most of the time what we grab on the devil's hook has already been freely given by God or soon will be.

From the Dust of Mistrust

Do you remember that couple in the garden? They had everything their hearts could desire. And what they had not yet obtained, they soon would obtain as they extended their domain and God increased their boundaries. At this point the story takes a horrendous twist. It is abrupt. It happens with little warning. This is no fairy tale. A sinister fisherman appears suddenly and begins stirring the waters in Eden, intent on filling his stringer with the day's catch. The root meaning of Eden is "abundant waters," and this dark angler is intent on fishing in it.

Up until this moment, the tranquil garden has been a place for the man and the woman to learn, experience, and practice God's Plan A. The only creature the couple had ever spoken to was God. Now, all of a sudden, the safe terrain of Eden has become Ground Zero for testing their trust, their obedience, and ultimately their love. Remember—love is a choice, and for a choice to occur two options must be present.

A nightmarish creature is introduced into this idyllic garden in Genesis 3:1 as the serpent. *Nahash* slithered right up to the woman and started speaking—no introduction...no explanation... no nothing. Here in the midst of the meeting place of God and man, an intruder attempted to gain center stage. The Bible does not explicitly tell us that this is Satan, but it seems implicitly clear from the whole of biblical revelation that they are one and the same creature. A second option is about to be presented. A temptation unfurled. A choice required. A destiny determined.

"Indeed, has God said, 'You shall not eat from any tree of the garden'?" (Genesis 3:1). That question must have stunned the woman. The serpent was asking her a question; he was misrepresenting God. His statement distorted a plain God-stated fact (do not eat of the tree of the knowledge of good and evil), but was said in such a way that she would be forced to answer in the affirmative or the negative. The snake questioned God's goodness and grace toward the woman. He implied God was holding back on her—that she had not received all of it. The temptation was in full swing. The deceiver was attempting to lure the woman out of the safe place God had provided and into a place he could get her to take the bait.

She responded, "From the fruit of the trees in the garden we may eat; but from the fruit of the tree which is in the middle of the garden, God has said, 'You shall not eat from it or touch it, lest you die'" (Genesis 3:2). Every time I read this response, I have a desire fueled by primal fear to yell at the top of my lungs, "Run for your life! Go to the toolshed and get the hoe! Cut that lying snake's head off!" It wells up in me. I don't like snakes—I hate snakes!

Her response revealed that Satan's bait had caught her eye. Her memory of God's gracious benevolence seems to have dimmed or at least become confused. The temptation was working because now the tree of the knowledge of good and evil had taken center stage. She had forgotten the tree's significance and had become fixated on its location. It was becoming the center of her world. A desire was awakening deep within her (a mistrust of the dust) as this deception progressed. The bait had taken the woman, and now all that was left was for the woman to take the bait.

When fishing, you sometimes adjust the speed that you retrieve the bait, or tug a little to make it move differently, or just stop it dead in the water for a moment. The purpose of these maneuvers is to make the fish crazy with desire so it will take the bait. And that's exactly what the serpent did here with the woman.

"You surely will not die!" (Genesis 3:4). Creation must have gone silent because the snake just called God a liar. It now directly impugned God's veracity. That should have shocked the woman back into reality as the alarms of her personal experiences with God—that relationship of unconditional love—began to go off in her mind. But…it did not.

The serpent followed quickly with the *coup de grâce* (French for "a baseball bat to the side of the head"—i.e., the killing blow), "For God knows that in the moment you eat from it your eyes will be opened, and you will be like God, knowing good from evil" (Genesis 3:5). There it is. That's the genesis of the tempter's cheap promise, the counterfeit. The man and woman were already like God. They were created in God's image and likeness. Plan A gave them the license to endlessly reproduce that likeness and fill the earth. She already possessed ownership of the exact copyright the serpent was attempting to sell to her, except his product was a cheap knockoff.

Consider all the cut-rate promises the enemy peddles and calls opportunity. He loves to dress death in pretty clothes and bright lights, but pull back the beautiful wrappings and a closer inspection will always reveal a rotting pile of decay. The woman did not read the contract. She did not inspect the package she was about to purchase. She reached out and swallowed the bait—hook, line, and sinker.

The woman's desire became obsessed with the tree and its fruit. She believed the lie of the serpent, reached out and "took" illegally what was not hers to take. And, according to 1 Timothy 2:14, the woman, being quite deceived, fell into transgression. She stepped out of bounds, from paradise into perdition, ate from the fruit, and gave it to her husband. Likewise, the man ate.

Perhaps the saddest part of this story is the silence of the very one who heard the prohibition first fall from the lips of God. The man said nothing. He did nothing. He joined his wife in the serpent's rebellion—the establishment of a counter-plan—against God. Their passion, once fueled by God's love, now morphed into lust, fired by self-love. Adam, the son of God, had now opened the door for sin to enter the physical creation. And it swept in, decimating everything in its path. Sin is not the result of the woman's deception. It is the result of Adam's direct disobedience.

Through an act of the will, Adam and Eve made a choice. Their eyes were opened, but what they had dreamed of seeing they did not see. And what they had once been able to see they could no longer see clearly. Fear (the chief emotion of a slave) engulfed them. The transparency of God's glory was gone, their covering of light darkened. As they stared at each other, for the first time they felt the guilt of disobedience and found themselves covered in the black muck of shame. The son had now become a slave, and he covered himself in the fig leaf of slavery.

Let's Make a Deal

In those crucial moments of temptation, the devil's purpose was to close the deal he had dreamed of since being kicked out of heaven and subsequently witnessing God's creation of his heir, Adam. The old serpent wanted his own kingdom, and since there was only one kingdom available, he was determined to have it. He was not powerful enough to take it by force, nor could he steal it. It had to be given over for him to legitimately rule it. The choice Adam and Eve made was far more costly than they bargained for. It was the precise choice the serpent had hoped for.

With their fatal decision, the deal was sealed and duly signed on the dotted line. The title deed was transferred and the grand plan seemed done—finished before it ever really had a chance to take root. Here they were—the man and the woman—hiding in paradise, frantically looking for what they had foolishly given away.

The Dread of Disobedience

Disobedience multiplies dread. As kids, my brother and I fought like cats and dogs. Being three years older, several inches taller and pounds heavier, I usually won these childhood battles. It was a never-ending struggle, because Neal would not give up until he couldn't get up.

One day we were playing in the basement, and we got into an argument. The fight broke out and the inevitable happened. Except this time, as I was making my way up the stairwell leaving his crumpled body in a heap, I saw him grab a gallon paint can.

Now, his mindset was to always get even—no matter what it took. I took off up the steps and he threw the can, but he didn't quite have enough muscle to hit me, and the can fell short. That black can labeled Rust-Oleum hit, bounced up in the air, and the lid flew off. Thick black paint poured out of the can, making its way down those unpainted wood steps like floodwaters pouring over the top of a dam.

We stopped breathing—both of us. Time stood still, if you know what I mean. Then, as if on cue, we both scrambled to wipe up that sticky paint with anything we could grab. The harder we wiped, the blacker those unpainted steps got. Try as we would, we could not get the paint off. The dry, unfinished wood drank it in. The more we wiped, the bigger the mess got. There was no way to hide this. No way to fix it. We were in big trouble.

All I could hear in my mind were my dad's words from earlier in the day just before he left for work: "Stop fighting!" Here we were with no way out and no place to hide, and to make matters worse, our mother stood at the top of the steps shaking her head. Her only words of comfort were, "Just wait till your daddy gets home."

My dad worked in the mines, and every day we would eagerly await his arrival, when his old blue Chevy truck pulled up to the house. We would follow him around the house and into the basement where he would hang his hard hat and sit down on the bottom step and remove his boots. That particular day, neither of us wanted Dad to come home, nor were we waiting in the driveway when he arrived. We were hiding, filled with dread, praying for something to happen—anything—maybe even the end of the world, if it would keep Daddy from finding the paint.

He found it, and then he called for us to come to the basement. The damage was done. For those steps there was no going back—no fixing them. That black stain remained on those steps until after we both married and left home. My dad finally painted all the steps, but not with black paint.

In the garden that afternoon, as the cool wind of the east began to blow in, the man and the woman were not in their usual places. Disobedience brought dread. Dread created fear, and fear drove them into the bushes to hide. They thought they could hide from God, and so do we. That's what the knowledge of good and evil does to you. It gives you loads of information without the wisdom to use it. Wisdom usually comes through experience. Knowledge without experience is a deadly dance partner. And when you've made a mess, there's no grass high enough to hide from God.

The Question

"Adam, where are you?"

Some questions really don't need an answer. So why ask them? When God asks a question, you can bet he is not asking to gain information or knowledge. He already knows all the answers to all the questions. That's the definition of omniscient. He asked the question so Adam and Eve would evaluate the position from which they had fallen. God's question was asked to evoke a confession, not determine a location.

There in that garden, the site of so many rapturous moments, the guilty couple must face their defiant choice and disastrous act. Like black paint on wooden step, the stain of their sin was evident, although they tried to wipe it away as hard as they could with fig leaves. Judgment fell and they were driven from the garden, but that may be the least of their worries.

Relationship, the centerpiece of God's Plan A, was now severed—ripped apart. Sin had distorted their hearts so badly that intimacy with God now seemed impossible. Shame had filled the void and with it a deep hunger that cannot be quenched. The couple had lost far more than what many might call the garden of God. They had ultimately lost the God of their garden.

Royalty was now no more than a fleeting wisp of a daydream. The divine gift of rulership had been traded for the bitterness of one bite of fruit—bartered away for a single moment of selfish, disobedient indulgence.

Their ability to reflect God's image was marred like a cracked mirror and became painfully evident in their pathetic ability to reproduce that distorted image. In fact, one of the saddest passages in all of Scripture is found in Genesis 5:3: "When Adam had lived one hundred and thirty years, he became the father of a son *in his own likeness, according to his image* [italicized to emphasize in the likeness and image of Adam, not God], and named him Seth."

Plan A seemed dead in the water. *Nahash* seemed to have gotten everything he wanted. God's plan couldn't be fulfilled now. No man existed who could listen carefully to his voice, constantly walk in relationship, and fully obey his directions. Nice try, but try again, God!

Content with his catch, old *Nahash* must have flicked his lips with his forked tongue as he crawled back into the darkness of the undergrowth. "If being cursed with an existence of dining at the dust cafe and enmity with these inferior humans is the best God can do, things don't seem that bad," he must have thought to himself as he pondered the echo of God's parting words: "Because you have done this, cursed are you more than all the cattle, and more than every beast of the field; on your belly shall you go, and dust shall you eat all the days of your life; and I will put enmity between you and the woman, and between your seed and her seed; He shall bruise you on the head, and you shall bruise him on the heel" (Genesis 3:14-15). "So what," he thought. "Your Plan A is still dead! Stone-cold dead!"

...Or is it?

CHAPTER 4
THE CURSE OF A CONFUSED IDENTITY

> There was always the feeling that
> something wasn't quite right.
> ~ Folker Heinicke

Power enables a person to put his dreams and plans into practice. In January of 1933, Adolf Hitler rose to power when he was appointed Chancellor of Germany. Ultimately, he would become the supreme ruler and exercise unprecedented control over that nation and much of Europe. To rid himself of all opposition, he set up *Konzentrationslager* (concentration camps) all over Germany to incarcerate those who were considered political subversives—Communists, Socialists, and others who opposed the Fuehrer. Soon ethnic cleansing and purges began with groups and races arrested and incarcerated who were considered undesirable—Jews, criminals, homosexuals, and gypsies. As Hilter's power increased and his enemies disappeared, the terminally ill and the physically and mentally handicapped disappeared from the hospitals and also ended up in these horrible camps. Some camps were for slave labor, and some were extermination camps.

Hitler's ultimate dream was to rule a world populated by blue-eyed, blond men and women of Nordic Germanic stock. His vision was two-fold: the creation of his superior race and the extermination of all the rest he considered inferior. The latter resulted in a holocaust. As the Nazi blitzkrieg raced across Europe, the extermination of the undesirables went into full speed. Millions of Jews, Poles, Czechs, and gypsies were packed like cattle into boxcars and sent by rail to the gas chambers and furnaces of death camps with infamous names like Dachau, Treblinka, Auschwitz, Ravensbrück, and Buchenwald. Atrocities and cruelties were perpetrated in these places at a level that are incomprehensible to the normal mind.

As the extermination was taking place, the creation process to re-populate was also being implemented. Young German men and women who met the Aryan criteria were chosen to participate in Hitler's insidious strategy like breeding stock on a farm. After sexual relations resulted in pregnancy, the men were taken away. Once the birth occurred, a mother never saw her child again. An estimated 5,000 to 8,000 children were born, and most were placed in affluent homes in the interior of Germany far away from the Allied bombing raids. These children have come to be known as the "Lebensborn Kinder," which is German for "source of life kids."

With the defeat of the Third Reich and the surrender of Germany in World War II, this program ended, but its devastation of the human heart did not. Thousands of innocent kids grew up feeling empty deep within their hearts and souls. They sensed something was wrong but were unable to formulate the questions that would bring the answers for which they hungered. Some of the parents shared bits and pieces with their adopted children as they grew into adulthood, but the scanty details only served to complicate their obscure origins. These kids realized they had no identity, and who they thought they were turned out to be a lie. Confused with conflicting stories and the irregularities found in their birth records, many of these men and women began a lifelong search for their identity and their origin.

One man, Folker Heinicke, described the sense of not having an identity in this way: "There was always the feeling that something wasn't quite right. It happens when you have no mother, no father—no roots." Identity is essential in understanding who you are, where you came from, and why you are where you are. Identity is your roots. But when you've lost your identity, you've lost yourself—you've lost your soul—you've lost it all.

Something Is Not Quite Right

As Adam and Eve exited the garden, they did so with the shards of a shattered identity clinging to their garments of animal skin. God never abandoned his children, but their recollection of exactly who they were and what their relationship with God meant slowly dimmed as the years passed and generation replaced generation. Time can be a thief, stealing the most important details and leaving us with only generalizations of what something should be or could be. The primary issue of relationship with God became a pseudo-responsibility with the children of Adam to serve, placate, and earn the favor of an angry God.

The beauty of being was replaced by the slavery of doing. Rules replaced relationship. Works substituted for worship. The real elements of paradise were truly lost, misplaced in the bushes when we reached for those pesky fig leaves to cover our nakedness rather than being transparent with our sinfulness. We embraced a plan God never commissioned or endorsed—a Plan B of sorts. If we can be good enough or work hard enough, perhaps the angel with the flaming sword will allow us back into paradise.

That plan has been the curse of confusion that has left us without roots—without a safe harbor or mooring we can depend on in understanding our true identity. In love, and out of a deep sense of compassion, God gave Moses the Law to guide men and women back to an intimate relationship with him. It was designed to keep people from hurting and destroying themselves as well as their neighbors. Their utter inability to keep the Law's requirements in their own strength was God's way of driving them back to him—of forcing them to depend on him again for every need. It was never intended to be a measuring gauge for personal righteousness, but the original intent was hijacked by our insatiable lust to do it our way on our terms in our own time. It was a tutor to lead us to maturity, but we turned it into a goal to achieve, a mountain to climb, a list to check off. We took God's tool to help us with the weeds and the briars outside the garden and made it the totem centerpiece of our faith. Salvation—our deliverance from the penalty and power of sin through Christ—became a work of our hands instead of a gift from God's.

The confusion in our heads became chaos in our hearts. We've lost our identity as God's son and daughters. I'm not talking about the people who don't know Jesus. The Bible classifies them as "lost," and God is still beating the bushes searching for their hearts. They act the way they act because for them it's their only choice. I'm talking about the average Adam and Eve Christian. I'm talking about the person who has experienced Jesus as Savior and Lord. Perhaps the person

I'm describing is you.

Consider again the words of Folker Heinicke: "There was always the feeling that something wasn't quite right. It happens when you have no mother, no father—no roots." This happens when we don't understand our identity or experience our legitimacy. On a spiritual level the same thing occurs if we don't understand our identity in Christ and our legitimacy as a son or daughter of God. Ignorance leads to slavery, and slavery leads us right back into the place where we strive in our own strength to garner the gifts which God alone can and must give in his strength. We can't gain them; God must give them. That striving to gain illegitimately what can only be given is slavery, because we have no real relationship with our heavenly Father. No Father relationship means we have no roots. No roots—no identity. No identity—no legitimacy. Sadly, no legitimacy communicates the lie that we have no value or worth. And though our citizenship is in heaven, we waste our earthly existence searching for an identity that will somehow make us valuable to God.

The Confusion Factor

Homer and Langley Collyer were sons of a very wealthy and respected New York physician. Both men graduated near the top of their class in college, and their future seemed limitless. Not long after their graduation, their father fell ill and died, leaving the sons his fortune, his home, and the family estate. In the prime of their life, Homer and Langley were now financially secure. All they could ever want was theirs to enjoy.

Instead of using their college degrees or visiting exotic places around the world, the two men chose a rather peculiar lifestyle for men of their class and financial standing. They never married. There was little contact with the outside world. They lived in almost total seclusion in the house on the estate their father had left them. They became recluses. They boarded up the windows and padlocked the doors. They rarely went out.

Eventually, the utility companies were forced to cut off their power, their gas, and their water because all attempts to contact the Collyers for payment went unheeded. No one ever saw either of them outside the house. The house appeared empty to most who passed by.

Years later, on March 21, 1947, the police received an anonymous tip from a caller who claimed that a man had died in the Collyer home. When the police arrived to investigate the report, an awful odor greeted them, but no one responded to their repeated knocks on the door. Several attempts to get in the front door were made, but the officers failed each time. They finally entered the house through a second-story window. There they found the body of Homer, his matted grey hair reaching past his shoulders, clutching a twenty-year-old magazine, although the autopsy showed he had been blind for years. Homer had died from the combined effects of malnutrition, dehydration, and cardiac arrest ten hours earlier.

As the police searched the house, they found an immense collection of worthless junk—car parts, broken machinery, appliances, musical instruments, rags, and large bundles of old newspapers. Dirt and debris filled every room. But Langley was nowhere to be found, and the stench remained.

Three weeks later, as workmen were completing the arduous task of removing the trash, they discovered the badly decomposed remains of Langley buried not more than six feet from where Homer had been found. He was the victim of his self-made booby trap constructed to protect and crush anyone who tried to steal the Collyers' worthless treasures. He had tripped a wire and was crushed to death while crawling through a tunnel carved out through the garbage to bring food to Homer.

The rubbish removed from the Collyer brownstone in Harlem weighed 140 tons. The salvageable items were later auctioned for less than $2,000, but the cumulative estate of the Collyer brothers in today's money would be worth over a million dollars. Homer and Langley lived their whole life and died in squalor because they had forgotten who they were—the university-educated heirs of a wealthy New York physician. They became hoarders, a nice word for garbage collectors. The life they chose is shocking, but it is a perfect illustration of the life most people choose to live once they come to Christ. As heirs of God and joint-heirs with Jesus Christ, most never access their inheritance because they have no clue what their true identity affords them. Therefore, they live out their spiritual lives ingesting the garbage of this world. They live like slaves instead of living as sons and daughters of the King because their thinking is confused.

The Slave Mentality

Every person who knows Jesus Christ as Lord and Savior is a son or daughter of the King. That is an eternal fact established in the mind of God, but not a reality the majority ever experience. The disparity rests in the way we think. Most Christians act and live with a slave mentality because they think like a slave. The primal instinct of survival outside the garden guides our choices far more than does the surrender of self in the passionate pursuit of our relationship with the Father.

Let me define what I mean by "slave" and "slave mentality." A slave is my term for a believer driven by the need to survive. That person knows facts about God but has not moved from the immaturity of hesitation into the maturity of a heart relationship with the Father. Do you remember that picture of Adam and Eve crouching in the bushes, hiding as God approached for a time of intimate fellowship? Just remove their heads and Photoshop ours into place, and that ageless snapshot would represent the relationship most believers have with God. They are headed for heaven, saved from their sins, but have no clue of what God really looks or acts like. They are serving an angry taskmaster rather than a loving Father or a passionate lover.

Personal survival drives a person with a slave mentality. "I, Me, and My" often reign as king on the throne. Their present mentality has been formed by their past experiences BC (before Christ) rather than by the finished work of Jesus on the cross and their new identity in Christ. If we never embrace our new identity, we will never experience the benefits of it. Unfortunately, most of the Church dines out of the devil's garbage dumpster, rather than at the banquet table of their King. She has become satisfied with the crumbs and the scraps she can get, rather than the riches she has been given. She survives—yes. Jesus promised the gates of hell would not prevail against her (Matthew 16:18), but survival is not enough. Hanging on is really not an option if you understand your true identity and God's Plan A. But, for the most part, the Church has been camped out at the gates of hell for almost seventeen centuries, content with eating the garbage dumped over the wall, instead of finishing the siege and kicking down the doors.

This kind of thinking stinks, but what we think eventually becomes who we are because this is what we act out. We have become victims instead of victors—slaves instead of sons and daughters—a people confused about our identity. The enemy, with the same craftiness he used on Eve, has convinced us God has another plan—a better one. Early on in the pages of Scripture God paints a transparent picture of this inward conflict of confused identity—slavery versus sonship.

The Way Out

True freedom is one of the byproducts of a personal relationship with God. The ability to be everything God intended is a solid definition of true freedom. As the intimacy of that relationship deepens, the experience of true freedom expands and is expressed in every area of a person's life. As this takes place, the revelation of our identity as a child of God shines through in experience and expression. When that relationship remains surface level, there is a tendency to revert to the old mindset of bondage.

The nation of Israel went down to Egypt, seventy strong, at the invitation of Joseph, Pharaoh's regent, who was himself a son of Israel. Hunger, fueled by famine, was the vehicle that carried them there, but God was the driver who drove them. They enjoyed the favor of God for a time, but after Joseph's death, the Egyptians slowly enslaved the Israelites and became their taskmasters. The ideals of freedom and relationship promised by God to the Patriarchs back in Canaan Land were in time forgotten, as a slave mentality of survival seeped in and washed away their identity. The people of God—his sons and daughters—became the slaves of Pharaoh. Time has a way of erasing the truth, but the only way truth can be lost is if we let it slip through our fingers. There were a handful of Israelites who held on to the promises God had given Abraham, Isaac, and Jacob, and they cried out in prayers of anguish and desperation.

God heard the whimpers of his children and sent Moses as their deliverer—the one who would save them from their slavery and set them free from the bondage of Egypt. On the exact night God had scheduled them to leave, he required them to do something in faith.

He ordered each family to kill a lamb without spot or blemish and apply some of its blood over the doorpost of their quarters on slave row. That night God judged Egypt. Their sin brought death to the first-born of every house in Egypt, except the ones where the blood was applied. Today, the Jews still celebrate that event as the Passover, the moment in their history when the death angel saw the blood and passed over their homes.

This Old Testament picture foreshadows what Jesus would later do for us on the cross. We deserve death, but if the blood of Christ has been applied to our lives in faith through grace, we are redeemed—bought with a price. That is exactly what God did that night for the nation of Israel. He redeemed them. He purchased them with blood. The first-born of all who were in Egypt was slain unless a substitute's blood was applied over the door and atonement made. That act pictured the substitutionary atonement of Christ. He died in our place so that we might live life on the basis of his finished work instead of on the basis of our own righteousness or strength.

That next morning the children of Israel marched out of Egypt as free men and women. God had called them to step into all the promises he had given their forefathers. He promised to be their God and they would be his people. With his promise of provision and protection, they stepped out of the bondage of slavery, so that they might step into the freedom of relationship with God.

Slavery is far more than a condition one is held in. It is also a mindset one becomes mired in. This army of almost two and a half million men and women would need more to erase the mindset of slavery than making their way over the border and out of Egypt. It is not where we end up that sets us free, but rather who we understand ourselves to be—who we believe we are that eventually leads to freedom. It's not location but identification.

Instead of leading this ragtag family of brick makers, shepherds, house-servants, and stone carvers straight to the Promised Land, God took them on an arduous detour into the desert to shake off the residue of slavery, which like dust had blanketed their spirits. God's plan was to provide everything they might need as they took a long walk with him and learned what relationship was all about. This tale has the same plot and similar elements as the garden story. As they walked with

God, his shade fell over them to protect them from the harshness of the desert sun, the glory of his presence illuminated their nights, food fell from the sky, meat was delivered by the wind, and layers of solid rock were split to become their oasis watering holes. God's provisions and protection were given to assure them that he loved them. He met their needs so that trust would germinate, relationship would blossom, and true abiding love would come to fruition.

But one of the harbingers of an inbred mindset of slavery is mistrust. Over and over, they complained about their lack, instead of asking for provision. They griped and fussed and accused God and his servant Moses of trying to kill them. That slave mentality tends to hang on like a rusty fishhook and always causes more pain than an ingrown toenail. The more God expressed his love, the more they reverted to a long-held belief instilled as mistrust in the dust of their original DNA by an ancient serpent in paradise lost—"God is holding out on you! You can't trust God!" Instead of forging a relationship with God in the heat of the desert, they were re-forging the chains of slavery on the anvil of mistrust with the hammer of fear.

God eventually led them to an arid setting at Mount Sinai for a marriage ceremony complete with covenant rather than a prenuptial agreement. Israel would be his bride, and God would be her Bridegroom. All those dos and don'ts were designed to shake the mold of slavery off the wedding dress of his bride. They were designed to bring freedom so that Israel might be what her Bridegroom had designed and planned for her to be (Plan A). The stipulations of the covenant were designed to lead these former slaves into a new level of freedom. Fear always arises out of the unknown—not knowing what will happen next. God wrote down his likes and his dislikes, communicated them clearly, and signed it in stone. No hidden agendas. No surprises. A love letter rather than a document of servitude.

Sadly, they misunderstood because they embraced God's marriage covenant with the idea that he would love them more if they kept the covenant. For Israel, their identity and legitimacy depended on their abilities instead of their hearts. In the ancient world, slaves were kept as long as they were able to produce. The Law of Moses was seen as a production opportunity that would gain the approval of God, rather than a marriage covenant that would open a doorway to a genuine relationship with God. For God it was all about freely being who he had created them to be. Tragically, for Israel it deteriorated into doing everything they could to earn God's love and favor. The distance was insurmountable—the difference between a passionate lover and a pathetic slave. The lie of the serpent still reverberated deep in the canyons of their collective soul, and with each echo the fear of failure and the terror of abandonment slowly calcified their hearts.

The Exodus had been a way out of slavery on the way back to God's heart. Their choice, like Adam's, resulted in what seemed like another impenetrable wall further separating God and humanity. If you listen closely, you will probably hear old *Nahash* laughing. "Give it up, God. Plan A is dead!"

Today's Reality

You may be thinking, "That's ancient history—yesterday's news. Jesus changed all that when he died on the cross." I would argue "changed" really isn't what he did. To change something is to admit someone made a mistake in or about the original action, and therefore it must be fixed. God made no such mistake. Jesus came to fulfill the Law (Matthew 5:17), meaning he came to fully obey God through the power of the Holy Spirit, which was something no one had ever done. The Law was given as a tutor to lead people to Christ (Galatians 3:24), to point them to the heart of God.

Instead, it became an idol—the holy grail for perfectionists, hypocrites, and religious leaders looking for opportunities to exercise power and exorcise grace. God sent it to steer people toward freedom; Satan used it to suck people back into slavery.

Why is that important for you and me? Almost thirty-five hundred years has passed since God wrote the Law on tablets of stone with the tip of his finger, yet little has changed in the heart of humanity. A people who refuse to learn the simple lessons of history are doomed to repeat them again and again. We have learned little. The mindset of modern believers has changed little since Egypt.

God set Israel free, but few ever experienced the joy of that freedom. When the choice had to be made between slave and son, more often than not, they chose the comfort of what they knew—slavery. They knew how to work—to do; but they never learned what it means to be—to enjoy the pleasures and perks of a new identity as beloved sons and daughters of God. They carried that dust with them out of Egypt, from the mountain of God to the Tabernacle, to the Temple, through the shadow of the cross, into the early church, through the dark ages, into the Reformation, and dropped it into today. Like an ancient relic that has taken on a miraculous standing, it continues to perpetrate the same confusion in the mind of God's saints. Far too many of God's sons and daughters still live in the confusion of slavery rather than the comfort of their radical new identity in Christ. We have majored on what to do when God was only interested from the beginning in whose we are. God never placed humanity under a curse, but the curse of confusion has dogged our every step since Adam stepped over the threshold and out of the garden.

I, for one, have come to the place where I refuse to walk in the chains of my predecessors, groping about trying to find another way—a better way to appease an angry god. I have chosen to throw off those chains of religion, for I was never created to bear their crushing weight. I was created for relationship with God—and you were too. I have been given a brand new identity, and so have you. I am not a slave. I am not a victim. I will no longer drink the confusion caused by the serpent's Kool-Aid. God is not holding out on me—or you. His plan has not changed—not since he inaugurated it by breathing his life into Adam. Everything we need to live that quality of life God has already provided.

Everything?

Yes, everything!

Section 3
God's Plan Restored

Jesus Christ is the last Adam. The Son became flesh through the Incarnation and restored everything Adam had relinquished as a man completely dependent on the empowerment of the Holy Spirit and fully obedient to the will of the Father. As a man, Jesus enjoyed the intimacy we were designed for, the identity we long for, and the inheritance we dream abot. In Christ, God's Plan A is now fully restored.

Chapter 5
The Last Adam

> It is done. I am the Alpha and the Omega.
> The beginning and the end.
> ~ Jesus Christ

I grew up in church. My parents never wasted an opportunity to go, so we were always present if the doors were unlocked. Some of my earliest memories are snippets of scenes that took place in the little brick church that my family's property surrounded. We lived so close we could walk to services. In that little Methodist church I was first introduced to Jesus and indoctrinated with the message of the gospel. Through godly men and women who loved Jesus with all their hearts, I learned who he is and what he had done. They taught me what they themselves had been taught. It was a message that transcended both generations and centuries—a message that had persevered through persecution, warfare, famine, pestilence, migration, and the ocean crossings of conquest and immigration.

But it was a message that majored on the deity of Jesus and minored on his humanity. As a little kid, Jesus assumed the position of the ultimate superhero in my mind, and his exploits were the unimaginable feats that only God performs. That's what I was taught. Those great miracles contained in the biblical accounts of Matthew, Mark, Luke, and John were performed to validate both the deity of Jesus and the message of the gospel he proclaimed. I did not question what I had been taught; everyone I knew believed the same thing.

Sunday school lessons, sermons, Bible college, and seminary studies all supported this presupposition, and it became engrained as dogma in my mind. I did not question it, for to do so was to question the deity of Christ, my salvation, my mentors, and my whole belief system. Therefore, I majored on the deity of Christ in my own teaching and preaching and minored on his humanity. I simply could not grasp how important his humanity is or how it works. Jesus seemed to be a mysterious paradox—the God/man, meaning he was one hundred percent God and at the same time one hundred percent man.

I began to wrestle with a passage from the Bible that appeared to be a discrepancy in what I had been taught and what I was then reading. That passage of Scripture was John 14:12. This verse was not something someone else said about Jesus. This verse was written in red letters, a direct quotation of Jesus, something he said about his disciples. "Truly, truly, I say to you, he who believes in Me, the works that I do shall he do also; and greater works than these shall he do; because I go to the Father."

It seemed at first reading that Jesus was saying we could do everything he had done and even more. That caught my attention. It caused my mind to race and my imagination to go wild. I read the verse again and again, thinking that I had read it incorrectly, but that's what it said in my New American Standard translation. So I got out my Greek New Testament and translated the verse and discovered what I had read was a clear literal interpretation of exactly what Jesus said, but in my mind, based on what I had been taught, that was impossible. Either Jesus really didn't mean what it seemed he was saying, or my theology was all messed up. How could I do the things only God can do? Only God can raise the dead, give sight to the blind, know the thoughts of others, or walk on water. How can I do that? I'm not God, and what's more, I never will be.

God, am I missing something here?

The God/Man

The Incarnation, that historic instant where God became flesh, where deity joined with humanity, is the single most important moment in human history. Some might argue it was the birth (the Incarnation actually occurred at the moment of conception), the crucifixion, the resurrection, or the ascension of Jesus Christ, but without the Incarnation none of those other events could take place. Redemptive history hinges on the Incarnation.

A great deal of ink has been put to paper in an attempt to explain it, but how can we explain or comprehend something so incomprehensible? Pagan mythology is filled with stories of gods and goddesses appearing as humans for short intervals of time. There are also myths in which pagan deities cohabitated with human beings, and their offspring was half divine and half human. But there is only one account where God became flesh, and we find it in the Incarnation.

In his infinite wisdom, God never seeks to explain all the details of the Incarnation scientifically—or spiritually, for that matter. The explanation we have is enough. Dr. Luke, a man of both science and faith, records this rather succinct statement from the angel Gabriel in response to Mary's question: "The Holy Spirit will come upon you, and the power of the Most High will overshadow you; and for that reason the holy offspring shall be called the Son of God" (Luke 1:35). Matthew, in his gospel, records a similar angelic explanation to Joseph, Mary's fiancé: "For that which has been conceived in her is of the Holy Spirit" (Matthew 1:20). The apostle John gives us a very concise yet astonishing explanation by declaring, "In the beginning was the Word, and the Word was with God, and the Word was God" (John 1:1). "And the Word became flesh, and dwelt among us" (John 1:14).

The Incarnation took place before the virgin birth, at the moment of conception, as the Holy Spirit inexplicably united the divinity of the Son with the humanity of an egg in Mary's womb. As those two elements united into one cell and divided into two and the process of gestation began, God the Son was united with humanity for eternity.

For the first four hundred years of the Church, church fathers, bishops, theologians, and councils debated, argued, and occasionally waged war in an attempt to explain what seemed unexplainable. Ultimately, the orthodox position on the person and nature of Jesus Christ was hammered out by the Council of Chalcedon in 451 AD. After much debate they issued the Creed of Chalcedon:

> *We, then, following the holy Fathers, all with one consent, teach men to confess one and the same Son, our Lord Jesus Christ, the same perfect in Godhead and also perfect in manhood; truly God and truly man, of a reasonable [rational] soul and body; consubstantial [co-essential] with the Father according to the Godhead,*

> *and consubstantial with us according to the Manhood; in all things like unto us, without sin; begotten before all ages of the Father according to the Godhead, and in these latter days, for us and for our salvation, born of the Virgin Mary, the Mother of God, according to the Manhood; one and the same Christ, Son, Lord, Only begotten, to be acknowledged in two natures, inconfusedly, unchangeably, indivisibly, inseparably; the distinction of natures being by no means taken away by the unity, but rather the property of each nature being preserved, and concurring in one Person and one Subsistence, not parted or divided into two persons, but one and the same Son, and only begotten, God the Word, the Lord Jesus Christ; as the prophets from the beginning [have declared] concerning him, and the Lord Jesus Christ himself has taught us, and the Creed of the holy Fathers has handed down to us.*

This is a very precise explanation of who Jesus is and who he is not. I know the verbiage is similar to reading the small print in a legal document, but it is essential for us to understand why it is so exact. Jesus is one hundred percent God and one hundred percent man—true God united with true man in one person. He is the God/man. Jesus is one person with two natures—one divine and the other human, and at no time have these two natures mixed, changed, divided, or separated, nor will they ever. That is essential because it declares that Jesus was not some sort of hybrid mutation, half God and half man. It affirms that as God, his divine nature remained infinite, eternal, and almighty, and as man his nature was limited and finite. Each nature was full and complete, meaning Jesus did not assume a human body without a human will, mind, soul, and heart. Finally, it confirms that while the divine did not become human—nor the human become divine—there was by unity of person an inner connection between them which was constant and which continues in Jesus Christ. All of this allows Jesus to be the perfect revelation and manifestation of the God of our salvation and the perfect sacrifice who could suffer in both body and soul the wrath of God for sin as a substitute for us.

This is essential in establishing that Jesus is one hundred percent God and one hundred percent man. He is not a freak or a creature with a split personality. He is God, which my teachers and mentors labored so hard to instill in me. But he is also man, and this is very, very important in the scope of God's Plan A, and we must understand it.

The Lights Come On!

You may be wondering why I included the preceding section on the Incarnation. I believe it is foundational in helping us understand the ingenious plan of God. There is no denying Jesus is God; rather, we may struggle to understand the corresponding extent of his humanity. We have no trouble believing he died on the cross for the penalty of our sins as a man, but what we don't realize is that he also lived out his daily life as an example for each of us, so that we might enjoy victory over the power of sin. We see that example in both his words and works. Yet we stumble over the central details of how Jesus did it.

As I pondered and meditated on John 14:12 and all the questions it raised, the Holy Spirit led me to Philippians 2:5-8: "Have this attitude in yourselves which was also in Christ Jesus, who, although He existed in the form of God, did not regard equality with God a thing to be grasped, but emptied Himself, taking the form of a bond-servant, and being made in the likeness of men. And being found in appearance as a man, He humbled Himself by becoming obedient to the point of death, even death on a cross."

This passage validates and supports the incarnational fact that Jesus is truly God and truly man in one person, but it is also a treasure map that will lead us into a deeper understanding and appreciation of his humanity. This passage also sheds some light on *how* we as mere human beings can do the works Jesus did, as well as the *greater ones* he referred to.

As I dug into this passage, a switch flipped and the lights came on for me. All of a sudden the exploits and deeds of Jesus became even more amazing to me. I was dumfounded when it dawned on me that everything Jesus did for the 33 and a half years of his life, he did as a man, not as God.

You read that correctly. Everything Jesus did from the moment he entered this world through the birth canal of a virgin to the moment he offered up his spirit on the cross and died, was done out of his humanity, not his divinity. He never ceased for a millisecond to be God, but what he did—his body of work—was accomplished as a man.

The apostle Paul tells us in Philippians 2:7 that Jesus emptied himself and took on humanity. The word Paul uses is *ekenosin*. It means "to empty, to make empty, or to make of no effect." It does not mean Jesus emptied himself of his deity like one might empty a pitcher of its contents as some have wrongly argued throughout the history of the Church. He never for one moment ceased to be God, but in his humanity, Jesus chose not to use his God-attributes. He chose to lay aside his privileges as God. He did not use his divine power, and instead he lived life as a real human, just like you and me.

That's why Jesus became hungry, thirsty, tired, and sleepy. God never sleeps, and the limitations that we experience as humans have no effect on him. As God he needs nothing, but as a man Jesus experienced the same limitations we experience except for one thing—he was without sin. He had no sin nature.

This is a critical point for us to understand. Jesus had no sin nature because he had no human father, only a human mother. The sin nature comes from the father's side of the family, not the mother's. Scripture is clear that sin entered this world through Adam, not Eve. "Therefore, just as through one man sin entered the world, and death through sin, and so death spread to all men, because all sinned" (Romans 5:12). Since Adam, every father has given his children the gift that keeps on killing. Therefore, every person descended from Adam has been infected with sin, the result of one act of disobedience—a single bite of forbidden fruit. Humanity has no answer, solution, or remedy for stopping or even slowing the mounting death toll caused by the plague of sin.

Genesis 3 records that God had already made provision for this seemingly insurmountable problem. God revealed it as he passed judgment on *Nahash* (the serpent) in Genesis 3:15: "And I will put enmity between you and the woman, and between your seed and her seed; He shall bruise [or crush] you on the head, and you shall bruise him on the heel."

Biologically speaking, a woman has no seed. The female produces eggs, and the male produces the seed or sperm. Yet God clearly declares that there will be enmity between and ultimate victory over the serpent's seed by the woman's seed. This verse is called the *protoevangelium* or the first gospel by many theologians. Contained in the verse is the key to how God will restore the full potential of Plan A. In this verse is the harbinger of the Incarnation and the virgin birth in "seed" form. It seems a man will be born of woman who is like the first man before his fall, but different from every other man born since the Fall. He will be a man who is born of woman but who is not born of man. A man born without a sin nature. A man who can now choose again to fully obey God as he is guided by the voice of the Holy Spirit.

This man has the potential to fulfill the demands of God, if he fully obeys and does not sin. Those are big ifs—no man had done or could do this since Adam. That man is Jesus Christ—the God/man—but to fulfill the requirements of God, he could not exert his God-attributes even once. Instead he had to work within the limitations and weaknesses applicable to every man. The last Adam had to finish the work of the first Adam for Plan A to be attainable for the rest of us.

Are the lights starting to flicker? Are you beginning to grasp the brilliance of God's plan? We (human beings) could never return to the garden on our own, so the God of the garden came to us—as one of us. Jesus was a new kind of man—a new prototype—the last Adam with a mission to restore all the benefits and resources of God's Plan A.

A Crucial Detail

The majority of Jesus's life is hidden. We have few details of his childhood, adolescence, or early adulthood, with the exception of a trip his family took to Jerusalem when Jesus was twelve years of age (Luke 2:41-52). We can deduce from what we know of first-century Jewish culture that Jesus grew up like every other Jewish boy or girl of his day. His parents would have schooled him in the Torah, the Psalms, and the Prophets. He would have memorized long portions of the Old Testament, like every other Jewish child. He would also have learned a trade from his stepfather Joseph so he could support his family. As far as we know, Jesus did no miracles of any kind during this time.

No Plan B

At age thirty, there is a radical shift, and Jesus comes charging onto the stage at a bend in the Jordan River where the prophet John the Baptist was preaching and baptizing those who were repentant. John had been prophesying that one was coming who would be greater than he and this one would baptize with the Holy Spirit and with fire (Matthew 3:11). All of a sudden, Jesus stepped into the water for John to baptize him, and John recognized Jesus as the Messiah. John hesitated, but Jesus assured him that it was necessary to fulfill the details of God's plan.

As John plunged Jesus into the cold, green waters of the Jordan and lifted him back out, the Holy Spirit descended bodily out of heaven and rested on Jesus, empowering and equipping him to do whatever he saw or heard God his Father doing. This is a crucial detail we often miss. This moment is recorded in all four Gospels because its importance is vital in our understanding of how Jesus was able to do the works he did. Every miracle, every sermon, every deliverance, every healing, every work—everything Jesus did from that moment until he offered up his spirit on the cross was done in the power of the Holy Spirit.

Without the power of the Holy Spirit, Jesus would have been forced to use his own attributes as God to do such miraculous works and would have effectively nullified any chance you or I have of duplicating his works, much less of doing even greater ones. That inherent power the Son of God exercised in heaven is not ours because we are not God. Instead Jesus submitted himself as a man to God the Father and was empowered by the Holy Spirit to accomplish everything God sent him to do. The key to his success was humility, obedience, and the empowering of the Holy Spirit.

That is exactly the way God intended Adam to live out his life—in full obedience and totally submitted to the guidance of the Holy Spirit. But sin deafened his ears and dulled his heart to the gentle voice of God's Spirit. The first Adam refused to listen, choosing to do it his way and in his own power. In contrast, the last Adam chose to do it God's way and was readily equipped with God's power.

This is a crucial detail in understanding why Jesus came. He most certainly came to die for our sins. There is no question about that. His sinless life made him a suitable and perfect sacrifice. But he also came to show us how to walk with God once again. He came to restore that relationship with God, but he also came to give us an example of what that relationship looks like fleshed out in real life. This can only happen if we are willing to do it through the presence and in the power of the Holy Spirit. Sadly, this aspect is missing in the lives of too many Christians. This missing element, this unwillingness to submit ourselves and surrender to the leading of the Holy Spirit, has resulted in a ton of excuses and an open door for the devil to convince us God has another plan—a Plan B.

Plan A Restart

I do not believe that Jesus ever gave up the powers he enjoyed as the Second Person of the Trinity; I believe he chose not to use them so he could fully experience what you and I experience every day. This in no way diminishes who Jesus is as God, but it demonstrates on a more majestic scale the depth of his grand love for us and how far he was willing to go to restore and restart God's plan for our lives.

Everything Jesus accomplished after his baptism by John was done as a man fully dependent on and in the power of the Holy Spirit, and not as a result of using his own God-attributes. To be the last Adam, Jesus was required to live life in the same way the first Adam and every other Adam (human being) since has lived. That is the only way he can be realistically called the last Adam. It's more than a name; it is the fulfillment of a mission. It's the restoration of a way of life unknown to the descendants of Adam. If the word *last* is affixed to something, it means "final, ultimate, occurring after all the others, or the end." If Jesus is the last Adam as 1 Corinthians 15:45 declares that he is, then there are no more after him. He is the ultimate Adam—the last one. Therefore, Jesus fulfilled—filled full—everything that God required of man. He accomplished what every other man had utterly failed to do. No other Adam will follow him. It is finished, which is exactly the victorious parting words of Jesus as he gave up his life on the cross, taking our place as our substitute and paying for our sin with his life (John 19:30).

Jesus, as the last Adam, demonstrated how to effectively walk with God as a man filled with the presence and the power of the Holy Spirit. That was God's Plan A—taken directly off the original blueprints of creation. It's certainly worth considering, especially if we ever hope to do the things Jesus did.

As the Holy Spirit rested on Jesus, God spoke these words: "You are my beloved Son; in you I am well-pleased" (Luke 3:22). In saying this, the Father did two things: (1) he identified Jesus as his Son; and (2) validated who he was even before he did anything. Every child hungers for those two things. Jesus knew who he was (God the Son), but the Father declares it so that all creation (both seen and unseen) will know. The devil could not mistake or wonder from this point on about the identity of Jesus and the intentions of his mission. This is a declaration of war uttered in different words, but carrying the identical meaning as the prophecy of the woman's seed in Genesis 3:15. God the Father drew a line in the sand and unveiled his secret weapon—a man (his Son) who has no sin nature. One who can now meet the serpent on a level playing field. The challenge has been uttered, and the battle will soon be joined.

A Spirit-Filled Man

The term *Spirit-filled* intimidates most Christians. It has picked up a great deal of unnecessary baggage in the last two thousand years and conjures up images in the mind that may or may not be true. Let's strip away all those layers and simply define "Spirit-filled" as a person filled or saturated with the presence and power of the Holy Spirit. That is the biblical definition.

Jesus was a Spirit-filled man from the moment of his baptism as he stepped from the waters of the Jordan River. Luke tell us he was "full of the Holy Spirit" and "led by the Spirit" (Luke 4:1) into the Judean wilderness for his initial encounter with the devil. Here Jesus was tested just as Adam had been tested. Adam experienced this testing in a garden as he enjoyed the fullness of God. Jesus experienced it in the wilderness as he fasted and leaned on the faithfulness of God. Adam failed, but Jesus succeeded. How? By listening to the voice of the Holy Spirit.

The devil understood who Jesus was. He must have marveled as God unveiled the brilliance of the God/man portion of his plan. Like a football coach in the press box after a game-changing interception, the evil one makes what he considers the necessary adjustments and moves to thwart God's last move. Drawing from the memory of the damning damage experienced in a prior head-on attack of God, Satan adjusted and attempted to play head games, not with Jesus's divinity but with his humanity.

Jesus spent forty days fasting in the Judean wilderness—alone. Forty days is a long, long time to go without food, long enough that if you allow your mind to wander, it will come up with some elaborate mental images of food, which only complicates the immediate hunger issue. Therefore, Satan attacked both the soul and the flesh of Jesus's humanity. He struck a blow at his identity and his physical hunger.

"If you are the Son of God…" is the classic probe. Satan knew full well that Jesus was the Son of God. The voice of God had declared it in no uncertain terms. Its veracity was unquestionable. You could even translate Luke 4:3 this way: "Since you are the Son of God, use your God-power to turn these stones into bread." In other words, meet your human need out of your divine prerogative. Use your power as God—nobody will ever know. You are God! Satan is playing one nature against the other. His desire was to create a civil war, a rebellion between the human nature of Jesus and his divine nature.

The initial response of Jesus was to ignore the devil and listen carefully to the Holy Spirit. Then he responded with a verse of Scripture, likely memorized as a child but brought to mind by the Holy Spirit. Jesus overcomes not because he was God, but rather as a man by resting in God and allowing the Holy Spirit to fight the battle. Luke 4 records two more attempts by the devil, and both are met the same way.

We overcome the enemy's attacks and temptations the same way. We must listen to the Holy Spirit. Otherwise, we will lose every time. We cannot outthink the enemy. Our intellect is insufficient to face even the least of his temptations. Jesus quoted verses of Scripture; he did not engage in an intellectual sparring match. The last Adam refused to be drawn into the same trap that destroyed the first Adam. He overcame the temptations of the enemy as a Spirit-filled man who chose not to sin rather than doing it as God. If he overcame these temptations as God rather than as a man filled with the Spirit, then in reality there was no temptations because "God cannot be tempted by evil" (James

1:13). Yet Hebrews 2:18 is clear: "For since He [Jesus] Himself was tempted in that which He has suffered, He is able to come to the aid of those who are tempted."

Spirit-Filled Miracles?

Let us consider the miraculous works that Jesus demonstrated during his 3 and a half years of ministry. Can those works be duplicated by people like us? Can we really do even greater works than Jesus? That's what Jesus unequivocally declared in John 14:12.

In his hometown synagogue in Nazareth, Jesus affirmed the source of his power and anointing: "The Spirit of the Lord is upon Me because He has anointed me" (Luke 4:18). He was filled with the Spirit, and because of this, every work he would do was the result of the Spirit's working through him. Every miracle, every act of compassion and kindness, every "thing" Jesus did was a result of being filled with the Spirit. He fulfilled (filled full) the mission Adam abandoned.

Do you mean Jesus healed the sick in the power of the Holy Spirit rather than because he was God? That is exactly what I mean. His healing miracles were Spirit-filled miracles. He caused the lame to walk, fevers to disappear, the blind to see, the deaf to hear, and lepers were cleansed and their flesh regenerated. Disease, sickness, and infirmities fled when he spoke with authority through the Spirit's power and touched those bodies racked by pain.

The early Christians did the same works with the same power. Peter and John spoke with the Spirit's authority in the name of Jesus, and a beggar—lame from birth—leaped, walked, and danced in praise of God (Acts 3:1-10). Peter's shadow was used in Jerusalem to bring healing (Acts 5:15-16). Philip healed the lame and the paralyzed (Acts 8:6-7). God used Ananias to heal Paul's blindness (Acts 9:17-18). Paul healed the father of Publius who suffered with a recurrent fever and dysentery (Acts 28:8).

This miraculous activity did not stop with the apostles (Philip and Ananias were not apostles). It continued and was a significant part of the ministry of the early church for the first three hundred years. Regular Christians like you and me who were filled with the Spirit performed the same healing miracles Jesus did. But unbelief, compromise, and bad theology (not biblical theology) embraced by the clergy slowly shifted the right and authority to use the power of the Holy Spirit out of the hands of all Christians and into the hands of a select few (primarily the bishops). Over the centuries, the belief that all could imitate Christ was lost, persecuted, or spiritualized. And yet Jesus has given us his authority and his ability in the power of the Holy Spirit to participate in these kinds of Spirit-filled works.

Jesus also cast out demons. It was a normal part of his everyday ministry. How did he do it? He performed these deliverances as a man filled with the power of the Holy Spirit. Yes, the demons recognized that he was the Son of God, because he never ceased to be God. But if he did the exorcisms as God, we can't duplicate them because we are not God. He delivered those in bondage and set the captives free as the power of God—the Holy Spirit—flowed through his yielded humanity.

The ministry of casting out demons did not stop with Jesus. He empowered his followers to do the same with his authority and in the power of the Holy Spirit (Luke 9:1; 10:17). Peter ministered deliverance (Acts 5:15-16). Philip did so as well (Acts 8:5-7). Paul also had a deliverance ministry empowered by the Holy Spirit (Acts 16:14-18). Exorcism was an integral part of the ministry in the early church due to the prevalence of paganism and witchcraft. Like healing, it continued on a regular basis until unbelief, compromise, bad theology, and intellectualism forced it into the shadows or compromised its value with elaborate ritualism. Deliverance from the oppression of demons is a Spirit-filled miracle, and Jesus demonstrated this during his ministry on numerous occasions.

What about raising people from the dead? Surely, only God can do that. Jesus must have used his God-powers to accomplish that—didn't he? Jesus certainly raised several people from the dead, with Lazarus being the most spectacular demonstration of his power (he had been dead four days). But like healing and deliverance, if Jesus did it as God rather than as a man fully obedient to God and acting in the power of the Holy Spirit, we could never imitate his works in this area. Peter raised Tabitha, a young girl in Joppa who had fallen sick and died (Acts 9:36-42). Paul raised Eutychus, who had fallen three stories to his death during a rather lengthy sermon by the apostle (Acts 20:9-12).

There are many credible accounts of this miraculous work taking place throughout the centuries—and yes, even today. Sadly, our unbelief and skepticism has relegated this Spirit-filled miracle into the realm of the unbelievable. Yet our disbelief does not do away with the fact that Jesus and others accomplished these miracles through the power of the Holy Spirit.

What about the ability Jesus had that allowed him to know what certain people were thinking? Isn't that the omniscience of God at work? Perhaps, but it could also be a word of knowledge, wisdom, or the prophetic gift, all of which come as an enablement of the Holy Spirit. Jesus listened, and the Holy Spirit gave him exactly what he needed to deal with those situations. Peter did a similar thing as he discerned the lie of Ananias and Sapphira (Acts 5:1-10).

What about the miracles of nature? Walking on water and commanding the waves and wind to calm down is impossible, right? Only God has dominion over the forces of nature, doesn't he? Prior to the Fall, Adam and Eve were given dominion over the earth. The first Adam lost that right in the Fall, but the last Adam restored it through his obedience to the Father. Jesus acted and spoke in faith and exercised the power of the Holy Spirit, and creation obeyed. Peter walked on the water. His walk was short, but its distance was proportional to his faith. But the fact still remains—Peter walked on water!

Every miracle, every sermon, and every act Jesus participated in was empowered and enabled by the Spirit of God. Jesus was not a carnival act doing a miracle a minute on the midway to draw a crowd or even to prove the power of an omnipotent God. He never demonstrated his power as a means of coercing people into belief. Faith, not a miracle, is the essence of belief. The Incarnation enabled Jesus to be the last Adam who fully obeyed the Father in every thought and act. Everything Jesus did prior to the Resurrection, he saw the Father doing (John 5:19-20) or heard the Father giving permission to do (John 5:30-32). Jesus came to do what Adam failed to do—partner with God through the power of the Spirit in a relationship that would allow him to be everything God had created the man and the woman to be.

Restored and Reclaimed

Everything Adam lost has been restored in Jesus Christ.
Everything?
Yes, everything!
What about the garden? You certainly can't believe God has restored the garden! In a manner of speaking—yes, not yet, and definitely. The garden setting was simply the place God met with his kids. So in that respect, wherever you meet with God is your garden. It is important to understand what the priority is here. It's not the garden that's the end-all and be-all, and it never was. It was the identity God gave Adam as a son and the relationship he was granted to experience the intimate presence of God. That identity has now been restored through the finished work of the last Adam, and that relationship can once again be experienced as fully as we desire. Remember, it was not the garden of God, but rather the God of the garden who makes all the difference.

And yes, eventually when everything is complete, and God's eschatological clock has run its course and the presence of sin has been cast into hell with the devil and his angels, we will once again dwell in the literal garden from which the garden of Eden was modeled. That is the promise of the last Adam: "To him who overcomes, I will grant to eat of the tree of life, which is in the Paradise [i.e., the garden] of God" (Revelation 2:7).

> *And he showed me a river of the water of life, clear as crystal, coming from the throne of God and of the Lamb, in the middle of its street. And on either side of the river was the tree of life, bearing twelve kinds of fruit, yielding its fruit every month; and the leaves of the tree were for the healing of the nations. And there shall no longer be any curse; and the throne of God and of the Lamb shall be in it, and his bondservants shall serve Him; and they shall see His face, and His name shall be on their foreheads. And there shall no longer be any night; and they shall not have need of the light of a lamp nor the light of the sun, because the Lord God shall illumine them and they shall reign forever*

and ever (Revelation 22:1-5).

The word *last* can also mean *finally,* as in "at last" all things are restored. God's Plan A is complete, fully and finally in place. History will return again to the place where it was derailed, and the Designer and Engineer of this magnificent plan "will give to the one who thirsts from the spring of the water of life without cost. He who overcomes shall inherit these things, and I will be his God and he shall be My son" (Revelation 21:6-7).

This is the promise of the last Adam for all who place their faith in him and live out their faith through him. We are the sons and daughters of God, who once again have the capability restored to reflect, reproduce, and rule out of our relationship with our heavenly Father. That identity has been reclaimed by the last Adam and is available to us right now. Definitely!

Chapter 6
A New Species

> And Jesus is the image of the invisible
> God, firstborn of all creation.
> ~ Paul, the Apostle

The lion is known universally as the king of the jungle—the king of beasts. This majestic cat, through the centuries, has been idolized as a symbol of power, royalty, and strength. Tyrants, emperors, and kings have metaphorically linked themselves and their kingdoms to these great cats for centuries. Jesus Christ, our King, is called the Lion from the tribe of Judah (Revelation 5:5).

An interesting discovery was certified in 2012 in the scientific community concerning lions. It would almost seem a no-brainer that as populated as the world is and as large as lions are, all the species of lions would have already been discovered. If you are like me and that's what you thought, you would be wrong.

We now know that the scientific community has discovered a new lion species hidden right under their noses in, of all places, a zoo. You read that correctly—in a zoo! And of all the biospheres out there, a zoo in Ethiopia! They have suspected it for several years, but the tests are conclusive. A new lion species will be designated and listed under the binomial nomenclature of *Panthera Leo*.

These lions are the descendants of a population of cats that were originally placed in the Addis Ababa zoo in 1948 by Emperor Haile Selassie, perhaps as living symbols of the lion wearing a crown and carrying a cross that emblazoned the Ethiopian flag during his reign. Over the past 65 years, these lions have bred and reproduced in captivity, producing a robust pride of distinctively dark-mane cats. They have raised eyebrows and questions in the scientific world for several years.

The Addis Ababa lions have a regal, distinctive dark mane that grows from the head, neck, and down under the chest, making them unlike any other lions in the world. These lions are also a bit smaller and more compact in stature. The belief for many years was that these characteristics might have occurred due to inbreeding in captivity, but that theory was dispelled after careful testing in 2012.

DNA samples were taken from eight males and seven females and put through a battery of extensive testing. As a result, international researchers have used the results of that testing to declare the dark mane lion of Addis Ababa a new and special species of lion. These lions are similar to all the other lions in the world, yet distinctively different.

And as always, it is this distinction that makes one unique! Unique is always the fingerprint of God and the handiwork of his magnificent plan.

A Brief Science Lesson

I was an average student of the sciences in high school and college, and as such took only the required courses. In high school, biology was required, and we were given a choice between physics and chemistry. I chose physics (not realizing it was math in wolves' clothing) for the simple reason that I had no desire to memorize the periodic table of elements, which was required in chemistry. It was a dismal choice because it was far into the second semester before I ever solved a physics problem satisfactorily.

On the other hand, I enjoyed the study of biology. My teacher, Miss Etta Pearl Bradley, was a wonderful single woman, married to the sciences and her chosen profession of education. She inspired me with the required insect collection assignment and her love of the pickled creatures we used as she taught us the fine art of surgical dissection. Oh, I can still smell the formaldehyde, feel the *ooey-gooey* consistency of the fetal pig entrails, and hear the squeal of delight Miss Bradley would utter when a student finally found the assigned element of our dissection exercises. It is from the recesses of my faint memory of things learned in her class that I now speak.

All organisms are biologically classified in groups. Originally these classifications were grouped in species with shared physical characteristics. A species is a group of organisms with a shared closed gene pool. This makes each species unique, like the Addis Ababa lions. They may be similar in many ways to all the other lions in the world, yet they stand alone because of their unique mane and compact stature. Therefore, they are a new species of lion.

Biologists use several methods for determining the species of an animal. The most common requirement is that an animal is able to mate with another of like kind and produce fertile offspring. Another method in classifying species is by examining the animal's physical features, which is called morphology. The method used with the lions of Addis Ababa was the genetic species concept. Here the genes—the DNA—are tested and must be defined by using genetic markers, which is the principle behind DNA bar coding. Using these methods and many more, scientists are discovering hundreds of new species all around the globe.

As human beings, we fit rather comfortably or uncomfortably (depending on your world view) in this classification system. Personally, I believe human beings are created in the image and the likeness of God, not the other choice of the image and likeness of some ancient hominoid. Scientifically, human beings are classified as *Homo sapiens*. In Latin, *homo* equals "man" and *sapiens* means "knowing." The meaning of *Homo sapiens* is "wise or knowing man." Human beings, according to science, are the only living species of the genus *Homo*. Meaning, if you boil it down scientifically, only one species of human beings now exist on this earth.

But—is there a possibility that this belief is totally wrong? Could science ultimately be wrong? Could there be another species of human beings among us? Before you laugh and conclude I am mad, please hear me out. Animal biologists once thought all the lion species had been identified, categorized, and catalogued. Yet, located in a zoo, in plain sight of hundreds of visitors each week, were the Addis Ababa dark-mane lions, a new and unique species. What if the same is true in your community, or God forbid—your church? What if a new species of human being now walks this earth?

What if...indeed!

A Closer Look at Origins

The theory of evolution would tell us that human beings are descendants of an ape-like family of creatures known as *hominidae*, a branch of the primate family tree. It seems, according to that theory, this transformation has taken about sixty-five million years, give or take a million or so. Well, I'll be a monkey's uncle or my uncle was a monkey, whichever you prefer. I don't prefer either and don't buy what this theory is selling. The theory of evolution is diametrically opposed to biblical teaching and the creation account found in Genesis 1 and 2.

When a person investigates their genealogical tree, they are often drawn back to the origins of their family. As one searches for their true identity in Christ, that person must follow the branches back to their origin if he ever has any hopes of moving forward in discovering who he is in Christ. Rest assured, your journey back to your origins will not culminate on a limb filled with hominoids.

Genesis 1:26-28 is very clear where human beings came from—where you and I came from. God created Adam and Eve in his image and according to his likeness. God spoke everything else he created into existence, but he formed man and fashioned woman. Our origin is from the dirt, which in Hebrew is *adamah*, the basis of Adam's name. I know we have already discussed this, but bear with me. Adam was the first human being created. He was unique among all the other creatures God created. There was none like him, which is exactly why God created the woman. In God's own words, "It is not good for the man to be alone" (Genesis 2:18). Adam was the only human being formed from the dust of the earth. He was unique. God followed up the amazing feat by forming an equally astonishing partner whom we call Eve. Together, according to the Bible, they formed what scientists would like to call "the only extant species of genus *Homo*." To be biblically true, we must remove the term *extant*. They were it—the fountainhead of the human species.

As human beings, this amazing couple possessed all the same abilities and characteristics that are common to all human beings. All, that is, except one. Adam and Eve were created without a sin nature—in a state of holiness or spiritual and moral purity. They were a unique species.

God endowed them with the ability to choose, a gift of tremendous potential and gave them only one prohibition, which forbade them to eat from the tree of the knowledge of good and evil. With the prohibition came a penalty—death. If they ever tasted it, the extant would become extinct.

The moment their greedy little mouths enveloped the succulent allure of that forbidden fruit Adam and Eve died. Stone cold dead! Dead as dead can be! Dead as a door nail! *Wait a minute,* you may argue, *but they were still alive. They ran and hid from God. They were forced out of the garden. They had kids.* Concerning that, I would almost agree with you—at least in ninety-nine percent of it.

The moment the poison of the fruit entered their system, the species of human being God created ceased to exist. That species vanished. That is, they died. Theologically, we might refer to it as a spiritual death. They were no longer able to commune or intimately fellowship with God. Dead in their trespasses and sins as Ephesians 2:1 so succinctly puts it. Make no mistake about it, this couple—this unique species of human being—never made it to the Endangered Species List, thereby guaranteeing them special protection. They went directly to the top of the extinction list, the very first.

Their holiness was gone. What made them unique as creatures was lost. It could not be transmitted to the next generation. It could not be reproduced. The ability disappeared to reproduce the original package as created.

In the blink of an eye one species of human beings vanished and another replaced it. A species clothed in sin rather than holiness appeared, created through an act of disobedience. They appeared from all natural appearances to be the same. They looked the same—each with a head, two eyes, two ears, a nose, and mouth—a torso with two arms, two hands with five fingers each, two legs, two feet, with five toes on each foot. They spoke with the same voices. Inside their bodies a heart continued to beat and a brain assessed the sensations of senses and sent the appropriate electrical currents and commands for the proper response. But they would never be the same because the man and the woman, the one-of-a-kind species God created, had ceased to exist.

Some might call what was left a mutation, but whatever you call this species, it is not the same one God created. And yet God still loved *Homo sapiens* and chose to pour out his grace on them. His plan was to bring them back from the extinction list because extinction nullifies God's Plan A.

It is vital that we grasp the importance and the meaning of that one single choice made by our ancestral grandparents. Our seemingly backward journey over previously shared truth is really a step forward to help us grasp our identity. This is our origin, where we all come from. This is the root of our natural family tree. This is the soil from which we sprang. Each human being emerges from a mother's womb with the same stuff we find hiding in the deep bushes of Genesis 3. This is the species that every father reproduces and every mother has borne. That is, with the sole exception of a young Jewish virgin of the first century named Mary, who gave birth to a new species (technically the original species) of human being—the last Adam. We call him Jesus.

The Last of a Lost Species

While the scientists of today dream and discuss the ability and feasibility of cloning long extinct animals, a process called "de-extinction," God acted, not through cloning, but through a miraculous event called the Incarnation as discussed in Chapter 5. This supernatural de-extinction by God resulted in the arrival of the Son of God into the physical realm of planet earth. God the Son clothed himself in the flesh of man. And the flesh he took on was the same kind the first Adam was created with, down to the smallest of the original details. This dread extinction now becomes a dynamic intervention of grace. The last Adam now resumed the role abdicated by the first Adam.

Like Adam in his original state, Jesus the man was without sin. God is not the Creator of the sin nature, therefore it was noticeably absent in Jesus. He was knit together in Mary's womb in holiness, a unique purity in both moral and spiritual nature. Two separate and definitively different species of *Homo sapiens* now walked the earth.

As Jesus matured physically, emotionally, and spiritually, he was both common to and distinct from all the other people around him. If from a human standpoint you had been given the responsibility of identifying him out of a crowd of a hundred or fifty or a dozen, it is very likely you would not have been able to do so. Scripture is very clear that "there was nothing beautiful or majestic about his appearance, nothing to attract us to him" (Isaiah 53:2 NLT). In other words, Jesus did not stand out physically. As a Jewish male, he was of average height, weight, and looks, with dark hair, dark eyes, a beard, and olive-colored skin. His appearance was common with the other men of his race and historical period. Contrary to all the art work and iconography of the Middle Ages, Jesus had no luminous halo floating around his head that indicated his holiness to those around him.

Neither would his dress have caused him to stand out. As a Jewish man of the first century he would have worn a linen tunic held in place with a leather belt, cloth sash, or a simple piece of rope. Over his tunic, he would have worn a square mantel around his shoulders with blue tassels sown on each corner. Add to this outfit a pair of leather or wooden sandals, and Jesus looked like every other man you would have met in Israel.

No one, now or then, would have ever known with their natural eyes that Jesus was anything more than an average Jewish male. Yet Jesus was different (without even bringing in the God part of who he was) as a human being. That difference is demonstrated in his actions and understood through his words. He was a man fully surrendered to God in thought, word, and deed. No darkness resided in him. There is wisdom, yet innocence. There is gentleness, yet authority. There is unconditional love displayed, yet unconditional obedience demanded. There is holiness, yet a willingness to stoop down in mercy to take hold of a hand shackled with chains forged in the fires of sin. There is full acceptance, yet the demand of complete discipleship. There is power demonstrated, yet weakness portrayed. There is complete sacrifice, yet total victory.

Jesus, as a man, is the ultimate paradox, a paradox of species. He is what Adam was created to be. He did what Adam failed to do. He was like Adam in his original state, yet the utter opposite of what Adam became. Jesus was a new species of man alone in a world teeming with the dying species of fallen Adam. And that is why he is referred to as the last Adam. He was the last example of a species (humanity without the sin nature) long thought to be extinct. Nevertheless, here he was standing at center stage of the apex of both human and salvation history. Plan A is proceeding at full speed, and the mystery of the ages is about to be revealed for all to see.

A New Intruder in the Garden

For centuries Satan had done everything in his power to spoil God's plan. Beginning with the forbidden fruit salad of lies in the ancient garden up through the slaughter of all the baby boys in Bethlehem, he had responded quickly and decisively to every threat. He knew the prophecy. He had heard it clearly from the very lips of God that day in the garden. Over and over through the centuries, it had been restated by the prophets. He had listened to the prayers of the faithful over the centuries crying out for a deliverer they called Messiah, the one who would someday set them free. The serpent had worked hard to silence that nonsense by inciting extermination plots using the Egyptians, the Babylonians, and even the Romans as his henchmen. He had taken the Messianic teachings and perverted them so that most of the Jews dreamed of a mythological warrior who would restore Israel to the golden age of King David.

If there was one thing the devil was sure of, it was that God would keep his promise. He would send a Messiah. And knowing this, his relentless vigilance and the ability to strike quickly were essential. When the time came, he would either trip up this deliverer or, if need be, kill him and thus deliver the ultimate *coup de grâce*.

Suddenly the wait was over and the mystery One's identity became evident. As John the Baptist lifted Jesus from beneath the swirling waters of the Jordan River, God spoke, and his words echoed through both the spiritual and physical atmosphere verifying the identity of Jesus (Mark 1:11). The last Adam was now fully unveiled. God validated his identity and unleashed his legitimacy.

The next three and one half years would be a running battle between Jesus and Satan. Tripping Jesus up proved to be impossible. It did not work with the head-to-head temptations in the wilderness. The adulation of the crowds and their desire to make him king failed. Endless questions carefully crafted with a hope that he would incriminate himself by breaking a commandment failed to accomplish their purpose. The religious leaders failed to twist his words into a charge of treason. At every step in this cosmic life-and-death struggle, Jesus prevailed. Since that fateful moment in the garden, no man had stood face-to-face with the serpent and not blinked at some point in the battle. Jesus did not blink. He did not back up. He stood firm in the presence and power of the Holy Spirit.

The devil was frustrated. His temptations were useless against Jesus, as were the entanglements of sin. Therefore the only option left to Satan was to coil one last time, strike, and kill this intruder who had come into what he now considered *his* garden.

God's Altar

The death of Jesus on the cross was the dividing moment of history. As the last Adam, Jesus had fully obeyed God as a man filled with the Holy Spirit. He accomplished what God had envisioned and planned in eternity past, long before he created Adam or Eve. Jesus executed the one and only plan of God to perfection, and then he gave his life for the rest of Adam's seed. Many see the events of the crucifixion as a tragedy, a prophet who found himself at odds with the religious and secular governments of his day. Some see him as a religious zealot with a Messianic complex who forced the authorities to execute him, a sort of spiritual suicide. Neither is correct.

As the last Adam, Jesus did what no other member of the human race could do. As sinless, he could willingly offer his life for you and me, in our place. Remember the penalty for disobedience that resonates throughout human history from the moment God gave Adam that single command to this very moment: *"In the day that you...you shall surely die!"* Death is the end result of sin. "For the wages [the payment for the work rendered] of sin is death" (Romans 6:23). Sin kills us, but sin could not kill Jesus. It had no grip on him and no power over him. Jesus, in his humanity, was the last of a sin-free species. He was morally perfect and holy which made him the only sacrifice that could satisfy the righteousness of God. In his death, he would save many.

The cross of Calvary was the ultimate altar of the Levitical sacrificial system of lambs, goats, and bulls illustrated in the Old Testament. It is the same as the visual imagery and metaphor fleshed out as Abraham was poised to offer Isaac, the son of promise, on the altar in Genesis 22. It is the same picture painted through a repentant King David as he built an altar on the newly purchased threshing floor on Mount Moriah, previously owned by a Jebusite, and the future location of the Temple. And the enemy missed it. There in front of his nose since the moment God had slain the animals of the garden to cover Adam and Eve was the very means whereby the amazing plan of God would be played out. And Lucifer missed it!

All he could see was the final extinction of the species God had de-extincted. All Satan could think of was the extermination of this troublemaker. And in his zeal, the devil missed what was so obvious and thus sealed his doom at the hands of the very species he held in such disdain. A human being, an Adam, albeit the last Adam, defeated the devil at the cross.

Although Satan fueled the envious lust that enflamed the Jewish religious establishment, driving them to arrest and turn Jesus over to the Romans, Satan did not kill him. Although the Romans, cruel masters of both torture and execution, nailed Jesus to the cross, they did not kill him. Jesus was not killed or murdered. Rather he was sacrificed on God's altar. He was offered up by his Father as he willingly surrendered his own life like all those innocent lambs that had preceded him.

Isaiah 53 uses phrases like *smitten of God and afflicted* (v. 4) and *the Lord was pleased to crush Him, putting Him to death* (v. 10) in describing God's wrath for sin. God made Jesus "who knew no sin to be sin on our behalf, that we might become the righteousness of God in Him" (2 Corinthians 5:21). The sinless species literally became sin so that the sinful species could be set free. The last Adam died to liberate the first one plus all his posterity.

And—Satan missed it. He missed the mystery of the ages.

A Lion Species

Jesus was dead. The sinless One had met the same fate as every other human being before him, or so it seemed. Death had claimed its prize, and God's little rescue plan was thwarted—or so it seemed.

The resurrection of Jesus was the end of what the cross began. As God the Father breathed life back into his Son through the Holy Spirit, a new day dawned. A day that pointed back to that sixth day, when God had breathed his breath, his *Ruach*—his Spirit—into Adam and he became a living soul. The imagery of these two events is strikingly similar. The lifeless body of Jesus on that stone shelf in the tomb prefigures the lifeless clay that would become Adam in the garden. I use the word *prefigure* because the events that occurred in that garden tomb three days after Jesus's death on the cross had their origin in eternity past. That event took place in the mind of God before the literal site of the event was created by the hand of God. This had always been the plan of God—God's Plan A. There was no Plan B. This may boggle our minds, but God is not bound by time. He is not limited or empowered by the past, present, or future. He created time and is thus free of its constraints.

Throughout this chapter, we have spoken of a new species of man. At the resurrection that man was fully unleashed. The man—Jesus—arose from the dead, having overcome the power of sin, death, and the grave. He destroyed the unquestioned dominion the devil had enjoyed for centuries. The four horsemen (Satan, sin, death, and the grave) of the human apocalypse had ridden roughshod over humanity for centuries, but now they were vanquished. Everything that resulted from the first Adam's disobedience had now been conquered. It was now time to complete the plan, to implement the final few pieces of the puzzle.

Jesus, as the last Adam, had fulfilled God's original mandate of reflection, relationship, and rulership given to Adam at his creation. Jesus reflected God perfectly. We know this because "in Him all the fullness of Deity dwells in bodily form" (Colossians 2:9). Jesus is "the image of the invisible God, the first-born of creation" (Colossians 1:15). Over and over throughout the Gospels, Jesus would declare that he and the Father were one. Oneness is the hallmark of relationship. Oneness equals intimacy. As for rulership, the human lineage of Jesus is undeniably rooted in the house of King David. The blood of Israel's most famous and powerful king flowed through his veins. Jesus was the fulfillment of the perpetual promise given to David that his kingdom would never end. The only thing that remained unfinished was the reproductive aspect of the original mandate. God's fundamental plan had been for this new species to "be fruitful and multiply, and fill the earth" (Genesis 1:28).

It seemed that a new species of Lion, one from the tribe of Judah, now roamed the garden. But like the first Adam, after his initial breath, Jesus was alone, the only one of his kind. There were no others of his species. His humanity was unique before the resurrection. Now there are no words to describe his composition and being. He was without sin, now he is glorified.

But the issue of reproduction still remains. For a species to truly be a new species it must have the capability of reproducing—of producing offspring that are like the original, made in his image and likeness. Please understand I am not talking about you or me becoming a god. Human beings will never be gods. But remember, Jesus took on humanity, and his death on the cross and subsequent resurrection and glorification did nothing to diminish his humanity even though he is still God. He has always been God, but from the moment of his Incarnation, he will never cease being human.

For the plan to be complete, offspring must be produced who can reproduce. There was no Eve. There was no counterpart, no consort. Unlike all the pagan myths that fill antiquity, God had no mate. There was no Mrs. God.

Yet in the portrait God brushed into the details of the Eden's landscape, the creation of Eve does give us a picture that will foreshadow future events. It is a clue to the plan God was unfolding. God created a mate for Adam by taking the raw materials from Adam's own body. Eve was fashioned from flesh, bone, tissue, and blood out of Adam's side. The mate of Jesus would not come "out of" his body, but rather would be placed back "into him and become a body." Here is the reversal of the original, the mystery of salvation unfolded.

The Sons and Daughters of God

You may be thinking, *Where are you going with this? I thought this book was a tool I could use to find my identity, who I am and why I am here.* It is, but it is essential for you to understand where you came from if you want to learn where you are going. In this case the details of the trip are just as important as the destination. Tragically, most Christians have heard Jesus came, lived, and died so that their sin debt could be paid for. That is an amazing truth, but only a small part of God's plan for you. His plan includes far more. The last Adam came to restore through his obedience everything the first Adam forfeited by his disobedience. Identity must have stable roots to produce a tree that is capable of yielding a rich harvest of fruit. It is vital that we understand our origin, our root, if we hope to reproduce the fruit of Jesus and do the works he did and the even greater ones he promised in John 14:12.

God's only plan, his Plan A, is seamless and clear. Yet for the most part, we, as the Church, have convoluted its simplicity. And thus unwittingly, we have held its life-changing power captive and hidden its truths away from ourselves and others where we needed it most. We don't realize who we are in Christ because we have not grasped the message of the whole gospel. That is, we have only internalized a small portion of the good news.

One of the most powerful, yet mysterious, verses of Scripture is found in 2 Corinthians 5:17. It is often quoted and routinely memorized, but the problem is we have not taken time to grasp the reality it sets forth and the potential this reality holds. It could change your life and introduce you to the real you if you are in Christ. "Therefore if any man is in Christ, he is a new creature; the old things passed away; behold, new things have come." The New King James Version states, "Therefore if anyone is in Christ, he is a new creation; the old things have passed away; behold, all things have become new."

Throughout this chapter, we have used the word *species* to describe a person or animal that is unique in its characteristics and origins. The dark-mane lions of Addis Ababa are unlike all the other lions in the world, but they are lions. Jesus, prior to his resurrection, was like Adam in his original state. He was fully human. After his resurrection, he was unlike any other human being who has ever lived. He was a human being resurrected from the dead with a glorified body, a body designed and equipped for eternal life.

Paul, in 2 Corinthians 5:17, now describes the people who are in Christ as new creations. In other words, they are unique, they are a new species, unlike the *Homo sapiens* they are now rubbing shoulders with. Let that settle in for a few moments. If you know Christ, you are a new species of human being, alike in many ways, yet creatively different from those who have yet to meet Christ.

Attention! Attention! Here's a news flash you will not see on the cable or network news: Jesus is reproducing a new species of human beings who will be like him. He is creating a body for himself. This body is called the Church, as the apostle Paul so carefully describes it in 1 Corinthians 12:27: "Now you are Christ's body, and individually members of it." We know that language, but we have mistakenly endowed it on lifeless brick and mortar rather than on the *new creation* it was intended for. Every Christian is both a corporate member and an individual member of this body. Every believer is a part of that corporate unity, but each believer is also individually unique in manifesting the glory of Jesus.

The ability to produce offspring that can procreate is the key test if something is to be considered a new species. Being unique is not enough. And that is exactly what Jesus has done in the Church. He is spiritually reproducing himself every time a person comes to faith in Christ. Every time a believer shares the gospel, that person is sowing the spiritual seeds of Jesus Christ. Christians do not reproduce physically. In other words, just because your mother and father were believers does not mean you automatically become one at your birth. Every person must experience God's grace and place their personal faith in Christ's finished work to be born again. Every person is born in sin according to Scripture. At the moment of salvation, when by grace through faith a person comes to Jesus Christ and that person's sins are forgiven, the old person ceases to exist. That is the definitive testimony of 2 Corinthians 5:17.

But there's far more. Yes, one creature dies, but a new creature is created. Not a new creature in time, but rather a new creature in quality, created in the form and likeness of Jesus Christ. The old things are gone—finished, extinct. A new creature is created through the process of a personal regeneration through the power of the Holy Spirit. Jesus, in conversation with Nicodemus in John 3, called this being "born again," or being "born from above" or "born of the Spirit." With this language, Jesus designates our new birth as the handiwork of the Holy Spirit, who was also the initiator of Christ's own miraculous birth. The source is the same, with the results being astonishingly similar to the creation of a new species. Through the regenerating power of the Holy Spirit, the characteristics of the Lion of Judah are passed to a new generation, and his "pride" of young lions continues to increase. For two thousand years, the fountainhead of this new species has been quietly filling this blue planet with reflections of who he is so that they might in turn reflect the glory of God, which is exactly what the first Adam failed to do. Jesus has been repopulating creation with a new species, reproducing himself in them. "So it is written, 'the first man, Adam, became a living soul.' The last Adam became a life-giving spirit" (1 Corinthians 15:45). We have all borne the image of the first, but now as the sons and daughters, God lets us discover the image of the last Adam and bear it as well.

This is not some science fiction movie plot with undetected body-snatching aliens masquerading as humans. No, the Lion of Judah has loosed his offspring and is re-introducing them to a garden once again to be "fruitful and multiply and fill the earth." You are not just another human being stuck in a dead-end existence, waiting for death to set you free so you can experience the wonder of heaven. No, eternal life began for you the moment you met Jesus, but maybe you're not experiencing its abundance. If that's the case, it's time you discovered who you really are and what it truly means to be a genuine son or daughter of the King, a new species "in Christ."

Chapter 7
It's All about Location

> A place without meaning
> is no place to be.
> ~ W. G. Trotman

In May of 2011, I became a church planter. It was a dream God had placed deep within my spirit many years before at the beginning of my ministry. At that time, he had even given me the name for the church (Eagle's Wing) and assured me that it would be in the northern area of the county I had grown up in. But for whatever reason, mainly the sovereignty of God, he never opened the door to fulfill the dream he had planted within me.

Church planting is hard work—extremely hard—and I am no longer as young and energetic as I once was. In fact, I fully understand the old ministry maxim I had heard over the last couple of years from other pastors when I mentioned my dream of planting a church. They would say, "Young guys plant churches; old guys like us look for a place to retire from." In other words, experienced ministers rarely plant new churches. It's far too much work. Settle in to a church, put down some roots, and spend your ministry serving those people. Certainly there is nothing wrong with what my friends were telling me, as long as that's God's calling for you. But their calling was not my calling.

Hard cannot even begin to describe these last two years. Everything we've done as a church has been difficult. Nothing has been easy. Achieving the best often comes with a grueling price tag. Church planting is certainly not for pastoral wimps and ecclesiastical prima donnas. Two constant sources of encouragement have been my calling from God and the willingness of the people I serve to reach for God's best, rather than for what is good or easy. Together we are seeing Eagle's Wing Church become a place of refuge, restoration, and relationship.

Perhaps the issue that has caused me the most anxiety has been finding an adequate place to meet. I've spent countless hours praying about this issue and then putting feet on my prayers by chasing leads and making phone calls. God honors both when they're done in tandem rather than when either is done alone.

Eventually, before we launched on September 11, 2011, God opened the door for us to lease a cafeteria and a hallway in a local elementary school on Sunday mornings. Due to the rules of the local school board, we knew it would only be for twelve months. Every Sunday morning we transported everything we would need to have a service, nursery, and children's classes to the school in a delivery truck and a twelve-foot open trailer I pulled behind my pickup. And every Sunday after service, we would re-load the chairs, the musical equipment, the nursery and children's gear and prepare for the next Sunday, all the while praying for sunny skies. We looked like the Beverly Hillbillies on their way from the Arkansas Ozarks to Beverly Hills, California.

Location is a big deal in church planting. Visibility and ease of access are the types of advertisement money cannot buy. People have to know you're there if you have any hopes of reaching them. I never thought much about it because I was only concerned with finding a "place" to meet. God was interested in *the* location where we would meet. Our first year was spent in a school visible from Interstate 65 just off a major exit right outside the city limits of Birmingham. Months of planning and large amounts of money could not have secured a better location, but God did.

As our time in the school came to an end, the angst of uncertainty overwhelmed me again. Where do we go? What do we do? God already had a place picked out, we just had to find it, and eventually we did. For the past year we have been in a rented commercial space three miles farther up I-65. This space is the first building you see when you exit the interstate at one of the main exits just north of Birmingham. I could have dreamed and dreamed about such a location, but in my wildest dreams, a choice spot like this would not have crossed my mind. Yet God had us covered all along. He placed us in a location we would not have been able to rent a few months later due to the implementation of a new zoning ordinance by the local city government. Though this is still a temporary location, we no longer look like the Clampetts on Sunday morning with our trucks and trailer filled to overflow with the all furnishings required to stage a worship service and train children.

At Eagle's Wing, we have learned a valuable lesson about God. Location, location, location—God (not just the real estate agent or the savvy business person) is all about location. It's not the place you are at; rather it's the location you are *in* that really matters.

Moving On Up

Throughout much of the world today, the location of one's birth determines the destination and extent of one's life. In other words, a baby born into a wealthy family usually enjoys an affluent life and a baby born into a poor family struggles with poverty. In many places there are only two classes: the rich and the poor. There is no in-between, no middle class. A large part of that person's identity is then thrust upon them due to the location of their natural birth. *Who* they are and *what* they may be able to achieve are often limited by location factors that are geographical, social, religious, or economic. Often this is a sad but true reality of the world in which we live.

Many years ago, I was part of a mission team that spent a week in inner city New Orleans leading a Vacation Bible School for children. I still remember arriving at the Carver Center located on Annunciation Street around 10 PM that Friday night in June and seeing several children under the age of six playing all alone in the street. I later learned their mothers were prostitutes and locked their kids out while they worked. It was my first introduction to real poverty and the chains it forges on those who are trapped in it.

Many who lived in this neighborhood were extremely poor. Jobs were few and far between. Transportation was limited. Most could not afford their own vehicles, and public transportation was costly. Prostitution and drug dealing were commonplace. Real opportunity was almost non-existent. Poverty was more than an economic issue; it was a generational issue. Poverty was all the people who lived in this neighborhood had ever known. There in that place poverty was a reality.

I grew up in a rural area north of Birmingham, Alabama. My

father was a coal miner and my mother, a school teacher. We were not rich, but we had what we needed. I had been taught from an early age that if you worked hard, you could go far. If you wanted it badly enough, you could do anything. That was the American dream, a manifest destiny chock full of opportunity. It was why my immigrant forefathers left Scotland and came to this country. It was the promise of a hope and a future.

On our last night on Annunciation Street, I sat down and talked for several hours with a young man from the neighborhood who was working that summer as an intern at the Carver Center. Due to his amazing musical ability and the help of some influential people, he had been awarded a full scholarship to a prestigious music school in New England and would be moving to pursue a college degree that fall. As we talked, I asked him about the neighborhood and what would happen to the other kids we had learned to love. If I live to be a hundred, I don't think I will ever forget his reply. "Nothing changes here. Unless you get a lucky break and can escape it, what you see is all you will ever have. There's no hope here! You can't overcome it. If you stay here it will overwhelm you!" These were the words of a teenager, just barely eighteen years old, yet wise beyond his years with street experience.

Poverty had become a way of life, a hopeless condition in which far too many people are still trapped throughout this world. I naively believed if you worked hard enough you could rise above it, but in this case you had to escape it and leave it behind. That person had to get out of the place (often the trap is more mental and emotional than geographical) he was trapped in. It was more than a physical condition; it was a mindset of hopelessness engrained by tragic circumstances over decades. As we talked that night, I realized this young man's only hope for a better quality of life was to escape the location in which he had been born. He put it this way: "I have to get out! If I stay, I will become what you see out there. I have to get out, relocate, leave!"

Spiritual poverty is just as real as economic poverty. And many Christians are trapped in a kind of hopeless spiritual poverty that only allows them to rise so high. Many of the beliefs we hold are neither true nor biblical. We have bought the lies of the devil over the centuries and replaced the truth of God with a cheap facsimile.

Far too many followers of Christ believe that God is angry at them, just waiting for them to make a mistake so he can wallop them upside the head with the back of his divine hand. Some are trapped in the maze of works, believing if they can do just a little more, work a little harder or longer, then God will love them more. Others are convinced that most of the promises of God are for tomorrow, and like Little Orphan Annie sing that little song, believing one day soon the sun really will come up, but it's always tomorrow, never today. Some have dug foxholes or built survival bunkers they call churches, and are nervously sequestered or desperately awaiting the Rapture and/or the *Parousia* of Christ, hoping they can remain pure and thus not miss his coming. They are so afraid of being contaminated by what they have designated the sinners of this world that they have forgotten why Jesus came—for the sinners of this world.

Yet others are going through the motions of religious ritual without ever experiencing true life in Christ. And yes, there are many, perhaps legions, who dutifully believe God no longer does the things he once did in the Old and New Testaments—that he has somehow changed because we have the final revelation of his Word neatly printed on paper and protected with a supple calfskin binding. We have tossed the new identity Christ died to give us and instead embraced the poverty of a religious system that systematically beats us down, rather than one that steadily lifts us up. Jesus did not die on a cross so that you or I could enjoy this daily beat-down. He took our beating so that he might lift us up to a new level, i.e., a new location "in Christ." This new identity he has given us means everything. We are moving on up! And it's all about location, location, location!

Shackled to a Mindset

Like a child born into physical poverty, all of us were born into spiritual poverty. There is no class system, no hierarchy, no rich or poor, no differentiation with regard to our spiritual condition once we make our entrance into this world at our birth. We are not born Christians at our physical birth. The playing field is level for all of us—the first Adam made sure of that for certain. We were all born into sin, physically alive but spiritually dead, sinners who have inherited the sin nature of our forefathers and then willingly and willfully sinned as well on our own. That's depressing and not popular, but it is the truth.

And, according to Scripture, the truth sets us free. I, for one, am tired of witnessing the sons and daughters of God dragging around a ball and chain, shackled by the lie that spiritual identity is bound up in what we do or don't do. Our identity as a son or daughter of God is not composed of living out certain principles or committing certain doctrines or Scripture passages to memory. It is located in the Person of Jesus Christ. Our abilities and talents have nothing to do with achieving it. Without Jesus, we are doomed to a life of despair in a kingdom of darkness. But the original identity God desires for each of us to enjoy has been restored. His Plan A has been reinstated through Jesus, and that is the only set of plans God is working with. There is no Plan B!

"For He [God] delivered us from the domain of darkness, and transferred us to the kingdom of His beloved Son, in whom we have redemption, the forgiveness of sins" (Colossians 1:13-14). The poverty of helplessness and hopelessness has been broken through this relocation. *Delivered* and *transferred* are words that denote a change of location, from one address to another. This change of location demands a vehicle to provide the move, and Jesus was that vehicle. As the last Adam, Jesus rescued us from one place by his death and then through his resurrection relocated us to another. Ultimately, this is not about the plan of salvation, but rather the Man of salvation.

The apostle Paul explains this so eloquently in Colossians 1:15-22:

> *And He [Jesus] is the image of the invisible God, the first-born of all creation. For by Him all things were created, both in the heavens and on earth, visible and invisible, whether thrones or dominions or rulers or authorities—all things have been created by Him and for Him. And he is before all things, and in Him all things hold together. He is also the head of the body, the church; and He is the beginning, the first-born from the dead; so that He Himself might come to have first place in everything. For it was the Father's good pleasure for all the fullness to dwell in Him,*

> *and through Him to reconcile all things to Himself, having made peace through the blood of His cross; through Him, I say, whether things on earth or things in heaven. And though you were formerly alienated and hostile in mind, engaged in evil deeds, yet He has now reconciled you in His fleshly body through death, in order to present you before Him holy and blameless and beyond reproach.*

Paul's use of the term *first-born* does not mean Jesus was born first in some sort of natural or even supernatural birth order, as some heretical groups teach. They have mistakenly taken a Greek word with an exclusive meaning and attempted to force it into a very loose English translation (to prove a select doctrine they happen to be pushing). Paul chose a particular word out of the *Koiné* Greek to emphasize a specific meaning. That word is *prototokos*, which means "first-born according to priority or sovereignty." He is stressing the God-attribute of preeminence with an emphasis on the eternality and absolute pre-existence of Jesus as the Son of God. His point is that Jesus is God and God became flesh so that through his flesh—life, death, and resurrection—he could *deliver* and *transfer* us from one kingdom to another. It was done in and through "his flesh" to fulfill the requirements demanded of Jesus as the last Adam.

Again, everything Jesus did on earth as a result of the Incarnation was done as a man, totally submitted and filled with power of the Holy Spirit, and in full obedience to God. The transfer of the first Adam into the kingdom of darkness was the result of his own disobedience, but our transfer into the kingdom of light has occurred because Jesus was fully obedient. Jesus did not have to go to his kingdom, his kingdom came with him. And wherever he went the kingdom of God was at hand. This was a major premise of his preaching as witnessed by his own words: "Jesus came into Galilee, preaching the gospel of God, and saying, 'The time is fulfilled, and the kingdom of God is at hand; repent and believe in the gospel'" (Mark 1:14-15). The kingdom was there because Jesus was there.

Our reconciliation with God through the finished work of Jesus Christ leaves us not only in a new state (remember that new species of human beings that we are now a part of), but also places us into a new location where the accusations and penalties for our own sins have no legitimacy whatsoever. These accusations and charges no longer apply. No legal proceeding can be brought against us any longer. We are totally free. This new location gives us a fresh, new start on eternity, and it began the moment we came to Christ. This new location is the key in understanding who we are and whose we are. If we don't understand it, we will never walk in its fullness. If we don't begin to walk in its fullness, we will never enjoy the inheritance God has given us. If we don't enjoy our inheritance, we are doomed to live in spiritual poverty. If we choose to live in spiritual poverty, in essence we are denying our birthright. If we deny our birthright, we will never find our identity. Spiritual poverty can be far more than something you're born into. It can also be a mindset you refuse to toss in the garbage can.

The Key to Identity

Several important factors make location the key in both real estate and business. In real estate, the location of a property determines its price and desirability. The more desirable a property is, the more popular it is. The popularity of any property automatically makes it more exclusive. The more exclusive it becomes, the higher the price it will command.

The same factors are true in business. The location introduces your business to your customers. If the product or service you offer has desirability, your business grows. If you produce the best product or give the finest service available, you gain popularity, resulting in a higher demand for the exclusivity of expertise you offer in your field of business. And as a result, your business becomes very profitable. People are willing to pay for what they want.

Location is also the key to our identity as children of God. If we grasp this key and turn it, the lock that has shut away our understanding of who God says we are will vanish. We may then step freely into a very unique position. And once we step into this unique position of what I call identity, the Church will once again be what God planned in eternity past.

The key is found in the tiny first-century *Koiné* Greek preposition *ev*. This two-letter word packs a punch, but when combined with *Christos*, its meaning is a spiritual well unfathomable in its depth and exclusive in the purity of the water from which we may drink. It is mysterious, yet knowable. Fantastic in scope, yet readily available to every believer. There is no other location that comes close to this one on the earth or above it. It is the exclusive location that lifts one out of the pit of spiritual poverty and into the realms of inconceivable privilege and blessing. The location is not a place but a Person.

In Christ

Ev Christos when translated into English literally means "in Christ." Eve, the bride of Adam, was created when God took "out of Adam" the essential elements needed to fashion a woman. The Church, composed of individual believers like you and me, is the bride of Jesus Christ. God did not take out what was essential from Christ to form her. Rather, the Father placed us in the One who himself is essential. Eve eventually became the life-giver to the race of fallen humanity. On the other hand, the last Adam became the Life-giver to a new race or species of redeemed humanity. When we are born the first time, we come out of the womb of our mother. When a person is spiritually born again—"born from above" as Jesus put it in his conversation with Nicodemus in John 3—the Holy Spirit baptizes, plunges, or submerges that new creature into the body of Christ. In that moment, a person is placed in Christ. This immersion is the supernatural work of the Holy Spirit. We demonstrate this mystery every time we baptize a new believer in water. The symbolism of the death, burial, and resurrection pictures physically what has already occurred supernaturally. When a person is saved by grace through faith in Jesus Christ, they are not born out of something, but rather born into Someone. That Someone is Jesus. And when God looks at you, he sees you through Jesus. He sees you "in Christ."

Nowhere is this more clearly taught than in Paul's letter to the Ephesians. This is one of the most pregnant verses in the whole Bible. One of the keys to the believer's identity in Christ is found in this identifying blessing: "Blessed be the God and Father of our Lord

Jesus Christ, who has blessed us [every believer] with every spiritual blessing in the heavenly places in Christ" (Ephesians 1:3). I pray this verse, meditate on this verse, teach and preach this verse, and counsel with this verse, because I am convinced if we begin to grasp the depth of what the passage means to us, it will radically revolutionize who we think we are and how we act. This verse tells us that God has endowed us (the literal meaning of "has blessed"—*eulogeo*) with the ability to succeed in everything he has called us to accomplish. In other words, God has equipped every believer to fully succeed in their destiny, if we recognize and utilize our position in Christ. We are dressed for success in him. Everything we need to fulfill our calling is available. It has already been placed in reserve.

Yes, there are certain aspects of this blessing that will only occur when we are in the literal presence of Jesus. At that time we will enjoy a glorified body like Jesus on which the ravages of sin have no effect. But many of these blessings are for now. They have been given so that we might walk in the victory of the cross and the resurrection. In fact, if you read this passage closely, the tense of the verb indicates this blessing has already occurred. It is past tense. Therefore, the blessing is ours to embrace, unwrap, and experience to the fullest as we discover our identity. This has always been God's plan. He has restored humanity's true identity in Christ. Our position in Christ ensures that we now have access to the blessings Adam enjoyed in his original state. We have full access to God and the ability to have an intimate relationship with him. Our new position enables us to do the works of Jesus and even greater ones. The possibilities are endless.

On eleven occasions in the first thirteen verses of Ephesians 1, Paul clearly points to this marvelous location God has graced us with. He uses different phrases like *in Christ Jesus* (once), *in Christ* (four times), *in Him* (five times), and *in the Beloved* (once), all of which clearly show us not where, but in whom we find our source of identity. Further in Ephesians 2 and 3 we will find *in Christ Jesus* (seven more times), *in Himself* (once), and *in the Lord* (once). It seems the Holy Spirit is making a rather obvious point he does not want us to miss. This has always been God's plan. Yet most of God's children have failed to grasp this simple fact and its revolutionary union. We are united with Christ. Where Christ goes, we go, and where we go, Christ goes as well.

Flat Nelson

This concept may seem very technical, theological, and maybe a bit mystical, and yet it is so natural when we really think about it. Let me illustrate what I mean with a simple illustration I used while teaching at Eagle's Wing one Sunday morning. Perhaps you have heard of Flat Stanley. He is a one-dimensional character who had his start in the 1964 book written by Jeff Brown. The main character was flattened by a blackboard that fell on him, thus the name Flat Stanley. Since that time, teachers all around the world have inspired their students to read, research, and write letters chronicling this world traveler's exploits to other schools around the globe. You simply cut a Flat Stanley out of poster board and color in his facial characteristics and clothes. He is then mailed to another school with a letter, and his travels begin. Students exchange letters and pictures of Flat Stanley meeting with famous people and visiting fascinating places. I met Flat Stanley at a writer's conference in North Carolina, where he was posing for pictures with both the famous and not-so-famous authors in attendance.

I came home and created a Flat Nelson to use as a sermon illustration to explain our position as believers in Christ. I drew a rather comical self-portrait complete with orange checkered pants and a turquoise striped shirt. I am not a fashionista by any stretch of the imagination, but even I know checks and stripes are a fashion faux pas and were never intended to be worn together. But due to my limited artistic resources (all I could find was a black Sharpie, an orange highlighter, and a turquoise highlighter) I created what I could with what I had on hand. The next morning I introduced Flat Nelson to my congregation, and everyone had a good laugh at my expense. Then I turned the tables by putting on a biblical character's robe and posing as Jesus. I became Jesus and Flat Nelson became me. Things got very quiet as I explained what being "in Christ" really meant.

As a spiritual father to their church, Paul painted the Ephesians a magnificent yet simple picture of this position in Christ. "But God, being rich in mercy, because of His great love with which He loved us, even when we were dead in our transgressions, made us alive together with Christ (by grace you have been saved), and raised us up with Him, and seated us with Him in the heavenly places in Christ Jesus, in order that in the ages to come He might show the surpassing riches of His grace in kindness toward us in Christ Jesus" (Ephesian 2:4-7).

First, I explained how human Flat Nelson was. He struggled with being human and was very capable of doing stupid things, making bad decisions, and his amazing ability to fail miserably in the blink of an eye. I shared how Flat Nelson gets some things right and some things wrong. How he is strong one moment and miserably weak the next. Then I described how desperately he wants to live for Jesus. He loves Jesus with all his heart, yet he fails his Lord so often. In reality, Flat Nelson represents every believer. He could be you, and you are like him whether you want to admit it or not.

Then I said, "I am going to portray Jesus. Jesus is God. God is eternal, omnipotent, omniscient, and omnipresent. He is incomparable and infinite. There is no one like him. He is God but became flesh, that is, he became a human being like you and me. He was crucified for our sins and raised by the power of the Holy Spirit. When he ascended into heaven, he led a triumphant procession in which the devil and his demons were stripped of their power and totally defeated. He overcame humanity's other enemies as well—death and the grave. At this very moment he is seated at the right hand of the Father in heaven."

Ephesians 2:4-7 tells us we are in Christ, seated in the heavenlies with Christ. The feet of Jesus have been placed on the defeated necks of the devil and his demons. They serve as his footstool. Jesus has defeated them. The Bible tells us over and over that we are in Christ. That's our position right now!

To visualize the explanation, I placed Flat Nelson on my chest inside the fold of the robe with only his arms and head sticking out. Flat Nelson was "in Christ," placed there and kept there by the finished work of Jesus Christ. Everywhere Jesus went, Flat Nelson went. And wherever Flat Nelson went, he went in Christ. Upon the Lord's triumphal entry back into heaven, the Bible tells us he sat down (sitting is symbolic of a finished work) at the right hand (the right hand is a symbol of power) of the Father. This verse tells us very clearly that when Jesus sat down, we sat down with him. We are at this moment—this present moment—seated with Christ in the heavens. That is our position, and it does not change no matter our earthly circumstances, situation, successes, or failures. It is a fixed location.

It cannot change.

Afterward, many of those in attendance shared with me that they had never understood what being "in Christ" really meant until that humorous moment when their pastor, posing as Jesus, walked around the room, sat down in a chair, and preached his sermon with Flat Nelson perched in his robe over his heart.

That is our position, our location, our place from which we venture out into the cold, cruel world, proclaiming and demonstrating the good news of Jesus Christ. That is the never-changing position from which we face the onslaught and temptations of the devil. That is the ultimate location from which we face the normal struggles of living in the desert of a sin-cursed world, whether it is sickness, divorce, bankruptcy, prodigal children, or a thousand other obstacles or problems that demand we give up or give in. God created a safe place for Adam and called it a garden, but our safe place is the God of that garden. He is the One who comes walking through the desert to remind us that no matter the situation or circumstance, no matter the depth of the night's darkness or the terrors that stalk us during the day, he has us tucked inside his robe perched just above his heart. We are in Christ!

The Challenge

Although Adam lost his garden position, Jesus has restored our position in God. This position alone guarantees the power we need to live a victorious, fulfilling life, one that overcomes no matter what we face. This position demonstrates our legitimacy as the sons and daughters of God. It validates Christ's connection with us and our connection with him. It substantiates our reason for existing. This location cements and solidifies our true identity. Like an echo bouncing off the mountaintops, it repeats over and over who we are and whose we are to all creation. Our identity is contained in Jesus. This has always been God's plan. And now that plan has been restored.

In grace, God has restored the plan so that we might experience the mystery of relationship with God that Adam forfeited. He has reinstated all the privileges of life Adam wasted when he chose to pursue a lie. The beauty of the Bride is shining once again as she awakens from her slumber and recognizes the Groom's reflection in the mirror rather than her own.

There is no Plan B and there never has been. But sadly, God's people have been willing to settle for something that never existed. We have been duped over and over by the sly serpent Satan. Now the time has come for us to claim our birthright and our heritage as a son or daughter born into freedom, born through the power of the Holy Spirit. This marvelous position, this location "in Christ," has restored our opportunity to walk once again the garden pathways with God. It is an opportunity to discover who he really is and experience his great love fully. It is the privilege of being intimate with the One who knows us inside and out and always pursues, the One who never pulls back or turns away. He is calling our heart to a deeper, more intimate relationship than we thought possible. The time has come for us to answer—to come out of the religious bushes we've been hiding in and reclaim the blessings and the glory the last Adam has purchased for us with his own life.

The day has dawned for this new species to take the dominion God bequeathed at creation and become his regent rulers, to rise up as the reflections of the living God to all creation, and to reproduce his image and likeness by passionately pursuing and performing the works Jesus did and the greater ones he promised we would do. The time has come for the relationship for which we were created to become a reality. The last Adam has restored the promise and reproduced a new species by placing them in union—in Christ—with himself. The restoration is complete. The work of Jesus Christ is finished. Every "i" has been dotted and every "t" has been crossed.

One thing yet remains, and that is for us to reclaim our inheritance and step fully into our identity. The time has come for us to discover who we really are and fully embrace all that means.

Section 4
God's Plan Reclaimed

Jesus restored our identity, but every believer must reclaim his inheritance through a growing relationship with Father God. This means we must deal with the religious teachings and folk beliefs of the Church that enslave rather than liberate. Often what we believe and teach are opposed to what is biblically true. Jesus unlocked those chains but we must step out of them! Every believer must personally reclaim God's Plan A if we hope to walk in our true identity and enjoy our full inheritance in Christ.

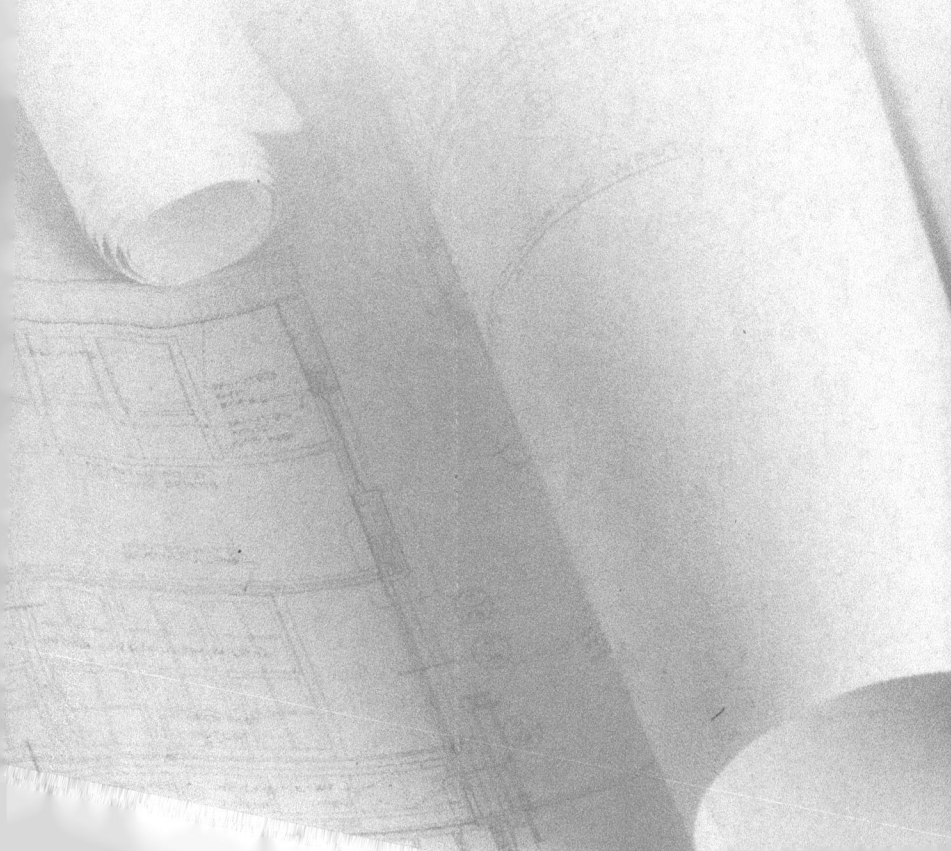

Chapter 8
The Chosen Unfrozen

> You did not choose Me,
> but I chose You.
> ~ Jesus Christ

For as long as I can remember, I have loved team sports. My father introduced me to basketball, baseball, and what I consider the greatest sport ever invented: football. Every afternoon when he returned home from work, we would spend a few minutes shooting hoops, snagging grounders to make the throw to first base, or running the post pattern and catching the winning touchdown pass. In my own backyard I was the elite athlete, the best of the best—or so I thought.

Many of you can relate to this. Eventually we graduate to backyard pick-up games, cow pasture stadiums, little league, middle school, and high school athletics. And there assembled on countless sandlots, grassy fields, asphalt courts, and in musty gymnasiums across this country are the greatest ball players ever to grace the sports stage, or so each one thinks. Here on these fields and in these gyms, little boys and girls will get their first bitter taste of reality.

I loved the friendships, the competition, the teamwork, and the life lessons I learned in sports. But most of all, it was the indescribable joy of achieving victory over an opponent and knowing personally that I had done my best and left everything on the field that fueled my passion.

Yet one thing terrified me, and that was the process of choosing teams. I think you know what I mean. It happens in organized leagues and in backyard pick-up games. A group gathers to play a game of whatever sport you like, and to do so, teams must be chosen. In its most rudimentary form two kids pick from the pool of available players. This simple method of choosing based on a set of skills will be used over and over again in almost every area for the rest of our lives.

As a kid, your greatest fear is that you will not be picked, left to watch the game from the sidelines, doomed to oblivion and, worst of all, unwanted. To be picked first is to be publically recognized for your superior talent as an athlete (or maybe it's because you're the best friend of the kid choosing). To be picked among the first validates you and makes you feel really good about yourself.

To be chosen in the middle only confirms what you already know deep down inside—you are average. Good, but not great. Solid, but not a superstar.

If you fail in your bid to be picked first, well, you cross your fingers and hope with all your heart you are not chosen last. Last is like being slapped in the face and told you are not very good. It means you will never have an opportunity to touch the ball unless you intercept a pass, fall on a fumble, make a rebound, or in frustration take it away from one of your own teammates.

But the ultimate humiliation is not to be chosen at all. As a kid, and often as an adult, not being chosen stencils a name on the jersey of your soul that blinks like a neon sign—*Worthless! Worthless! Worthless!* And nobody in their right mind wants to be classified as worthless and unable to measure up.

All through school, I made the team. I was rarely picked first, but thankfully never last. Sometimes it was just by a slim margin. I can remember sweating it out, awaiting the posting of the list or my name being called out at practice, and then breathing a deep sigh of relief as that tense moment passed.

And then I graduated from high school.

Since my earliest days of playing football in the backyard, I had nursed a dream deep within my heart. I wanted to wear the crimson and white and play college football at the University of Alabama, under the legendary coach Bear Bryant. During this time, they were perennial SEC champions and competed for the national championship every year with their high-powered wishbone style offense and smothering defense.

Only one letter of interest came to my mailbox, and it was from a small school that dropped football later that year. I received no phone calls requesting game films or possible scholarship offers.

Reality, not football coaches, began knocking on my door. I weighed a whopping one hundred and fifty pounds soaking wet dressed in full pads and played center on the offensive line and outside linebacker on defense. Size was not in my favor and neither was my speed. An inability to sprint forty yards with Olympic speed was a good bet I wouldn't get many offers or visits from schools interested in giving me an opportunity to play at the next level.

But I had a dream. So I tried to walk on at Jacksonville State, a smaller school that had won the national championship in their division the year before. I enrolled in school that fall, and on the specified day, showed up in my shorts and cleats for a series of timed sprints and kicking drills. The coaches were looking for wide receivers and punters. I had never played either position. I had snapped the ball to the punter in high school, but I possessed little or no kicking abilities. And nothing miraculous had changed with my foot-speed, which for a wide receiver was underwhelming. To make a short story even shorter, I did not make the list at the end of the day.

For the first time in my life, I had not been chosen. My dream gasped for breath, promptly spun around and around, and died. It was devastating. I felt worthless, useless, rejected, unwanted, and less than. Dreams often die tragic deaths, but life moves on. That's a tough lesson to learn.

I understand what it feels like to not be chosen. Since that moment forty years ago, those emotions have gripped me again and again, more often than I would like to admit. I have been rejected in friendships, job opportunities, social situations, as a writer, and as a pastor. I know what it feels like to want something, to do everything needed to achieve it, and still not be chosen.

And all of us do. At one time or another, we will be picked last or not picked at all. It is inevitable. Our abilities limit us because our abilities are limited. Our abilities are what we can do, and no one can do everything. Therefore what we can do must never be used as a gauge in determining who we are.

Ability and identity are two separate things. Ability defines what we can do and the level at which we perform. Identity is who we are. Be careful of trying to make them one. Our identity is determined by God, despite our abilities.

A Universal Hunger

One of the greatest longings we have as human beings, perhaps our ultimate craving, is to be wanted. We all want to be accepted or desired. Ultimately, that hunger can best be defined as being loved. All of us want to experience and express love with another person. That is not a mysterious part of some evolutionary process, random act, or accident brought on by a rogue mutation in the human gene pool. No, that is a priceless gift from God, one of the things that make us refreshingly different from all other creatures we share this planet with.

Love is both a characteristic and an attribute of God. It is his essence. God is love. And by virtue of being created in his image and likeness, we hunger for who he is and the ability to savor and reciprocate the love he has given us.

We were created in love to be loved and to love in return. And when we don't experience what we were created for, we feel unwanted, undesirable, and unworthy. We feel like the kid standing on the sidelines who never gets picked whose heart is empty and whose soul is racked with a craving that cannot be quenched. We understand. To be wanted, to be accepted, ultimately to be loved satisfies a craving God instilled.

It was put there by God to be filled by God. He did not delegate that responsibility to your spouse, your children, your parents, your sibling, your friends, or any other human beings. That satisfaction must be filled by the presence of God. We were created for this. Blaise Pascal phrased this hunger so eloquently when he said, "There is a God shaped vacuum in the heart of every man which cannot be filled by any created thing, but only by God, the Creator, made known through Jesus." We can look in every crack and crevice and search until life wears us out, but we will never satisfy this longing except through Christ alone.

The frustration we experience day-to-day in this world of being unwanted, not accepted or loved in a way that satisfies this longing, often finds its way into our relationship with Christ. We project the way this cold world treats us into our relationship with him. We should expect that kind of treatment from the world because it is filled with frustrated souls just like us. One starving soul cannot feed another starving soul. The blind can't lead the blind. If that happens, everyone goes hungry and falls into the pit. But we should never expect nor accept this as God's way.

A tendency to do this indicates that one is clueless about their true identity in Christ. The world judges our abilities and then chooses whether or not they will accept and laud (not love) us. Those one-minute intervals of fame or fortune rarely last even a moment in the scope of eternity and then we are dashed once again on the rocks of rejection, left picking the seaweed of unwantedness out of our hair, while lamenting the song of the unloved. As believers, our problem is we have succumbed to the belief that the level of our abilities determines the depth of our identity.

Trapped in the Cloud of Turmoil

This inability to separate ability and identity has resulted in bondage. This lie that what we do is who we are has created an opaque cloud of turmoil in which most Christians reside. As a pastor and counselor, I see it quite often. And from time to time, I find myself being slowly sucked back toward it, although I know the truth and have experienced the freedom that comes from living this truth.

Far too many sons and daughters of the King are lost in this hellish cloud of delusion. This single belief keeps them from experiencing the full love, acceptance, and grace of God. I often ask people to express how they think God sees them in only one or two words. Many of them have been Christians for decades. Some are church leaders—pastors, teachers, and deacons. Their responses usually sound like this: loser, failure, mess-up, sinner, disgusting, worthless, or pitiful. They are saying, "I don't measure up. I can't please God. Therefore, he could never love me."

This is not God's view! This is their clouded view because they are weighing themselves and their abilities through the eyes of the world system, rather than from their identity in Christ.

They may smile, carry a big Bible, know all the verses, and constantly work their fingers to the bone doing good things, and still not feel God would ever pick them for anything. I hear this belief system expressed when we have a prayer time in phrases like: "Oh,

I didn't voice my needs because the other ones were much more important." Or "God does that for others but not for me." Or "I wish I was a better Christian. I try, try, and try, but I just don't feel like I measure up." In other words, there is no way God is ever going to choose me—for anything.

Let's be honest, that's how most Christians feel. In fact, this may be the way you feel at this exact moment. If so, please read on—God has a gift he wants you to open, and he's allowed me to deliver it.

Yes, it is certainly true that none of us have anything God really needs. He is, after all, omnipotent, omniscient, and omnipresent. Yes, we have all been beaten and berated by the fact that our good works (those done in our power) and our own self-righteousness (goodness) are like filthy stinking rags in comparison to the holiness and righteousness of God. And all of us have been told, at least a million times, that we are nothing but dirty rotten sinners (a subject I will deal with in the next chapter). We know all this. For some reason many pastors are intent on driving this fact into the very marrow of our bones, often using it like a whip to batter their flocks into submission.

In reality this is only half the truth. Yet this half of the message has crept in over the last two thousand years and become the focal point of the whole message. A half-truth is not the whole truth. In fact, a half-truth is a lie. And a half-truth causes far more damage than a whole lie, which is usually apparent and recognizable over time. It is nothing more than a wolf in sheep's clothing, a deadly deception clothed in biblical words. A half-truth is death, and unless we learn the whole truth, we are doomed to live in a cloud of bondage, although God has given us a different identity.

If we are to reclaim our true identity—who God says we are—we must learn the other half of the truth and begin to live out the whole truth. We must embrace and experience God's Plan A and refuse to settle for the bogus Plan B. Only the implementation of God's plan will destroy the nagging bondage of rejection, failure, or feeling like we deserve last place—the belief that we are always the bridesmaid and never the bride.

The Slave Mentality

We've talked a bit about the slave mentality and the Israelites, but there is so much more to discuss. It is time to dispel the cloud and get rid of the stinking thinking of the slave mentality and the victim spirit. When the children of Israel came out of Egypt, they were free. God declared it, and he never lies. He sent Moses, the deliverer (or savior) to redeem them (to make sure the purchase price was paid) and lead them to the Promised Land (a new kingdom that would be both spiritual and nationalistic in nature). They saw the miraculous judgments God poured out on Egypt. They witnessed his power in the wilderness, yet they still thought like slaves.

These people had spent generations in slavery. Their mindset was the mentality of a slave. Their thoughts and actions were still mired in the mud of the Egyptian brick pits. All they had ever known was bondage. "Please your master and he will reward you...or at least not beat you" was the silent mantra that steered them. When God set them free, in their hearts and minds they simply exchanged one harsh taskmaster for another. They never fully believed the promises God had given them, so they never experienced them. The promises were available but never embraced.

Instead, they lived like slaves because they thought like slaves. Yet God said they were free. God sent prophet after prophet with promise upon promise, but the people never lost their slave mentality, and it eventually destroyed both them and the subsequent generations.

If we are not careful, this same lie will destroy us. We are not slaves, but as long as we think like slaves, we will act like slaves. Slaves serve because they are forced to, but true children live out their gifting and calling. Slaves try to appease their master out of fear and insecurity, but true children are confident, creative, and bold because they enjoy the security of their intimate relationship. They understand God is pleased with them, therefore appeasement is unnecessary. Actions speak louder than words. And this is a spiritual principle you can take to the bank: one's actions prove one's beliefs. What we believe is what we do.

Every believer has been redeemed by Christ. Our sins are paid for. God is no longer angry. He poured his wrath out against our sin at the cross on Jesus—every ounce, all of it. We have become new creations, new creatures. We are no longer slaves to sin. That is the truth, but we will continue to live like slaves unless we renew our minds and embrace the fullness of what Jesus has done and the revelation of the new identity God has endowed us with in Christ. We did not trade the taskmaster of sin for another taskmaster. We have received grace. We have been set free to experience all that God intended from the beginning.

For many of you, what you are about to read will feel like being thawed from a long freeze. You know something is wrong in your relationship with Christ, but you cannot put your finger on it. It's not sin or flagrant disobedience. You feel alone, like you're standing on the sidelines hoping and praying for more. You have witnessed other Christians who seemed to be experiencing true relationship with God. You can see it in their relationship, but the frigid ice that has encased your belief system would not allow you to reach out and touch it. That is no longer the truth. The chosen are being unfrozen.

He Said God Said but Did He Really?

God has an amazing ability to heal the dry, damaged, and wounded spots of our soul. Often the healing will come when we make a choice to believe what God's Word says over the things we may have been taught. All of us have preconceived ideas about what certain biblical words, phrases, and doctrines mean, due to the teaching and preaching we have accumulated. These preconceived ideas or prejudices are often those of the preacher, the teacher, or the writer we are listening to or reading, rather than what God actually said. They gradually slip in over time and become a part of our belief system and doctrine. All of us who yearn for the truth of God have them, and all of us who teach the truth of God fail to keep them out of our teaching. They are the results of what others have said God said, rather than what God actually said.

As teenagers we used to play a silly game at parties where one would whisper a sentence in another person's ear. That person would whisper it to the next person, and so that sentence would be passed around the room until it arrived back at its source. The final sentence never matched the original. As it passed around the room, it gained or lost vital parts and its meaning was altered. It was contaminated by what people thought they heard or what they thought was meant. It was totally different than the original.

This has happened again and again through the centuries with Christian doctrine. God spoke on a subject through an act of revelation. That revelation was collected, and we call it the Bible. Followers of God then attempted to interpret these revelations from God through the grid of language and grammar, context, historical usage and preference, customs, symbolism, and prior revelations of God. Next, an attempt is usually made to systematize the interpretations into some sort of doctrine with specific applications.

The problem is not with the revelation. God made sure the writers of Scripture got that correct through the direct mediation of the Holy Spirit. The words of Scripture were God-breathed, which is the literal meaning of the word *inspired* found in 2 Timothy 3:16. The problems arise in our interpretations and their ensuing applications. They are not God-breathed. That is why there are so many denominations and doctrines. This great teacher or that church father interpreted it this way, and his disciples carried that teaching to its next logical or illogical step, whatever the case may be. The idea of "he said she said he said" takes over in time, these doctrines become engrained, and people are willing to die for them. The problem is "did God really say this?" And if not, then why do I believe it?

One of the most important lessons I have learned is to question everything I hear or read, not in an arrogant or mocking way, but rather in a critical way—in a biblical way. Does this line up with Scripture? Did God really say this? What did God mean by saying this?

As believers, we must learn to think critically and biblically for ourselves once again. We can never simply accept what anyone says as "God said," without doing our homework and checking it out against the biblical record. This is how false teaching and heresy creep into orthodox doctrines. This is why one group ends up following an enigmatic teacher into the jungle and willingly sips poison Kool-Aid or another group barricades themselves in a fortress with a so-called messiah and perishes in the flames of a fire. At some point, they stopped thinking for themselves and allowed someone else to think for them. God has given us the Holy Spirit and a good mind, and both must be employed in our quest for truth.

A Plan with a Choice

So what does being chosen or thinking for myself have to do with God's plan or my identity? I would answer "everything." The biggest step we will take in discovering our true identity is releasing our false identity—who or what we thought or had been taught we were. In other words, we will never step into who we truly are without examining every thread of who we think we are in light of who God says we are.

The best place to start in this case is not in the beginning, but before the beginning (not in the garden of Eden, but rather before that in eternity past). That starting place was actually in the mind and heart of God. We can know what God was thinking then because he shared it with the apostle Paul through the revelation of the Holy Spirit. "Blessed be the God and Father of our Lord Jesus Christ, who has blessed us with every spiritual blessing in the heavenly places in Christ, just as He chose us in Him before the foundation of the world, that we should be holy and blameless before Him. In love He predestined us to adoption as sons through Jesus Christ to Himself, according to the kind intention of His will, to the praise of the glory of His grace, which He freely bestowed on us in the Beloved" (Ephesians 1:3-6).

Perhaps you are panicking a little because there are a host of biblical words in these verses that cause an argument if two or more Christians are gathered in one place. Sadly, those disagreements have clouded the simplicity of God's spoken revelation. I have no desire to grind an axe on the whetstone of Calvinism or Arminianism or stomp my way into the reformed or non-reformed camps. I simply want you to see with your eyes, hear with your ears, and understand with your mind and heart what God has stated in clear, simple terms.

God says he has chosen us! If we are Christ followers, God chose us to follow him. He handpicked us for his team. Out of all the people who ever lived, he chose us to be his sons or daughters. Before our mind starts to rebel against this statement with all the extra garbage that has been heaped on it, savor the truth that God chose you and me. Allow all those suppressed desires to be loved and wanted to float to the surface, and satisfy them with this—God chose you and me!

We did not choose God, rather he chose us. His choice had nothing to do with the level of our skills or abilities or the lack thereof. It had nothing to do with who we are, what we do, how well we do it, or how many generations our family has been doing it. This choice had nothing to do with how good we are or how bad we were. It had nothing to do with the wealth of our experiences or our lack of experience. It had absolutely nothing to do with us.

God did not look into the future and choose us based on anything we would do or not do. We had absolutely nothing to do with it. We were one person standing on the sidelines of eternity in the teeming crowd of billions who would populate this planet in God's mind, and God pointed at you and me and said, "I choose you!"

This choice did not take place when we surrendered our life to Christ either. This choice by God took place in eternity past, *"before the foundation of the world."* This was a sovereign act by a sovereign God in eternity past before time and space or matter ever came into existence. This selection occurred as God conceived in his mind this grand idea to bring creation into existence. His choice of us was an original part of the only plan he has ever entertained, his Plan A. In this plan God placed us and Jesus together in the same thought. He purposed it beforehand, before the foundation of the world.

This word *chose* means "to select from, out of, or away from." God called us "out of." It does not mean God chose some and left others. To get that meaning you must extrapolate and import other passages and meanings not given in this text. It simply means God selected us or he elected us. Since Paul recorded this amazing revelation from God, a ton of theological garbage has attached itself to these verses. Theologians may debate the sovereignty of God and man's freewill, but this verse does not. God does not debate, he declares, and he has declared, "I chose you!"

This choice of God is based only in his unconditional love. He chose us because of his great love for us. And he chose us for himself. That should set us free from our insecurities and fear. It should shatter the chains of competing for attention, the bondage of performance, and the need to achieve. We don't have to measure up, because Jesus did. That takes all the pressure off us and places everything on God's shoulders, which is what happened when Christ died on the cross.

Too many Christians are under the impression that the reason they are born again is that they chose God, that they picked him. That is not exactly what the Bible teaches. We are saved by grace through faith. Grace is the gift of God, not an investment of our sweat equity. Sovereignty and freewill work together in a mysterious way, but no matter what anyone teaches, they do work together. By God choosing us, he gave us the ability to respond to his love freely. His love and our obedience produce a partnership between sovereignty and freewill. Augustine, John Calvin, Jacobus Arminius, John Wesley, Charles Whitfield, Jonathan Edwards, and a vast host of God's servants have spent their whole lives attempting to explain this mystery. When I checked last, none had done it in such a way that all can agree. Neither can I. But my aim is not to explain all the minutia of sovereignty and freewill; my goal is to simply embrace both and enjoy the amazing fullness of being chosen by God.

God placed us in his mind in Christ and determined to set a plan in motion that would achieve this miraculous union in reality. Was he aware of what would transpire in Eden? Yes! So much so, that he made prior arrangements before he ever spoke Eden into existence. The why and how of it are questions we can ask in eternity. For this moment I want us to know our identity is wrapped up in Christ, and God handpicked us specifically for it. That one truth, if we choose to believe it, should quench our hunger for security and satisfy our craving to be wanted and loved. Through that choice God said in eternity past, "I love you. I want you. You are now secure in Christ."

Holy and Blameless

Most people struggle with this choice in the beginning. It goes against everything we have been taught since childhood. I struggled with it. I could not (and still cannot) grasp why God would chose me. I had nothing to offer. This passage (Ephesians 1:3-6) is not here to answer that question, but rather to declare God's amazing love for us.

Stop asking "why me" and start asking a better question: "Why would God do that for me?" The best place to find the answer is in this passage. God's desire was that we be holy and blameless. He chose us to be set apart for him. We were picked *out of* and then set apart for God the Father. Blameless is a word used to describe a sacrificial animal that had no defects. God determined in his mind and heart that his children would be his alone and spotless without sin or defect. The only way a sacrificial animal could be rejected was if it had a defect. We were not rejected, because Jesus pushed us aside and took our place on the altar.

I know, I can hear you thinking, "But...but...but..." Now is the moment we must choose to believe God's Word rather than the lies the devil is whispering to us. Yes, he will bring up all of our shortcomings in the past, present, and if possible even suggest some for the future. Who are we going to believe? God, who cannot lie, or the devil, who has been a liar since the beginning and who is aptly nicknamed *the father of lies*? Our choice at this moment will either move us into a more secure position of identity that God decided on long ago or back us into a pit with nothing to look at but pictures of our past failures adorning the walls.

According to God, his choice assures us that we have been made holy and blameless in Christ. It's that position thing again. Will we assume that position guaranteed by God's Plan A or acquiesce to the Plan B the Liar wants us to believe?

Reality check time here—there is no Plan B! We stand holy and blameless at this very moment because we are in Christ and he was, is, and forever will be holy and blameless. His position is our position. His standing is our standing.

The Ultimate Gift

To be chosen for God's team is utterly mind-blowing if that's all we had been handpicked for. But we were chosen to be far more than *a part of God's team*. We were chosen to be his sons and his daughters. God was not interested in building a team like a coach or a businessperson builds a team. His gift to us is far more than the satisfaction of being a member of a team, but rather the intimacy of being a part of his family. That makes it personal, and it completes his purpose in this miraculous selection.

Paul unfolds the ultimate gift of God's choice of us in Ephesians 1:4-6: "In love He predestined us to the adoption as sons through Jesus Christ to Himself, according to the kind intention of His will to the praise of glory of his grace, which he freely bestowed on us in the Beloved."

God's intention was to adopt us into his family. Imagine that! God wanted kids. I am a father who has an adopted daughter. If you have been adopted or are the parent of an adopted child, this passage is rich with experiential meaning. God chose us out of all the others to be his own flesh and blood. We who were not and could never be on our own become his son or daughter.

I will never forget the night I went to pick up our soon-to-be daughter after receiving a phone call telling me if we wanted her to come and get her. She was nine years old, and it seemed no one else wanted her. I can remember the way she walked, head downcast with eyes sad and empty. The trembling of her little body and the flood of her tears filled with both rejection and rejoicing as we drove away are etched forever in my memory. One minute she seemed unwanted and the next, she became our little girl, deeply loved and treasured.

I made a choice when I answered the phone that night that if I went to get her, she would not be going back to that place. For my wife Cathy and me, this was not a game. This was life or death for a precious little girl. Immediately, we secured temporary custody and began the legal process of adopting her. We chose her *out of* the situation she was in, and we then acted to make sure she never had to go back.

That is what God has done in our lives. He *predestined us to adoption*. That is, in eternity past, he acted so we would never have to return to the shadows of hopelessness and despair. A choice without an action is only a dream, and God is far more than a dreamer. God is a doer. He acted in a decisive manner.

Predestined, like chosen, has taken on a life of its own in theological circles. It is hotly argued and debated, but it simply means "to mark out with a boundary beforehand." It means to "foreordain," that is, "to ordain beforehand." God predestined you and me to be his children. He acted and marked out the boundaries of what that would look like long before the landscape he was dreaming became a reality. Our adoption as his children was a part of his plan before that plan was implemented. It is true; you were always on his mind.

These boundaries God marked out provide security and love, not a robot-like existence. Remember, sovereignty and freewill work seamlessly like a partnership. God is responsible for unveiling our destiny, but we must walk obediently into it. Life is not some cosmic puppet show where we are the puppets and God is the One pulling all the strings. God gives us choices to make, and we are responsible for those decisions. We must take care of our responsibilities because God will most certainly take care of his.

In reality, Ephesians 1:5 simply tells us that God made a choice and acted in eternity past to adopt us, to give us the gift of unconditional love, rather than control every move we would make. His goal: sons and daughters who would experience his love, a love that has no conditions placed on it and no end. In 1 Corinthians 13:4-8, Paul describes the very essence of this love: "Love is patient, love is kind, and is not jealous; love does not brag and is not arrogant, does not act unbecomingly; it does not seek its own, is not provoked, does not take into account a wrong suffered, does not rejoice in unrighteousness, but rejoices with the truth; bears all things, believes all things, hopes all things, endures all things. Love never fails." This is the ultimate gift, the love God has given each of us in Christ.

This gift leaves me speechless and dumbfounded. I struggle to comprehend the full depth of its meaning. God did not have to choose anyone, yet he did. He chose you and me knowing we would be born into a world polluted with sin, knowing we would be dead in our own trespasses and sin, and knowing that his Son, Jesus Christ, would have to restore our position through his death. And God also knew that we would be required to reclaim our destiny and inheritance from the depths of a seemingly bottomless pit of religious quicksand formed by the sludge of two thousand years of theological standoffs, sectarian infighting, and denominational ignorance. Knowing all this, he brought creation into existence.

Perhaps you are thinking, "Why—why would God go ahead with creation since he already knew what would happen?" I don't know the whole answer, but based on the passages we have explored in this chapter, God has something far better for us, a higher dignity than even creation could bestow.

Embracing the Obvious

Based on what we've learned up to this point, one thing is for sure: we must embrace what is obvious. God loves you and me. He loves us with a quality of love we cannot fully comprehend but desperately hunger for. Out of this love he chose us and acted on that decision by setting out the boundaries to adopt us as sons and daughters.

Therefore, it is high time we as believers in Jesus Christ stopped moaning and groaning about our inabilities, failures, or deficiencies. It is time we stopped blaming others for our present location or situation and ceased whining about what we deserve yet are unwilling to reach out and take. This fodder only feeds the voracious appetite of a slave's mindset, a mindset we may have embraced, but one that was certainly not foisted on us by God.

We have been given the opportunity to choose because that's one of the byproducts of the partnership between sovereignty and freewill. We must believe, obey, and act on the revelation of God's Word. We can no longer stand on the sidelines and in shame hang our heads claiming, "He said, she said, God said."

You have been chosen and chosen by a God who loves you. At this very moment, God is shouting the obvious: "I chose you in Christ in eternity past to be holy and blameless through Christ so that I could make you a son or daughter by the legal act of adoption for one reason only: I love you."

Will we embrace the obvious! Will we reclaim the position God chose to bestow and Jesus died to restore? The first step in discovering who we are comes by accepting whose we are. God chose us, therefore we are his beloved. Our true identity was gift-wrapped before the foundation of the world. Don't you think it's about time you unwrapped that gift? Perhaps the moment has come to explore those mysterious boundaries God marked out for you so long ago and reclaim God's plan for you.

Oh, Abba Father, I have labored far too long in the brick pits of slavery! You have chosen me to be your child in Christ before the foundation of the world were laid, and yet I have refused to explore the meaning of these new boundaries you have created for me due to unbelief, ignorance, and fear. Please forgive me, dear Father, and guide me as I step into this unfamiliar territory as a child chosen by you and for you in Christ. I embrace this choice that you made in love, and I now desire to walk with you into the destiny you ordained for me as your child. I make the choice to reclaim everything that Jesus restored. Thank you, Father—I desire to experience all of it! In Jesus's name, amen.

Chapter 9
Saints or Sinners?

> The only difference between saints and sinners is that every saint has a past and every sinner has a future.
> ~ Oscar Wilde

A person's name is very important. It is the initial monogramed into the fabric of who we will become once we are born. Those names are printed on birth certificates that identify us as we begin our life. They are signed countless times on a variety of documents as we live out our life. They are engraved on granite markers once we exit this life. A name follows a person from birth to death, giving that person some sense of identity.

A surname or family name links us to our past. It gives roots to our identity. The etymology (the original, literal meaning) of a surname unlocks the history of its meaning. European surnames originated sometime during the twelfth century as a means of differentiating between a host of individuals with the same name in the same location. Surnames developed from nicknames, locations and topography, vocations, physical characteristics, and a parent's given name. Eventually these names were inherited and passed from generation to generation.

My own surname, Hannah, has its roots in the Scottish lowlands found among the Strathclyde Britons, who were Celtic in origin. The name first appears around 1296 and has several variant spellings. My ancestors fled this region due to unrest, poverty, and persecution, passed through the Ulster Plantations of Northern Ireland, and eventually found their way to the shores of the colonial America to begin a new life with a new dream.

As a child, I would ask my father about our origins, and he would always reply, "We are a duke's mixture—Scots Irish." His surname was very important to him, a badge of honor to be treasured and respected. As a teenager, about to leave for my first adventure in the family car without direct parental supervision, my father warned me, "Don't do anything stupid that would bring dishonor or disrespect to your name. It is an honorable name. Bear it well." As I have grown older, I now understand what he meant.

We also have a given name to go with our surname. That given name designates who we are in our family. Many of these given names carry a specific meaning. They remember a special event or person or are family names passed from parent to child. I was given my father's name, although like all the men in my family, I go by my middle name. I rarely heard my first name employed with the exception of when I was in real trouble with my mother or once a year on the first day of school.

Names are often a guide into destiny. The ancient Israelites chose names for their children that memorialized events of the past or spoke prophetically about the child's future. The name Jesus means "savior or deliverer, the One who saves." It was given prophetically in anticipation of what he would do. Jesus became the Savior of the world. The name Ichabod means "the glory of God has departed" and was given by a mother dying in childbirth who had heard from the battlefront that her husband had been killed and the ark of God taken captive by the Philistines. I often wonder what happen to Ichabod.

Names are the first label we receive, but they are never the last. Inevitably, the labels we garner as we make our way through our formative years are the ones that stick and influence, limit, or loose us to be all that we were created to be. Unfortunately, if it is an unhealthy one, we can't seem to get rid of it.

By unhealthy, I mean names that were hung on us because of a mistake, a failure, a limitation, a disability, someone's anger, or a sick sense of humor. Often we are tagged with a nickname that belittles. Sometimes it comes through the frustration or rage of an authority figure or the ridicule of a playground. Labels like stupid, dumb, fat, ugly, four-eyes, failure, freak, worthless, and loser—the list is endless.

These labels are then stitched into the fabric of our soul and become part of who are, subtly influencing our belief system and our actions. They cause deep and painful wounds that never heal. For many, these names guide them into their future.

Who we believe we are is the person we will likely become.

Slaying Sacred Cows

This endless acquisition of names and labels knows no sanctuary. It transpires in the one place on earth where every person should be safe and free from judgment and condemnation. I am referring to the church. Church has come to mean different things to different people. For many, it is the building where they meet on a regular basis to worship. In reality, the church is the body of Christ, the redeemed of the Lord. It is made up of people who have been born again by grace through faith. It is a people of faith, not a place of worship.

I grew up in church. My earliest memories revolve around the church. I am a Southern boy, raised in the buckle of the Bible belt. I have a deep respect for the traditions of my culture, especially those related to my faith, as well as the cultures and traditions of others. So the path I am about to embark on may go against the grain for some. I have no desire to offend. Rather I have a deep desire to empower you to pick up the seam ripper of the Holy Spirit and rip out at least one label that you may have mistakenly affixed to your soul.

My desire in this chapter is to humbly expose a sacred cow of the Church, a misnomer in meaning and application. A sacred cow is an idea, belief, custom, or institution supposedly immune from criticism and therefore above questioning. A rather large herd of these mysterious cattle graze unchallenged up and down the hallways, vestibules, altars, and pulpits of most churches. Some are harmless, and others are downright deadly. They can be customs, traditions, or beliefs that may or may not be biblical. All must be questioned from time to time and their value assessed. Otherwise this herd becomes diseased and dangerous. Those that no longer serve a meaningful purpose should be put out to pasture, and those that are unbiblical or destructive should be slain with the sharpest knife available. It is likely that more believers are kicked, gored, or trampled by these so-called blessed bovines more often than by anything else they encounter out in the world.

Sacred cows die slow deaths. They are almost impossible to kill, and many are like a cat with nine lives. They keep coming back for more. The hardest sacred cows to kill are created from a misunderstanding, a wrong belief, or an out-and-out lie, yet wrapped in layers and layers of generations of belief and usage, while peppered with bits of truth here and there. They have been handed down and entrusted to us by our ancestors or from trustworthy preachers, teachers, and counselors. Each one affects some key component of our identity—who we *think* we are.

And that's the issue. This variety of sacred cows blocks our view of God and muddles his plan in our minds. The unimportant or the untrue becomes guarded, honored, and uplifted, while the truth lies buried in the fertilizer. Slaying sacred cows is all about reformation, refining, and reforming our belief system according to the truths of God's Word, while purging those elements that are questionable, unclear, or even untrue. It is not about an axe to grind or a vendetta to get even. It is all about reclaiming all of our inheritance in Christ and walking in the full identity he has given us.

The sacred cow I would like to expose is a little phrase that has become a part of the church culture. I grew up hearing it from the lips of preachers and teachers who I greatly respect and admire. It has been sprinkled in almost every testimony I've ever heard given by a person describing their life-changing experience with Christ. In the past, I have used this phrase in my own teaching and preaching. I accepted it because it rang true. It sounded biblical. It describes how most Christians see themselves, how they relate to themselves in their relationship with God. The old adage "if it quacks like a duck and walks like a duck, it must be a duck," just *ain't* true in this case.

That phrase is *"I'm just a sinner saved by grace!"*

The Question

No, I am not a heretic. Nor do I believe in sinless perfection while I still have a sliver of my foot still touching this sin-infected planet. I am well acquainted with myself, and I still sin by disobeying God. I am human just like you, with the same weaknesses and shortcomings.

I fail miserably. We all do! Yet, as a born-again Christian (there is no other kind), is it biblically correct to refer to ourselves as *"a sinner saved by grace"*?

I am questioning hundreds of years of Christian tradition here. I am exposing myself in print, knowing that some will ridicule my view and label me a biblical liberal or worse, a false teacher. I may receive some angry e-mail, be denounced in certain pulpits, and probably be uninvited to preach or teach in some places. Yet I believe the Bible is true and because it is true it will stand strong when it is questioned. Our questions don't threaten or change the truth. Our questions help us arrive at the destination where truth already exists. God is not somehow threatened when we ask questions. Yet our faith is questionable if we refuse to question it (by that I mean inquire, investigate, search out more understanding, and dig deeper in our discovery of meaning and application).

As a Christian, how should I refer to myself and others of the faith? Am I a sinner or a saint? What does God see when he looks at me? Am I a sinner saved by grace or a saint who sins occasionally? The answers to these questions are critical in discovering and reclaiming our identity in Christ. The label we choose to wear must be chosen very carefully. The name we bear must be the same name God calls us by or there will be utter confusion in our soul.

I believe the answers are found in Scripture. Paul tells us clearly that "all Scripture is inspired [literally *God-breathed*] by God and profitable for teaching, for reproof, for correction, and for training in righteousness" (2 Timothy 3:16). Throughout the history of the Church, many aspects and treasures of our inheritance in Christ have been lost. Some have been rediscovered, and others lie buried in the dust of misuse or no use, awaiting someone willing to ask the tough questions in the face of tradition and persecution.

Martin Luther was willing to ask the tough questions about ultimate authority in the Church and the source of forgiveness and salvation, and then seek the answers in God's Word alone. As a result, the Reformation was birthed. The driving doctrine of the Reformation was *Sola Scriptura*, meaning "by Scripture alone." We embrace this doctrine as Protestants, believing the Bible contains all knowledge necessary for salvation and holiness. The Bible, not tradition, not a preacher, teacher, church official, denomination, or writer, is the sole authority for faith and practice. Therefore, let us put this question to the *Sola Scriptura* test: Am I a sinner or a saint? And let us see what the Bible has to say.

Definitions are Indispensable

Most Christians are more at ease with being labeled a sinner than a saint. A large part of that comes from how tradition, culture, and groups have defined the terms. I have learned the hard way that not everyone defines a word the same way I do. Nor do they use a word in the same way I may use it.

While in seminary I offered to give a fellow student a ride off campus to a shopping mall. He was from Liberia, Africa, and had a good mastery of the English language. As we were finalizing the details for the trip the next day, in my best Southern dialect I said, "I will pick you up tomorrow at 10 a.m. and carry you to the mall." He began to wave his arms and shake his head in disbelief. So I repeated it again. He became more agitated, frantic, and animated. So, I repeated it again.

"No! No! No!" he shouted and stomped his foot.

I was totally dumbfounded by then, not knowing what to say, so I just stood there with my mouth open. Finally, he said, "You do not have to pick me up and carry me. I weigh too much for you to lift. I have no problem walking, but I do need a ride to the mall." Then it hit me. He thought I planned to lift him in my arms and carry him bodily to the store. We were using the same words, but they were endowed with different meanings. My Southern idioms failed to communicate as they were translated through the rigid English grid he had been trained in.

Words take on different meanings when they are translated. Often what they mean in one language has no equivalent in another. Sometimes new words must be invented or similar ones substituted to make a close equivalent. When this happens some of the word's meaning is lost. And that seemingly insignificant bit may possibly mean the difference. Such are the words *sinner* and *saint*.

A sinner, in common church usage, is anyone who sins. That's the definition most of us have grown up with and incorporated into our belief system. But this simplistic definition is a bit misleading if you appeal to Scripture for your definition.

The Greek term *hamartia* (sin) means "to miss the mark, to fall short of what God requires." It is the picture of an arrow shot from a bow that falls short of the target for which it was intended. When anyone falls short of what God requires, an act of sin has been committed. Everyone is guilty of this. All have sinned and fallen short of God's glory. It can be a noun (a thing) or a verb (an action).

The Greek word *hamartolos* (sinner) means "one who is sinful or devoted to sin." It describes a person whose life is filled with sin (sinful) or one whose life is characterized by a continual practice of sin, i.e., a lifestyle of sin. It is a noun describing the essence of a person, not a verb describing an action.

The term *saint* carries quite a bit more baggage and confusion. Saint is a word coined in the first century by Christianity. Over the centuries it has come to mean someone who possesses exceptional or extraordinary levels of virtue and holiness and has demonstrated that through their works and/or their devotion to God.

The Catholic Church defines a saint as someone who is in heaven, having been completely perfected and recognized as such by the Church, while the Orthodox Church defines a saint as anyone who is in heaven, whether recognized here on earth or not. Both churches venerate these saints, believing that prayer offered to them brings special assistance and also more influence with Jesus. These beliefs, along with multiple layers of pagan superstition and folk religion, have created a great deal of confusion among Protestants when faced with this word. It is far easier to apply it as the name of a mascot for a football team than utilize it to describe ourselves.

During the Reformation, the reformers threw out this definition of a saint, stopped their veneration, and destroyed the statutes and icons of the Roman Catholic saints. We have jettisoned what was considered unnecessary and unbiblical baggage, yet we have kept its definition in our collective religious psyche. For most of us, a saint is someone who lives at a higher level of goodness and holiness in their relationship with God. We might call Billy Graham or Mother Teresa a saint. But most Christians would never refer to themselves in that way. They don't feel like they measure up to this standard of good works and godly devotion. For most a saint is someone who never sins, who never does anything wrong, who oozes with love and floats a step or two above the ground with a shining halo hovering above their head.

I believe the Bible, not church tradition, is a better place to find a correct definition for a saint. The Greek word used throughout the New Testament is *hagioi* (plural). It simply means "holy ones," and the context determines whether the writer is speaking of people or angels. It comes from the root word *hagios* or holy, meaning "set apart or consecrated to God," thus making the item, place, or person holy or sacred and reserved for God and his service. Based on this, a saint is a person who has been sanctified and set apart unto God. To clarify it even further, a saint is one who has been cleansed by the blood of Christ and the renewal of the Holy Spirit, thus separated from the world and set apart unto God.

Now with these working definitions, perhaps we can answer the question: Are we saints or sinners?

A False Dichotomy

God never uses the phrase *a sinner saved by grace* to describe even one of his children. It is not found in the Old or New Testaments. So if God does not use it, it must mean he sees us in a different light than we see ourselves.

None of the writers of the New Testament when writing their gospels or epistles ever use the term *sinner* to refer to another believer. A sinner was an unsaved, unregenerate person. A sinner described the old species of humanity separated by sin from God, fathered by Adam. It is always used to refer to someone who had not come to faith in Christ, with one exception. The apostle Paul referring to himself said, "It is a trustworthy statement, deserving full acceptance, that Christ Jesus came into this world to save sinners, among whom I am foremost of all" (1 Timothy 1:15). Paul understood the awful path he had traveled, a persecutor and murderer of Christians, before his encounter with Jesus Christ on the road to Damascus and his subsequent appointment with Ananias whom Jesus sent to share the message of the gospel. He understood apart from Christ, he (as well as each of us) was the worst of the worst. He knew the depravity of sin and its capabilities. Likewise, we remind ourselves often of its deadly danger.

I understand fully what is meant by being a sinner saved by grace. Every believer was once a sinner. But that was a description of our life BC, before Christ. All of us have a common story marked by being born with a sin nature and then choosing to willfully sin over and over. We were sinners dead in our trespasses. Sinner (full of sin) describes who we were.

But at a moment in time every believer was born again. At that exact instant, we could truly say, "I am a sinner saved by grace." Yet a second later, the statement should change to, "I *was* a sinner saved by grace." In that moment of salvation, you and I were changed by an act of the Holy Spirit through the atoning work of Jesus Christ.

Perhaps some may feel that this is just a game of words, an exercise in semantics. How does this affect my walk with God or my identity in Christ or God's plan for my life?

That's a great question. It affects us when it is the lens through which we view God and what he has done for us. Our belief system is our theology of God, no matter our denominational pedigree.

Biblically speaking, a sinner is anyone living a lifestyle of sin. Is our life marked by a life filled with sin? A Christian cannot practice sin, that is, live in a constant and continual lifestyle of sin. What we practice proves who we are, according to 1 John 3:7-8. "Little children, let no one deceive you; the one who practices righteousness is righteous, just as He is righteous; the one who practices sin is of the devil; for the devil has sinned from the beginning."

The scope of our lifestyle is based on whose we are and who we believe we are. As a Christian we belong to Jesus, yet most believers still see themselves as sinners. Thoughts create concepts, and concepts are woven into a belief system. What we believe is what we are currently living out. Actions always mirror beliefs. Change a belief, and we change an action. The change comes internally before it is ever realized externally. What we believe is what we become.

If we believe we are saints and understand what that means, we will likely commit fewer sins. If we believe ourselves to be sinners, we will likely maintain our present status because we believe it is the best we can do. We will try harder and harder. We will be frustrated because our best doesn't seem to be good enough. When, not if, this happens, we will give up and go through the motions of religion without ever tasting the wonder of relationship with God. But the reality is it's not about our best, it's about Christ's best, which he fully gave on the cross.

Most of us have been lambasted with this phrase all our Christian life. Good pastors and teachers have thundered this phrase like they were quoting it from Matthew, Mark, Luke, and John. It is not there! It has been driven like a nail into the construction of our belief systems. Most Christians view themselves as "a dirty, rotten, stinking sinner." That's what we've been told we are. In Protestant circles it is viewed almost as the sacrament of humility. This view does not make us humble; it robs us of the dignity God has bestowed on us. He does not see us this way, so why should we? What purpose does it serve?

The religious system of Jesus's day viewed the average Jewish man and woman, the common person, as a sinner. These common people simply could not know God because they could not keep the laws of the Torah perfectly. They could not know God because they had not sat at the feet of Rabbi So-and-So and imbibed the life-giving words that poured from his lips. Two classes developed: (1) the religious elite, made up of the Pharisees, the Sadducees, the scribes, and the lawyers; and (2) the rest of the people, the sinners. Jesus came to destroy this false dichotomy and did so with the cross.

The early church flourished because they recognized one another as holy ones, as saints. But over time the same false dichotomy crept in and infected the Church. Pride, power, fame, and finances spurred it along. And a few hundred years after the cross, it was fully entrenched again. The religious leaders were popes, bishops, priests, kings, and princes—and everyone else composed the group known as the sinners. The Word of God was taken from the hands of the common people and entrusted to the so-called spiritually mature. The cup of the Eucharist was withheld from the common people because they were considered sinners and unworthy of it. The Humpty-Dumpty class system of religion that Jesus had shattered managed to put itself back together again.

And here we stand, twenty-one centuries later, looking back...and not much has changed. The false dichotomy still remains. The same slave mindset that has dogged God's people since they exited Egypt still resides deep within our consciousness. In the minds of most believers there are saints (those who can do nothing wrong) and sinners (the rest of us who can do nothing right). It is the same Humpty-Dumpty of the first century and the Middle Ages.

Yet the Bible knows of no such division in the Church. The time has come to jettison this stinking thinking forever and embrace our full inheritance in Christ. The Church is composed of regenerate men and women who make up the fellowship of the saints. Every Christian is a saint.

Therefore, you are a saint!

Simple Proof

If we see ourselves as sinners rather than as saints, our belief system denies the testimony of Scripture and the finished work of Christ. Our beliefs must have their source in the truth of the Bible or our theology will be muddled and confusing.

Saint is not a description of perfection; it is a declaration of identity. It is God's declaration that we have been set apart by him, for him, and made holy in Christ.

I hold a very high view of the Bible. I believe it to be God-breathed, which makes it inerrant and infallible. I also believe the Holy Spirit guided the writers of Holy Scripture as they chose every precise word and penned them. The words we read reveal God's heart and mind. They demonstrated his Plan A. One of the most obvious proofs of this is found in the salutations of many of Paul's epistles.

As he wrote to the church at Ephesus, he opens with this statement: "Paul, an apostle of Christ Jesus by the will of God, to the *saints* who are at Ephesus, and who are faithful in Christ Jesus" (Ephesians 1:1, emphasis added). The apostle is addressing all the believers who make up this local body. He greets them as saints, as holy ones. The Holy Spirit chose this specific word to communicate the true identity of every believer.

I often use this verse and the ones that follow to counsel depressed and defeated Christians who see themselves as "dirty, rotten, stinking sinners." This is what they've been told and this is what they believe, so this is all they can hope for. This sort of thinking produces a smothering cloud of hopelessness and defeat. To become healthy they must first see themselves through God's eyes.

In this verse, the Holy Spirit gives us a glimpse from God's viewpoint. If you look very closely, this is not what we have been told and certainly not what most have believed. Yet it is the truth from God's vantage point.

This declaration of identity also occurs in Paul's greeting to the believers in Rome (Romans 1:7), Corinth (1 Corinthians 1:2 and 2 Corinthians 1:1), Philippi (Philippians 1:1), and Colossae (Colossians 1:2). It appears over fifty times in the New Testament, referring to Christians in different locations. Once would be worthy of our attention, but the Holy Spirit uses this term of God's endearment over and over. Perhaps God wants us to understand and embrace our new identity in Christ? Perhaps, indeed!

If God, communicating through his apostle Paul, had wanted to use the term *sinner* when addressing the Church, the church at Corinth would certainly have given him ample ammunition. They are one of the most dysfunctional groups of people in the New Testament. The epistle of 1 Corinthians is a letter of correction for a multitude of sinful behaviors perpetrated by Christians on one another and their community.

This behavior included a believing man who was living in an immoral relationship with his stepmother. Others were involved in endless civil lawsuits against Christian brothers and sisters. Some were involved with prostitutes, not understanding the sanctity of marriage, and others were willing to get a divorce at the drop of a hat. Still others would arrive early for the Lord's Supper and eat all the food and guzzle the wine, getting drunk and leaving nothing for those who arrived later. To make matters worse, if that's possible, that dangerous dichotomy of saint (the spiritual ones) and sinner (everyone else), the class system of antiquity, was clawing to regain ascendency through the exercise of spiritual gifts, which the Holy Spirit had given to build up the Church, not tear her down. Certainly if any church could be labeled First Church of the Sinners, it was Corinth.

However, Paul sends this letter of correction to a seemingly different address: "To the church of God which is in Corinth, to those who have been sanctified in Christ Jesus, saints by calling, with all who in every place call upon the name of our Lord Jesus Christ, their Lord and ours" (1 Corinthians 1:2). Paul, in his greeting, defines a saint and then applies it to this church and connects them to all the other saints and to himself. In other words, the address on the envelope clearly read: *To the saints—yes, the saints—at Corinth!*

The Transforming Process of Salvation

Too many Christians have been born again without understanding the simple facts of what occurred at that supernatural birthing by the Holy Spirit. Perhaps it would make it easier to embrace being a saint if we could watch the sinner disappear into Christ's death on the cross and then appear as saint with Christ in his resurrection.

At the cross, Jesus paid the sin debt of the whole world, from Adam to that last person who will be born up to the beginning of eternity. He died for you, me, for everyone. We were sold into the slavery and bondage of sin for a bogus promise and a taste of forbidden fruit. We were separated from God, dead in our trespasses and sin.

Nonetheless, God's Word is very clear. "In Him, we have redemption through His blood, the forgiveness of our trespasses, according to the riches of His grace, which He lavished upon us" (Ephesians 1:7-8). Redemption, which is the purchase price required to free a slave, came through Jesus. He substituted his life for ours. He became the sacrifice, dying in our place, for the sins of the world.

We learned in Chapter 8 that as believers we were chosen by God in Christ before the foundation of the world. He chose us to be his sons and daughters before creation came into existence. He knew that Adam, and subsequently each of us, would fail and be infected with sin. He planned for it in Christ. That was his Plan A. There was no other plan.

"For while we were still helpless, at the right time Christ died for the ungodly....But God demonstrates His own love toward us, in that while we were yet sinners, Christ died for us" (Romans 5:6, 8). *While we were yet sinners* describes our existence prior to the moment of salvation. While still in our sin, Jesus became our substitute and died in our place, releasing the floodgates of God's love and grace.

Paul writes "for by grace you have been saved through faith"

(Ephesians 2:8). God's grace brought salvation. It brought deliverance to us. We did not deserve it nor could we earn it. Apart from God we were helpless and our condition was hopeless. Every sinner who receives this grace through faith disappears in the shadow of the cross. As Paul says in Galatians 2:20, "I have been crucified with Christ; and it is no longer I who live, but Christ lives in me; and the life which I now live in the flesh I live by faith in the Son of God, who loved me, and delivered Himself up for me." The sinner has disappeared, swallowed up in the grace of God displayed in the Lord Jesus Christ.

At that moment of salvation several remarkable things occur in rapid succession, perhaps even simultaneously. We were, through the Holy Spirit, born again through the process of regeneration. "But when the kindness of God our Savior and His love for mankind appeared, He saved us, not on the basis of deeds which we have done in righteousness, but according to His mercy, by the washing of regeneration and renewing by the Holy Spirit, who He poured out upon us richly through Jesus Christ our Savior, that being justified by His grace we might be made heirs according to the hope of eternal life" (Titus 3:4-7). In that moment of time, a sinner is redeemed, reconciled to God, forgiven for sin, delivered from the kingdom of darkness and translated into the kingdom of God, accepted in Christ, justified and glorified. The sinner ceases to exist. A saint is the result of regeneration.

Let's take one aspect of this process, the gift of justification, which is a part of this regenerating work of the Holy Spirit. *To justify* is a legal term which is unfamiliar to most people. It means "to secure a favorable verdict," which in our case would mean acquittal and vindication before the judicial bench of God, rather than the death sentence we deserve. That kind of verdict would render us righteous in God's eyes, as though we had never sinned, even though all of us have. Yet by the grace of God through the death of Christ, we received this amazing judgment, a verdict of not guilty. We are no longer sinners. And to complete it, we receive God's gift of Christ's righteousness. It is imputed, charged to our account. All this takes place by grace through faith. It is God's gift.

At the completion of this magnificent, yet miraculous process, Paul sums up what takes place with these words: "Therefore if any man is in Christ, he is a new creature; the old things passed away; behold, new things have come" (2 Corinthians 5:17). A new creature lives a new lifestyle. The sinner has disappeared, and a new saint stands upon the old creature's ashes.

When God says you are no longer a sinner, you are no longer a sinner. We are covered in Christ's righteousness, and that is the person God now sees—a holy one, a saint. For a son or daughter of God to continue referring to themselves as *"a sinner saved by grace"* might sound quite noble and humble, but it is in reality a denial of what God has done for that person through Christ. It contradicts what the Bible clearly teaches and ultimately calls God a liar.

The Challenge

The word *liar* is a faint past echo of Adam's sin. He too believed a lie. And lies always obscure the truth and rob us of the most important aspects of our inheritance in Christ. That is, they steal our true identity. The name we claim will be the name we proclaim. The label we accept will either limit us or launch us as we seek out and embrace this intimate relationship with God.

The enemy knows that we will only live out what we believe. Because of this principle, he has convinced the vast majority of Christendom to bear the name of sinner rather than Christ. Jesus Christ is the Holy One, and we have been called by his name to bear his image, his righteousness, his holiness. Let us bear it well and in doing so, walk as saints, not sinners.

> *Abba Father, I have listened too long to the lies of the enemy and the shame of my own soul. Please forgive me. On the cross of Jesus my sins were forgiven, and you no longer remember them against me. I confess in faith you have bestowed on me the righteousness of Christ and because of that alone I am a holy one. I renounce the name of sinner and cast it off as a label of false humility and secret pride. In ignorance and unbelief I received it, but now I choose to reject and release it. I humble myself in Jesus's name and receive the name you have bestowed in your great love and grace—the*

name of saint. I reclaim all that it means. May my life from this moment forward bring honor and glory to you as I live out the fullest meaning of this wonderful name. In Jesus's name, amen.

Chapter 10
Total Salvation

And may your spirit and soul and body be preserved complete, without blame at the coming of our Lord Jesus Christ.
~ Paul, the apostle

My father was born during World War I, grew up during the Great Depression, and emerged into manhood as a sailor in the U. S. Navy looking for German U-boats on a submarine chaser in the north Atlantic during World War II. His views, opinions, and beliefs were forged in the fires of world confusion, economic chaos, and a Southern agrarian society in transition, and formed on the anvil under the hammer of a staunch Baptist faith.

Raised on a farm in rural Alabama, he understood hard work. And over the years, he had developed a maxim he lived by whether he was working, relaxing, or worshipping. *If it's worth doing, it worth doing right.* In other words, everything a person does should be done to best of one's ability and to completion.

Nothing bothered John Olen Hannah more than a half-done job, except one that had been finished in a haphazard manner. In his mind both were worthless and shameful. If something required an investment of time and an exertion of effort, he believed it should be done with quality and professionalism. My father instilled this belief in me from an early age.

As a father, I sought to instill this same principle of living through a relationship of encouragement and love with my own daughter Amber. One of those moments came in the fourth grade soon after Amber came to live with us.

One of the major requirements of the fourth grade is that every student in Alabama is required to learn all fifty states, their abbreviation, and each state's capital. I remember it was a daunting assignment for me almost forty-eight years ago when I was a fourth grader. I will never forget the day Amber came home with that assignment.

She was convinced she couldn't do it because it was too hard and too much for her to remember. She was on the verge of tears. She lacked self-confidence. She had had very little help with her school work and no encouragement whatever before we adopted her as our daughter. As her father, I offered to help her with the assignment, and her sky blue eyes lit up. I told her I believed in her and I knew she could do it because I recognized how smart she really was. Later that evening we got out the list and broke it down into manageable portions. We decided that we would learn five at a time. I encouraged her to study those five by writing them down—each state with its capital and abbreviation, over and over. After several minutes of doing this we would have a mock test. I would call out a state and she would write it down with its abbreviation and capital.

After we had taken our first mock test, I noticed that several of the states and capitals were misspelled. I encouraged her, but I also suggested she pay closer attention to the spelling. That's when I heard her utter these words, "Daddy, the teacher told us that as long as we were close she wouldn't count off for the spelling."

I was flabbergasted. "As long as we get the spelling close..." That sounded a little fishy to me and unlike any teacher I had ever had. All I could hear in my head was my father's voice: *If it's worth doing, it's worth doing right!* Before I knew it, those very same words tumbled out of my mouth.

"But Daddy, that's too hard! That's too much! The teacher said..." Amber argued.

"It is far easier to spell them correctly than it is incorrectly. If we do it as we learn them it will be a piece of cake. I'll help you. I believe you can do this," I replied. Tears welled up in her eyes and trickled down her cheeks, but she realized I was serious and the argument ended.

Every night we worked on the assignment together, and every step of the way I encouraged her. Slowly but surely she learned every state, every capital, and every abbreviation. As she learned, our relationship grew, and she began to trust again. She began to bloom, and her protective shell began to crack.

The big day of the test finally arrived, and Amber headed to take the test that would change her life. I will never forget that afternoon when she and Cathy returned home after school. Amber burst through the door with a smile on her face that stretched from ear to ear. Her blue eyes were sparkling, and she vigorously waved a piece of theme paper at me.

"Daddy! Daddy! I got all of them! I made an A+! I did better than anyone else in the class! I spelled all of them perfectly! Every last one of them!"

"I knew you could do it! I told you so! I am so proud of you!" I replied.

And then she threw her arms around my neck and hugged me with all her might. I will never forget that hug as long as I live. That sense of accomplishment and experience of doing the job right gave her a renewed confidence in herself that propelled her into trying things throughout her middle school, high school, and college experience that no one thought was possible.

I now realize my dad's motto was taken and adapted from the Bible. It was God's Word demonstrated by God's own personal example. "Whatever you do, do your work heartily, as for the Lord rather than for men; knowing that from the Lord you will receive the reward of the inheritance. It is the Lord Christ whom you serve" (Colossians 3:23-24).

When God does something, he does it right. He never leaves a job half-finished or completed with shoddy workmanship. Just look around at the countless examples of the amazing intricacy of creation. He has spared no cost and cut no corners. Observe the intricacy of a butterfly's wing, the complexity of the human brain, or how the carbon dioxide we exhale becomes oxygen once again through the sophisticated process of photosynthesis by trees and plants.

God left nothing to chance. He went to great extremes to make sure it worked correctly. He had a plan. He put it in motion. And none of his labor will be wasted. *If it's worth doing, it's worth doing right!* Nowhere is this more clearly illustrated than in our salvation.

More Than We Have Believed?

In God's mind, our salvation was worth doing. Therefore, it was certainly worth doing right. He did not scrimp or try to pinch pennies. Instead, he was extravagant. He sacrificed his beloved Son that we might become his children once again. That kind of love is indescribable, yet infinitely desirable. It compels a person to take notice once they have encountered it.

God could not simply wink at sin. Its dreadful price had to be paid, and it had to be paid in full. In the waning moments of the crucifixion, Jesus cried out in a loud voice, "*Tetelestai*—It is finished!" This was an accounting term in New Testament times, a word written on a business document or a receipt when full payment was received. The work of salvation that required Jesus to die for our sin was completed on the cross two thousand years ago, but its results continue forever. It has no expiration date. It was worth doing, so Jesus did it right.

I believe Jesus meant far more than most of us have been taught. Salvation has a fuller meaning than what we have believed. It encompasses far more than we may be aware of. And the time has come for every believer to enter the fullness or totality of the salvation Christ purchased with his life on the cross. Otherwise, we will never fully embrace God's Plan A for our lives or experience the fullness of the identity he sent his Son to restore.

We have all been taught that Jesus died on the cross to pay for our sins and the sins of the whole world. This is absolutely true and unarguable. First John 2:2 declares this: "He [Jesus] is the sacrifice for our sins. He takes away not only our sins but the sins of all the world" (NLT).

The problem is the payment was far more comprehensive than we have believed. Most Christ followers have at least a partial understanding of its spiritual aspects, but what about the emotional and physical ones? In most Christian circles, these are neglected, yet Christ died to give us more than partial salvation. He died to give us total salvation. The sin debt infected all the parts that compose who and what we are, the totality of a human being. Sin did not kill a portion of Adam; it claimed all of him. And to restore humanity, this salvation must redeem and reclaim all of Adam—his created fullness.

Otherwise that salvation is only partial. Abundant and eternal life must be experienced in totality, or it is not really abundant or eternal.

I don't believe God stopped with the spiritual aspect of salvation. If he did, then our salvation is only one third finished, and God always completes the work he starts.

Remember, *"If it's worth doing, it's worth doing right!"*

Buried but Not Lost

We are three-part (tripartite) beings, meaning we are spirit, soul, and body. There are many godly men and women who love God who would disagree and hold the position that we are two-part (bipartite), with the spirit and soul being synonymous. I respect them and my purpose here is not to dishonor them or attack their position as unbiblical. I simply hold a different view. As followers of Christ we can agree to disagree without burning one another at the stake or labeling another believer a heretic.

I would readily agree that there are numerous verses where the differences between spirit and soul are certainly ambiguous. But in my personal study and interpretation of Scripture, there seems to be clear differentiation between the spirit and the soul in certain verses. One of these is found in Paul's first letter to the church in Thessalonica. "Now may the God of peace Himself sanctify you entirely; and may your spirit and soul and body be preserved complete, without blame at the coming of our Lord Jesus Christ" (1 Thessalonians 5:23). According to this verse, God will sanctify or set apart and make holy all of us, and all of us entails our spirit, soul, and body.

We were created in the image and likeness of God, according to Genesis 1:26. God is one, yet he has revealed himself as Father, Son, and Holy Spirit. Since we are made in his image and likeness, we must mirror this Trinitarian reality in some way. One of the major ways I believe we do this is through our makeup as spirit, soul, and body. Our creation reflects our heavenly Father.

The writer of Hebrews also delineates between the spirit and the soul. "For the word of God is living and active and sharper than any two-edged sword, and piercing as far as the division of the soul and spirit, of both joints and marrow, and able to judge the thoughts and intentions of the heart" (Hebrews 4:12). If the soul and the spirit can be separated, then each is a separate entity, like the joint and the marrow. They cannot be synonymous or this allusion is faulty. The Holy Spirit does not waste words nor does he make spurious insinuations.

Many of the early church fathers of the first three centuries held a tripartite view of humanity. Church fathers such as Irenaeus, Tatian, Melito, Justin Martyr, Clement of Alexandria, Origen, Gregory of Nyssa, and Basil of Caesarea made references to the distinction of the spirit, soul, and body.

By the third century AD, several historical errors or heresies arose that caused a prejudice against the belief that we are trichotomous beings. All had to do with doctrinal disputes and explanations over the humanity and nature of Jesus. The early church fathers believed Jesus was both human and divine, but often struggled in finding the right terms to satisfactorily define or explain it. These definitions and explanations were an ongoing process as they wrestled with the words of Scripture. We often take this for granted.

During this time Augustine of Hippo burst on the scene, becoming the champion of orthodoxy as he fought and wrote against a heresy advocated by a British monk called Pelagius. Pelagius claimed that man had the capacity to seek after God apart from any movement of God or the Holy Spirit, and thus salvation could be affected by man's efforts. It denied the existence of original sin and gave man the ability to choose good on his own. Augustine argued that man was incapable of doing good apart from the sovereignty of God's grace due to the damage done to human nature as a result of original sin. Pelagianism was condemned as heresy, but its teachings persisted.

Augustine was a dichotomist, believing that the spirit and soul were the same. In his opinion, any distinction between the spirit and the soul was unprofitable. He rejected it as mystical. He also found it hard to defend and an open door for heresy. The Church began to veer toward Augustine's view as heresy after heresy arose with regard to the question of Christ's humanity and nature.

A compromise known as Semipelagianism pushed the majority of the Church into the dichotomous camp of Augustine. It held that the human spirit is excepted from original sin which only affected the body and soul. As such, human nature is essentially good and retains freedom of the will to initiate salvation. Augustine gave no ground, standing firm in the doctrine of original sin and his belief that apart from God's grace man is incapable in his fallen nature of choosing good. His view won out and over time, the spirit and soul became synonymous, and an intricate piece of our identity and inheritance was misplaced—buried beneath the fine dust of orthodox defense and doctrines.

Jesus restored our position as sons and daughters made in God's image and likeness—made to reflect the Trinity of God through spirit, soul, and body. God had created these three components of humanity as good, but all three had been affected by the Fall. Therefore, it was necessary for Jesus to redeem all three to bring a comprehensive or total salvation.

Spirit, Soul, and Body

We were created to mirror the Father, the Son, and the Holy Spirit as spirit, soul, and body. Each component is vital if we hope to reclaim our true identity in Christ and our inheritance from Christ and walk out God's Plan A. It is therefore crucial that we understand our makeup and how each affects who we are and what we become. The following delineations are not etched in stone. They are not always fixed and easily distinguished as the particular attribute of one or the other. The spirit, soul, and body have elements that do overlap. For instance, worship is something that all three participate in, but our spirit must lead in that worship. The sanctification process is being applied by the Holy Spirit in all three areas. Our task is to discover the proper balance of their partnership as we walk out the total salvation Jesus purchased on the cross. That is God's Plan A.

As a believer, our spirit is that immaterial part of us that has consciousness and appreciation for God. It is from our spirit that the Holy Spirit works and dwells. Here we are regenerated—born from above and receive the ability to commune with God once again in the intimacy of relationship. Here true fellowship—the ability to walk arm-and-arm with God—takes place.

Within the regenerated human spirit God shines the illuminating light of his presence. According to Solomon, the spirit of man is the lamp of the Lord, searching all the innermost parts of his being (Proverbs 20:27). Faith, hope, reverence, prayer, and worship are incubated in our spirit and released to bring glory to God. Jesus said to the woman at the well, "God is Spirit, and his worshipers must worship in spirit and truth" (John 4:24). God created the human spirit to guide and lead the human soul and body in a union that fully reflects the image and likeness of God.

When Adam disobeyed God, this light of God was extinguished in the human spirit by both sin and Satan. It became darkened, and its sensory ability to commune or even understand the things of God was deadened and deafened. The exact thing God had promised took place immediately in Adam's spirit. "If you eat its fruit [the tree of good and evil], you will surely die" (Genesis 2:17 NLT). Humanity's ability to connect with God died.

We are also a living soul. The soul is who we are, and through it we are recognized by others around us. It is our personality, what makes us singularly us! It is the immaterial part of a person where imagination, conscience, memory, reason, affections, will, and emotion reside. It includes our mind. Here all our experiences and memories combine to make us the person we are at this very moment. The soul is the seat of our passions, feelings, and desires. It is the rational thinking part of us, as well as the experiential sensing part of us.

The soul is often the point of the spear for Satan's attacks. Here the enemy seems to work his hardest as he appeals to our desires and our affections through temptation. Here he condemns us by reminding us of past failures and sins. Here he also pokes the painful wounds of the past, stirring up fear, insecurity, and shame.

The mind, which is a part of our soul, is the battlefield on which we daily battle the devil. Here God is working out day-by-day our sanctification by renewing our mind, memories, emotions, and affections as he conforms our will to his.

When Adam sinned and the light of the spirit was dowsed, his fallen soul took the leading and guiding position his spirit had once held. The soul was not equipped or created with the appropriate hardware to be in the lead. Perhaps this is the real reason Adam and Eve hid in the bushes after their disobedience. Their spirit shorted out, and the soul and body responded in the only way they knew how.

Unable to hear God, the selfish soul does what it desires, which is a deadly way to live. It always defaults into self-survival mode.

Finally, our body is the physical shell that houses the spirit and the soul. God created it as he did our spirit and soul in his image and likeness. In its present form it is temporal. The moment we are born, our body begins the aging process which culminates in the dying process because of both Adam's sin and our own.

Most of us are far more familiar with our bodies than we are with our soul or spirit. Our body houses our sensory perceptions—our ability to see, taste, touch, hear, and smell. Our bodies are composed of numerous systems like the cardiovascular, digestive, immune, respiratory, muscular, skeletal, and nervous systems. Together with other amazing systems we experience physical life.

Sadly, the body is subject to sickness, disease, injury, and wear and tear, whose ultimate cause is the sin-cursed environment we live in, as well as the sinful choices we or someone else has made. All sickness is the result of the entrance of sin into the world through Adam and the proliferation of sin by all his descendants. That one disobedience morphed into the Pandora's Box of the malevolent and malicious mess we presently reside in.

Sin's Paycheck

Evil was not God's handiwork. He did not create sin, disease, illness, or sickness. Murder, rape, war, hate, suicide, and ethnic cleansing were not a part of his masterpiece. These things were the result of disobedience multiplied ad infinitum and have become the toolbox of Satan to destroy the human race. Death, which is the culmination of these things, claims its eventual due. The wages for sin really is death.

When Adam fell, his spirit, soul, and body were infected with sin, which always results in death. His spirit could no longer commune with God in a Spirit-to-spirit manner. It was dead to God.

Adam's soul, without that Spirit-to-spirit connection with God, took control of what was left and turned toward what he thought was right or what would best meet his needs. He became selfish and prideful, something we all struggle with if we are gut-level honest. This inward turn rather than upward, along with a warped self-dependence, became tools that were easily manipulated and controlled by the enemy to destroy his soul one experience at a time.

Adam's body did not escape either. He may have lived nine hundred and thirty years, but God had originally created his son to live forever at the peak of spiritual, emotional, and physical health. From the moment the illegal fruit touched the man's rebellious lips, his body began the physical process of wearing out until it eventually shut down, decomposed, and returned to the dust from which it was created.

Death is separation from God, not just cessation of life. In that infamous moment, Adam's spirit was separated from God, walled up in a prison cell without a door out or an ability to do what it had been created to do. His soul became infected, and he died over and over as tragic events and pain-filled memories crowded his mind and crippled his emotions, further separating him from the joyous intimacy he had once experienced. And if this were not enough, his body which served as the means to express spirit and soul started to fail and shut down. His strength diminished and his eyes dimmed. His pace slowed as his hair grayed. Deep lines formed around his eyes and on his forehead as the weight of the world pressed him down. His arteries filled with plaque, and arthritis squeezed the fluidity out of his joints. He was dying daily, little by little, until everything God had made was fully separated from the true Source of life.

And that is the human condition apart from Jesus Christ—dead and separated from the One who created us for intimacy and whose intent was that we have an identity as sons and daughters. Instead—apart from Christ—we return to the dust from which we were created. And you and I are powerless to stop it or change even an iota of the final result in and of ourselves. Helpless and hopeless, we cannot find Christ on our own. We desperately need a Savior who will save the spirit, soul, and body!

Partial or Complete?

One sin sold the whole of humanity into bondage. We and all our ancestors before us became its slave—sold over and over to do its bidding. This bondage was holistic. It placed our spirit, soul, and body in spiritual, emotional, and physical chains that seem unbreakable.

Augustine was right when he taught that humanity apart from God's grace is hopelessly lost and unable to find God on its own.

But God came looking for us. He pursued us, the ones who were dead in our trespasses and sin. He stuck to his plan. He never wavered. "But when the fullness of the time came, God sent forth His Son, born of a woman, born under the Law, in order that He might redeem those who were born under the Law, that we might receive the adoption as sons" (Galatians 4:4-5). Jesus came to redeem us. Again, the word *redeem* means "to pay the asking price for a slave." Jesus purchased you and me, redeeming us from the slave market of sin we were imprisoned in. By *purchased*, I mean he paid for *all* of us—spirit, soul, and body.

The question then arises: Was his work of salvation partial or complete? Most Christians would stand to their feet and declare with an emphatic voice, "Salvation is complete!" I also believe that. When Jesus cried out from the cross, "It is finished," it was finished and he meant it.

If we believe this, then why do we preach, teach, and live in our actions only one third of that salvation? Most people have no issue with the spiritual aspect of salvation. But when it comes to the emotional and, yes, the physical aspects, for some reason we want to defer those to the future. That is, one day in the by-and-by we will enjoy health of soul and body. We say we believe salvation is complete, but we live as though it is partial, which means we don't really believe what we say.

Instead, we make excuses for God as though he has somehow changed and is now unable or unwilling to do the things he once did. These excuses go like this: God no longer does that anymore. Or, when we get to heaven we will finally be healed. Or, health is not the same as salvation. Or, we have the complete Bible now, which is all we need.

None of these excuses are legitimate. As a friend of mine says, "That dog won't hunt." They are bogus and will not stand up under the truth of Scripture. We tend to believe them because we don't see the results the early church saw, so the excuses sound really plausible. For most, a physical or emotional healing is no longer expected or anticipated. We have little or no faith in what God has done for us in Christ. Therefore, we are ecstatic about the spiritual aspect and willing to settle for less than the full amount Jesus purchased. We have allowed our experiences to dictate what God will or will not do, rather than allowing the witness of his acts recorded in the revelation of his Word.

The early church expected God to move, but do we? Really—do we? Somewhere along the way the biblical meaning of salvation lost two-thirds of its meaning. Perhaps through misuse, abuse, or lack of use the fullness of its meaning was lost. We must recapture its full meaning if we ever hope to live in God's Plan A.

A Fuller, Biblical Meaning

God sent his Son on a mission that had been planned before the foundation of the world was laid. He came to make right what had gone so terribly wrong—not part of it, but all of it.

Jesus's mission was to redeem humanity from the bondage of sin, reclaim Adam's lost inheritance, destroy the works of the devil, and restore our full identity as sons and daughters of God. John says, "The Son of Man appeared for this purpose, that He might destroy the works of the devil" (1 John 3:8). Luke declares, "For the Son of Man did not come to destroy men's lives, but to save them" (Luke 9:56).

Jesus came to break the stranglehold that Satan held over the human race. Luke tells us Jesus came to save us. He uses the Greek word *sozo*, which is translated "save." This word is rich in the fullness of its meaning, but sadly most Christians have only a partial understanding. Yet it is a comprehensive word that paints a clear picture of all God intended.

The most common meaning of *sozo* or save/salvation is forgiveness of sins. At salvation our spirit is freed from the darkness sin brought and once again made alive to God. The Spirit of God makes his abode—his temple—in our spirit. Salvation enables a person to once again commune and enjoy the intimacy of relationship God intended from the very beginning. We can once again hear God, talk with God, and follow the Spirit's leading.

But forgiveness of sin is not the lone meaning of *sozo*. There's far more. We are not just a spirit; we are also a soul and body. We need salvation in all three, and as you dig deeper into the meaning, it becomes evident that we do indeed have total salvation.

Sozo also carries the meaning of deliverance from torment. True salvation is deliverance. Jesus is called Savior, that is, he is the

Deliverer. The words are synonymous. The devil inflicts torment on our soul. Emotional wounds and hurts, wrong choices, failures, disappointments, betrayals, traumatic experiences, and shortcomings all find their home deep in our soul.

Here the enemy punches the replay button of our mind over and over as he torments us with condemnation and confusion. The more we believe his lies, the more tormented we become. Jesus brought salvation or deliverance from torment for our soul. He brought total healing for the soul—for our mind, our will, our emotions, and our memories. He died on the cross to deliver us from sin's effect on our mind.

Salvation is being worked out day-by-day in the soul. God is redeeming every wound, every wrong belief, every warped affection, and every painful memory—one at a time. This is why Scripture tells us to "work out your salvation with fear and trembling; for it is God who is at work in you, both to will and work for His good pleasure" (Philippians 2:12-13). Our soul is being transformed by the renewing of our mind according to Romans 12:2, so that we might actually live out God's will, which is good, acceptable, and perfect.

The *sozo* of Christ has one more aspect that is vital to total salvation. It carries the meaning of the healing of diseases. We can spiritualize this away, which is what the Church has done for almost seventeen centuries. Or we can blow away the dust of centuries of disuse and rediscover an element of our salvation that has been lost.

The ravages of sin on the human body are evident. All of us are experiencing these effects at this very moment. Yet Jesus came to save our body just as he came to save our spirit and our soul. Sadly, most Christians have accepted the belief that the body is evil and therefore a temporary container unfit for eternity. While it is true we will have a new body, the prototype is the one we have right now. This body will ultimately be transformed as this perishable puts on the imperishable. My point is our natural body is the seed from which our spiritual body will eventually spring. If we wish to grasp this future more fully, we need to spend some time studying the post-resurrection appearances of Christ. The body he now has is like the one we will eventually receive.

But Jesus came to die for this physical body all of us inhabit right now. He redeemed all of us, not just part of us. This body is important to God. He created it. It's his handiwork. I don't fully grasp nor can I explain why, but when God chose to give a visual picture to creation of who he is, he created Adam in his image and likeness. This image and likeness of God is mirrored not only in our spirit and soul, but also in our body. Jesus came in a genuine human body. Many of the heresies of the early church could not grasp this. His body was just as human as ours is. When pinched, Jesus felt the same pain we feel. When his body was pierced by thorns and nails, he bled just like you or I would.

Sozo meant healing the physical body, and when Christ pronounced from the cross, "It is finished," he also purchased physical healing. God's desire for us was never sickness or disease. He did not create them; they are the byproducts of Adam's sin. Jesus came to reverse the curse and redeem us fully from its effects.

I don't entirely understand physical healing, but my ignorance or lack of experience does not limit God. One of his names is Jehovah Rapha—the God who heals. God's names reveal God's character, and these never change. I don't see everyone I pray for healed, but I continue to pray because I believe salvation is complete—that is, a total work that includes the body, as well as the spirit and soul. I don't have all the answers. In fact, in this area I have more questions than answers. But my questions will not cause me to draw back or retreat from pursuing this truth.

Old Testament Roots

Roots are important. They provide a solid foundation on which a plant, a tree, or even a belief system can grow and produce fruit. Without deep roots all will shrivel up and die. This belief that as human beings we are spirit, soul, and body and that God has provided total salvation for each part has deep roots. These roots reach far back into the Old Testament.

The work of the Suffering Servant, the Messiah of Isaiah 53, is prophetically proclaimed at least seven hundred years before Jesus died on the cross. Here in this passage God reveals what his Messiah would do in his sacrificial work for humankind:

> *Who has believed our message? And to whom has the arm of the Lord been revealed? For He grew up before Him like a tender shoot, and like a root out of parched ground; He has no stately form or majesty that we should look upon Him, nor appearance that we should be attracted to Him. He was despised and forsaken of men, a man of sorrows, and acquainted with grief; and like one from whom men hide their face, he was despised and we did not esteem him. Surely our griefs He Himself bore, and our sorrows He carried; yet we ourselves esteemed Him stricken, smitten of God, and afflicted. But He was pierced through for our iniquities; the chastening for our well-being fell upon Him, and by His scourging we are healed. All of us like sheep have gone astray, each of us has turned to his own way; but the Lord has caused the iniquity of us all to fall on Him* (Isaiah 53:1-6).

Translating is a tricky process. Every translator approaches the task with some personal bias—it is inevitable. It is very interesting how verse four is translated and what words the translators chose to use. In other Old Testament passages the Hebrew words for *sorrows* and *griefs* are translated differently on a consistent basis. The word for *sorrows* is "pain" and the word for *griefs* is "sickness." In fact, the NASB offers these as alternate reading. Isaiah 53:4 can also be read this way: "Surely our sickness He Himself bore, and our pains He carried; yet we esteemed Him stricken, struck down by God, and afflicted."

This extended passage from Isaiah 53 has been used to describe the spiritual payment Jesus made, but it also includes the emotional and physical as well. Jesus was a man who knew sorrow, which is physical and mental. He was intimately acquainted with sickness and disease for it was all around him. Verse four tells us clearly he bore our sickness and carried our pains on the cross. He was pierced through for our transgressions (the sin of stepping outside the bounds set by God). He was crushed for our iniquities (thinking that God's law does not apply to us and teaching others to ignore it). Jesus was chastened for our peace (the Hebrew word is *shalom*, which means "wholeness of spirit, soul, and body"). And by the scourging he received at the hands of the Roman soldiers we are healed.

This passage in Isaiah graphically describes the essence of the salvation Jesus purchased on the cross. It was total, not partial, so that he might bring healing and redemption to our spirit, soul, and body. He was crucified so that our rebellion, transgression, and iniquity could be paid for, bringing us healing in the spirit. He was chastened and disciplined in our place so that we might experience wholeness in our tortured mind and soul. Jesus was beaten—scourged beyond recognition—so that by those stripes our physical healing might come and our bodies be redeemed. The atonement of Jesus was complete. It was for the total healing of our spirit, soul, and body, which corresponds exactly to the total loss Adam suffered when he tasted the forbidden fruit.

Salvation is more than a fire insurance policy that keeps a person out of hell. It is the one thing that gives life back to our spirit, soul, and body. Jesus came to save us from all the ravages of sin, not just one or two. He came to provide reconciliation with God so that we might once again commune spirit to Spirit and heart to heart. Jesus paid the entire debt so you and I can experience all the benefits. Sadly, in most cases we fail to experience what we don't know or don't believe.

Accessing the Totality of Salvation

The totality of salvation begins first in our spirit. Here the Holy Spirit comes to live and make us alive again unto God. But we may not be experiencing the fullness of our salvation.

Perhaps you know Christ as your Lord and Savior. He has healed your spirit and you hear his voice from time to time. But your soul—your mind, emotions, desires, affection, and memories—is messed up. Perhaps you are filled with hurt, wounds from the past, a betrayal, a rejection, a failure, or a disappointment, and you have allowed anger—or jealousy, envy, hate, rage, thoughts of murder, depression, anxiety, unforgiveness, or fear—to unknowingly give the devil a foothold in your life. Due to this you are being tormented, and there is no peace, no answers, and no way out. Perhaps you feel you are going insane, and if something doesn't happen soon you will lose it. If so, you are in bondage.

Perhaps you have taken another path and become cynical and silent, toxic to anyone who tries to get close. Perhaps you find it impossible to drop the walls of your defense system so that you can express real love and receive it. If so, you are in bondage.

Perhaps you have an addiction. It could be physical, emotional, or mental, and you are a slave to it and feel you can't live without it. You are in bondage.

It may even be demonic. Perhaps you refuse to give up something God has clearly told you to put down. Perhaps you've hardened your heart and won't forgive. You are in bondage.

Jesus endured unfathomable suffering so that you might experience peace in your soul at this very moment. If you will surrender that issue, no matter how far back it happened or how awful or traumatic it was, or how embarrassing it is—God will heal it. That's his promise based on the total salvation he purchased for you in Christ.

But the healing of the spirit and the soul is only two-thirds of the equation. Perhaps you are physically sick and need healing in your physical body. Jesus purchased that on the cross as well. Every person who came to Jesus in the New Testament and requested healing received it. Check it out for yourself.

In Jesus's day, and for most of the history of the Church, it was believed that sickness and disease were the handiwork of the devil. But somewhere along the way, the Church started to believe and teach that God either sends sickness or allows it so that it will make us better people as we learn character from suffering. The New Testament speaks of suffering for our faith in a hostile environment but not as a result of God giving a saint some type of sickness as a faith builder.

All sickness has its birth, its genesis, in Adam's sin. Sin spawned sickness. Some sickness is the direct result of sin in our life—of doing what we know we shouldn't do or not doing something we know to do. Some sickness is the result of someone else's sin. And some sickness is the result of living in a sin-cursed environment contaminated to its very core with sin.

Please hear me! I am not saying that you or someone you love is sick or has a disease because of personal sin in your life. I am saying God is not the source of that sickness or disease. Can he use it? Certainly he can, but he did not create it or send it to your address. That goes against his very nature and name. Remember his name always gives us a picture into his character or nature. "For I, the Lord [Jehovah], am your healer [Rapha]" (Exodus 15:26).

Clearly the Bible teaches that we are spirit, soul, and body. Clearly it teaches that the redemptive work of Jesus was complete. The real question is: Do we really believe it enough to pursue it with all our heart and access its fullest meaning? If salvation really means forgiveness of sin, deliverance from torment, and healing of diseases, why would we ever stop pursuing our inheritance until we receive all of it? Why would any Christian stop one-third or even two-thirds of the way there?

God's Plan A was to make us whole in the totality of our being, just the way he created us. He wants each of us to walk in the fullness of the salvation Jesus died for. We must press in for those things he has purchased and given us access to. The dust may have settled on yours, but if you rise up and blow it off, it is still yours and its benefits are yet to be discovered.

If you do, you will see the broken-hearted restored. You will see the shattered put back together. You will see the demonized delivered and the sick healed. The issue does not rest in whether God wants to do this or if it is his plan. The issue rests with those of us who are the redeemed of the Lord. Will we believe God's promises and access our God-given inheritance of total salvation?

Just remember—*if it's worth doing, it's worth doing right!*

> *Abba Father, you sought me out and pursued me with your love. I confess I cannot fully comprehend a love so deep. You created me spirit, soul, and body as an expression of who you are. You redeemed all of me—spirit, soul, and body—not just part of me. I will pursue that salvation in every area of my life. I will reclaim all that is mine with your help. Thank you for blowing away the dust that has hidden my inheritance and hindered my access to the totality of your salvation Jesus purchased on the cross. I receive it! I believe it! I will walk in it! In Jesus's name, amen.*

Chapter 11
Sealed, Spirit-filled, and Saturated

> You might as well try to see without eyes, hear without ears, or breathe without lungs, as try to live the Christian life without the Holy Spirit.
> ~ D. L. Moody

A catalyst is a change agent. It can be any subject that accelerates a reaction. It might be an element, an event, or even a person. Ninety percent of all commercially produced products including foods, cosmetics, fuels, and chemicals involve a catalyst at some point in their manufacturing process. Without a catalyst a change might never occur.

God is the ultimate catalyst. Everything God touches is changed, yet he never changes, which is the definition of a catalyst. The changes God initiates are always for good not evil, always for better not worst. He does not introduce change just for the sake of change. He gets no secret thrill from turning things inside out or upside down. He causes change because change is necessary to fulfill his plan.

There had to be a tree of the knowledge of good and evil to test Adam's heart. It was necessary for Abraham and Isaac to visit a lonely altar on the wind-swept slopes of Moriah. Jacob had to wrestle with the angel of the Lord. It was essential that Moses encounter the burning bush. It was crucial for David to endure the persecution of King Saul. The path that Jesus walked ultimately intersected with the necessity of a cruel wooden cross.

There had to be a catalyst of God's touch in each of their lives. Otherwise, there would be no experience or expression of real love. Faith would be a concept rather than a reality. God's promise would have only been a hope-so, his covenant just another broken contract. Without persecution, there would have been no king who was a man after God's own heart. And ultimately, without Moriah's second altar formed in the shape of a Roman cross, there could be no Savior to redeem humanity.

God has the plan. It was fixed in his mind in eternity past, and through history the catalyst of his touch has guided the fluidity of its flow toward an ultimate fulfillment. Since creation, the imprint of his fingerprint in both the visible and invisible world has been the Holy Spirit.

The Indwelling

As followers of Christ, we have the unique privilege of hosting the Holy Spirit's presence within us on a permanent basis. He indwells every believer and comes to reside in the temple of our human spirit at the very instant we are born again. In Ephesians 1:13, Paul asserts, "In Him [in Christ], you also, after listening to the message of truth, the gospel of your salvation—having also believed, you were sealed in Him with the Holy Spirit of promise." This sealing takes place at the precise moment when "by one Spirit we were all baptized into one body, whether Jews or Greeks, whether slaves or free, and we were all made to drink of one Spirit" (1 Corinthians 12:13).

The indwelling presence of the Holy Spirit is *the* decisive factor in determining whether or not a person is truly a believer. But if anyone does not have the Spirit of Christ, he does not belong to Him (Romans 8:9). It is not the aisle we walk down, an altar we kneel at, a prayer recited, or one's name on a church roster that defines us as Christian. The proof is not what we have done, but rather *who* lives within us—*who* has sealed us. The proof really is *in* the pudding.

This privilege is unique, and not every follower of God has experienced it. Prior to Jesus, only Adam and Eve enjoyed this distinction. At their creation God breathed his *Ruach*, his Holy Spirit, into Adam and he came to life. Eve was fashioned out of the living spirit, soul, and body of Adam that was indwelt by the Spirit, thus I believe God bequeathed the same gift to her as well. When Adam and Eve sinned, the Spirit of God departed.

The Scriptures do not tell us God *indwelled* those who followed him in the Old Testament. It tells us that the Spirit was *in* a handful, *came upon* many, and *filled* a few, but his personal relationship was very limited, and not every follower of God experienced his work or permanence in their lives.

Yet this indwelling was an original part of God's A Plan. Adam and Eve were able to commune with God prior to their fall due of the indwelling of the Holy Spirit—his living presence within them. They could relate, understand, and experience all that God is because of this. God was setting down the pattern that he intended all humanity to follow. The catalyst was not an outside force but the indwelling Spirit. Moment by moment this couple would be empowered by God with a guidance system that would provide the capability for them to carry out the precise plan of God for their lives—if they were willing to listen and obey. But sadly, as we all know, that unique pattern was shattered as the stench of sin replaced the fragrant aroma of the Spirit.

That is, until Jesus came!

The Biblical Pattern

For Jesus to fulfill, to complete the calling of the last Adam, he needed the Holy Spirit. In Chapter 5, I have shared my own belief and one I think is proven by Scripture that although Jesus is God, everything he did while here on earth before his death on the cross was done as a man indwelt by and filled with the Spirit of God. Every touch, every expression of compassion and love, every sermon, every teaching, every healing, every miracle, and every deliverance were the direct result of Jesus depending on the guidance and power of the Holy Spirit. Apart from the Father's direction and the Spirit's empowering, Jesus could do nothing. The Holy Spirit was the catalyst for every work Jesus performed.

Remember Jesus was reinstating and fulfilling the original plan of God that Adam failed to carry out. As the last Adam, that was his purpose. This is somewhat like a running back in a football game who fumbles the ball as he attempts to run the ball down the field to score. As that ball bounces around, anyone can pick it up. Jesus picked up the bouncing ball Adam fumbled, continued the play that had been called in the huddle and carried it into God's end zone for a score. When God called that specific play in eternity past, he knew it would go for a touchdown. And we live in the aftermath of the celebration and its rewards.

God often works in patterns. For example, the Holy of Holies, found first in the Tabernacle of Moses and later in the Temple at Jerusalem, was patterned after the original throne room of God in heaven. There are patterns or types of Jesus found throughout the Old Testament. Joseph was a type of savior to his family and the nation of Egypt. Moses was a type of deliverer as he led the people of Israel out of bondage. Joshua was a type of salvation as he opened the door for Israel to step into the Promised Land. All of these represent a picture Jesus fulfilled.

At the moment of Adam's creation, God breathed his *Ruach*, his Spirit and breath, and Adam became a living soul. God breathed into Adam's nostrils the breath of life. He was equipped to carry out the mandate of reproduction, rulership, relationship, and reflection. The Holy Spirit was the catalyst that brought Adam to life and whose presence would provide the power needed to live the life of God. This God-quality of life came not from the fertile soil but from the Spirit.

This same Holy Spirit acted in a similar way at the conception of Jesus, at the precise moment of the Incarnation. When God was made flesh, Luke records exactly how it would take place with the words of the angel Gabriel to Mary: "The Holy Spirit will come upon you, and the power of the Most High will overshadow you; and for that reason the holy offspring shall be called the Son of God" (Luke 1:35). Truly this is a mystery whose depth we cannot adequately plumb or understand, but perhaps God breathed his *Ruach* once again and God the Son was joined to flesh as the last Adam. It seems the Spirit of God was the catalyst of the Incarnation.

Perhaps this would be a bit of a stretch were it not for an event that John recorded in his gospel. A sense of uncertainty had fallen on Resurrection Sunday and the disciples, who were filled with fear and uncertainty, had bolted the doors to the house in which they were hiding. We don't know how many were there. All we know for certain is that Thomas was absent. All of a sudden, the resurrected Lord Jesus was standing in their midst. A moment before he had not been there and now he was.

John recorded an event that none of the other gospel writers recorded. These words are often ignored or debated by scholars, teachers, and preachers because they don't fit a pattern the Church has become comfortable with and perhaps tried to impose incorrectly. Please allow your spirit, heart, and mind to hear these words:

> *When therefore it was evening on the first day of the week, and the doors were shut where the disciples were, for fear of the Jews, Jesus came and stood in their midst and said to them, "Peace be with you." And when He had said this, He showed them both His hands and His side. The disciples therefore rejoiced when they saw the Lord. Jesus therefore said to them again, "Peace be with you; as the Father has sent Me, I also send you." And when He had said this, He breathed on them, and said to them, "Receive the Holy Spirit. If you forgive the sins of any, their sins have been forgiven them; if you retain the sins of any, they have been retained"* (John 20:19-23).

Did you catch verse twenty-two—"He breathed on them, and said to them, 'Receive the Holy Spirit.'" Do you see a pattern? Every time God breathes the Holy Spirit something new happens. Adam became a living soul. God the Son became flesh. The disciples became new creations. The payment for their sin had been made on Friday as Jesus died on the cross. Sunday had now arrived, and the validation of that transaction was stamped on human history forever as God the Son breathed new life into his little group of followers.

Jesus gave them the indwelling gift of the Spirit at that moment. It is the same gift he had promised them just a few days earlier when he said, "And I will ask the Father, and He will give you another Helper, that He may be with you forever, that is the Spirit of truth, whom the world cannot receive because it does not behold Him or know Him, but you know Him because he abides with you, and will be in you" (John 14:16-17). Jesus is saying, "I will give you one who is like me, *another of the same kind*. He is the Helper who comes to advise, exhort, comfort, strengthen, encourage you and who will intercede for you at all times. But now, he will be in you!"

This may be a different perspective for you, but I ask that you consider the pattern. It seems to be the pattern of creation, the Incarnation, and perhaps even the new creation. One thing is for certain—the catalyst of God is no longer on the outside. He has gained entrance once again to the inside of every member of this new species birthed by Jesus Christ through faith.

A Filling with Power

Most believers have been taught that the Church was birthed on the Day of Pentecost, and that may be true, but the first believers were indwelled by the Holy Spirit on the evening of the resurrection. New life came through the Father by the Spirit to Jesus that morning, and he breathed that same new life by the Spirit into his disciples that evening. This new life was both a quantity of life and a quality of life. It was eternal and abundant. Both were to run concurrent with the other. Eternal does not mean when you get to heaven. Your eternal life began the moment you came to Christ. *Abundant* describes its quality—in essence, more than is necessary. Jesus promised both when he said, "The thief comes only to steal, and kill, and destroy; I came that they might have life, and might have it abundantly" (John 10:10). The disciples had been baptized by the Spirit into the body of Christ. They had been placed there through the indwelling of the Spirit.

Fast forward forty days and listen to the instructions Jesus gives to his followers. As he prepares to ascend, he promises them the power they will need to do the task he had been preparing them for the last three and a half years. The last words of a person are very, very important, and these are the Lord's last instructions before he ascended into heaven.

> *And gathering them together, He commanded them not to leave Jerusalem, but to wait for what the Father had promised, "Which," He said, "you heard of from Me; for John baptized with water, but you shall be baptized with the Holy Spirit not many days from now." And so when they had come together, they were asking Him, saying, "Lord, is it at this time You are restoring the kingdom to Israel?" He said to them, "It is not for you*

> *to know the times or epochs which the Father has fixed by His own authority; but you shall receive power when the Holy Spirit has come upon you; and you shall be My witnesses both in Jerusalem, and in all Judea and Samaria, and even to the remotest part of the earth"* (Acts 1:4-8).

Jesus had given them the person of the Holy Spirit, now he would fulfill God's promise to pour out the power of the Holy Spirit without measure. The Spirit of God had baptized them into the body of Christ, and now the reigning Christ would baptize them in the power of the Holy Spirit. John the Baptist had prophesied this exact thing in Mark 1:7-8 when he said, "After me One is coming who is mightier than I, and I am not fit to stoop down and untie the thong of His sandals. I baptized you with water: but He will baptize you with the Holy Spirit."

I don't see this as two separate works, as some others do, but rather as a continuation of one work completed through the partnership of the Son and the Spirit. This was God's plan and his purpose all along. The indwelling of the Spirit signifies our authenticity in Christ, but this baptism by Jesus in/with/by the Spirit endows us with the capacity to demonstrate the power of Christ, and thus it validates our authenticity. You can sew the Carhartt label in any pair of pants you want to, but if those pants don't perform up to the level of that name in the work place, they are not Carhartts. We can call ourselves Christians, but we must also demonstrate Christ through the Spirit's empowerment if that label is to fit.

Yet many who profess to be authentic possess little or no capacity to demonstrate their validity. They cannot prove what they proclaim. A powerless Christian is an oxymoron. It does not compute with the witness of the Scriptures.

Adam was created to be a visible representative of God to creation—created in God's image and likeness. Every Christ-follower is re-created in the image and likeness of Christ. We are then filled with the Spirit so that we can do the works Jesus did and even greater ones (John 14:12).

On the Day of Pentecost, Jesus poured out the Spirit and baptized his followers in the power of the Holy Spirit, which is reminiscent of his own baptism by John when the Spirit rested on him. Even a casual look at these misfits will show even the most hesitant that something amazing happened to them that day. They went from fear-filled to fearless, from hesitant to bold, from self-focused to laser-focused on the King and his kingdom. It is obvious that the baptism of the Spirit—this filling of power—changed them.

Sadly, it is not so evident in most believers today. Perhaps the problem is we have settled for less than what God intends. Perhaps we have accepted "a form of godliness but denied its power" (2 Timothy 3:5). In the early church, spiritual power validated one's authenticity. In the modern church it seems we would rather proclaim the message than demonstrate it. Jesus and the early church did both. It seems in our day much of the Church has neglected this divine model of both proclamation and demonstration and is following a pattern (*a form of godliness*) handed down from generation to generation, but not the *powerful* pattern bequeathed to the bride of Christ by God, and certainly not the one demonstrated by her Bridegroom.

Perhaps we have not obeyed God's Plan A and tarried until the catalyst has come: "But you shall receive power when the Holy Spirit has come upon you" (Acts 1:8). Have you received the power you need to live the life Christ has called you to live? Only you can answer that question, and answer it you must. If you have not received his power, then ask and keep on asking. Seek and keep on seeking. Knock and keep on knocking. This is the heritage of those who are called by Christ's name, a vital part of his promise: "If you then, being evil, know how to give good gifts to your children, how much more shall your heavenly Father give the Holy Spirit to those who ask Him?" (Luke 11:13).

No Pattern Available

This baptism or filling has no pattern, though many would like you to believe it does. Scripture is always the best teacher, and if a pattern existed, certainly it could be found within its pages. The book of Acts provides us with the eye-witness accounts of the first Spirit baptisms or fillings. Perhaps we should look there first instead of denominational dogma and sectarian doctrine.

On the Day of Pentecost, Jesus poured out his Spirit on his followers who were praying and waiting. Now you would think if God intended for us to develop a pattern, surely it would come from the account of this as found in Acts 2:1-4. But there is no pattern—no "one plus one always equals two." Some argue this passage provides for a specific pattern, and others would explain the lack of a pattern as a one-time event that now happens to all believers without their even knowing it. I don't accept either explanation.

In Acts 2, the believers waited for ten days in an upper room, praying and worshipping, and then Jesus poured out the Holy Spirit. They were already followers of Christ. The Holy Spirit descended and all of them spoke in tongues, giving witness of the risen Lord in different languages.

> When the day of Pentecost had come, they were all together in one place. 2 And suddenly there came from heaven a noise like a violent rushing wind, and it filled the whole house where they were sitting. 3 And there appeared to them tongues as of fire distributing themselves, and they rested on each one of them. 4 And they were all filled with the Holy Spirit and began to speak with other tongues, as the Spirit was giving them utterance (Acts 2:1-4).

Here's the pattern: Believers + time span of waiting + Holy Spirit + tongues = empowerment.

The second occurrence happened in Acts 8 as the evangelist Philip went to Samaria and preached Jesus. Crowds showed up and multitudes came to faith in Christ. A true awakening broke out! They were unbelievers who believed and were baptized in the name of Jesus, yet there is no mention of the Spirit falling. Word got back to the apostles in Jerusalem, so they sent Peter and John to check it out. Pay close attention to what happened upon their arrival:

> Now when the apostles in Jerusalem heard that Samaria had received the word of God, they sent them Peter and John, who came down and prayed for them,

> *that they might receive the Holy Spirit. For He had not yet fallen upon any of them; for they had simply been baptized in the name of the Lord Jesus. Then they began laying their hands on them, and they were receiving the Holy Spirit* (Acts 8:14-17).

Here we have a different pattern. Unbelievers + gospel + faith in Jesus + water baptism + prayer and laying on of hands + the reception of the Holy Spirit (not evidenced by tongues) = empowerment. This is not the same pattern as in Acts 2.

There is yet a third pattern found in Acts 10 as Peter visits the house of Cornelius, a Roman soldier and a Gentile. As Peter was still preaching, the Holy Spirit fell:

> *While Peter was still speaking these words, the Holy Spirit fell upon all those who were listening to the message. And all the circumcised believers who had come with Peter were amazed, because the gift of the Holy Spirit had been poured out upon the Gentiles also. For they were hearing them speaking with tongues and exalting God. Then Peter answered, "Surely no one can refuse the water for these to be baptized who have received the Holy Spirit just as we did, can he?" And He ordered them to be baptized in the name of Jesus Christ* (Acts 10:44-48).

Here is the pattern: Unbelievers + gospel + still listening to the gospel when faith occurred + Holy Spirit falls + tongues and praise + water baptism (no laying on of hands) = empowerment. This pattern does not match either of the previous ones.

The fourth and final occurrence happened many years later in Ephesus as Paul arrives on a mission to evangelize the city. He met twelve men who had heard the message of John the Baptist concerning Jesus. They are called disciples. Paul does not ask if they know Jesus (that is, had they placed their faith in him); he assumes they do and are already believers. Instead he asks if they have received the Holy Spirit:

> *And he [Paul] said, "Into what then were you baptized?" And they said, "Into John's baptism." And Paul said, "John baptized with the baptism of repentance, telling the people to believe in Him who was coming after him, that is, in Jesus." And when they heard this, they were baptized in the name of the Lord Jesus. And when Paul had laid his hand upon them, the Holy Spirit came on them, and they began speaking in tongues and prophesying* (Acts 19:3-6).

Here we have another pattern that is different from the previous three. Believers + a clarification of the gospel + water baptism + laying on of hands + Holy Spirit fell + spoke in tongues and prophesied = empowerment.

My point is that there were four clear occurrences where the Holy Spirit fell and not one of them matches any of the others perfectly. The pattern is at best erratic and at worst non-existent. Two of the groups were already believers and two were not. Some spoke in tongues and others did not. Some received the laying on of hands, while some did not. Some were baptized in water and others were not. There is no set biblical pattern for this empowerment.

Perhaps there is an absence of a pattern because God is in charge and would rather not surrender his purpose and plan to some neat little configuration that we would likely turn into a theology we can argue, fuss, and fight over, or a prerequisite litmus test for being a *real* Christian (which is exactly what we have done).

I don't buy the argument that what took place in Acts were one-time events that can never be duplicated. If that is so, twenty-one centuries later we are getting short-changed, because we need the power of the Holy Spirit just as much as these early believers did. I don't ascribe to the belief that Acts was a transitional book and therefore you can't build doctrine based on it. That idea goes directly against 2 Timothy 3:16: "All Scripture is inspired by God and profitable for teaching, for reproof, for correction, for training in righteousness." Acts 1-28 certainly fits in the *all* of Scripture.

I also do not buy the belief that this was the same event and that it occurred three times to three different people groups—Jews,

Samaritans (half Jew and half Gentile), and Gentiles (if you forget about the Acts 19 account). I believe God promised to pour out his Spirit on all believers and that's his Plan A—his only plan. I believe Jesus desires to baptize (or fill) every believer in/by/with the Holy Spirit and thereby empower us to walk in the fullness of the Spirit. It may be concurrent with a person coming to Christ at salvation, and it may occur later. This is not a second work of grace but a completion of God's *only* work of grace.

The true key is not when, where, how, or if you spoke in tongues. The question is: Do you know that Jesus has baptized you in/by/with the Holy Spirit? As Paul asked the Ephesians, "Did you receive the Holy Spirit when you believed?" This implies they would have surely known it. It would have been evident. It seems members of the early church knew it the moment it happened. They were energized and empowered. There was a change and their lives were different.

Do you know? You should! If you don't, obey Jesus, ask him to fill you or baptize you (you choose the language you want to use although they mean the same), and keep on asking until you receive the empowerment you need to live out God's Plan A.

Saturated with the Spirit

God's Plan A for your life is that you be sealed, Spirit-filled, and saturated with his Holy Spirit. He was the catalyst in Jesus's life and ministry and he must be in our lives as well. Every work Jesus did was accomplished through the power of the Holy Spirit. He came to restore this missing element in the lives of God's people.

The Spirit of God no longer comes for a season or a work and then leaves as he did in the Old Testament. God's Spirit lives in us—he indwells us—and through his life we are made alive to God in Christ. We are the literal temple (the root meaning of *temple* is "to inhabit" from which we get the word *indwell*) of the living God—the habitation of God, which is a privilege that was totally unknown from Adam's fall to Christ's victory on the cross.

God's Spirit now seals every believer at the moment of salvation until the day of redemption. This sealing could be likened to an engagement ring—a binding promise that we belong to him and that he belongs to us. The Spirit of God guarantees our authenticity as a believer and will do so until we see Jesus face-to-face. It is a down payment on our soul made by God through Christ and validated by the presence of the Holy Spirit within us. We can rest assured that what God has paid for he will fully collect on that day when he comes for his bride. Not one person Jesus has paid for will be lost. That should give us peace of mind to know that we are eternally secure in Christ.

God did not simply seal us, he also desires to Spirit-fill us. That is, he wants to endow us with the same power Jesus exercised. There is no possible way to live the Christian life without being filled by the Holy Spirit. It cannot be done simply on obedience, perseverance, tenacity, and will power. If that were so, as some teach, we would be talking about the perseverance, tenacity, and the will power of Jesus. Instead, we have a prototype of a man *full of the Spirit, led by the Spirit*, and who worked *in the power of the Holy Spirit*. He came to fill the broken prototype of Adam and fulfill it as the last Adam. If it was necessary for Jesus to be Spirit-filled, then it is most assuredly a necessity for us. To fully reclaim our identity and inheritance in Christ, we need the same power that raised Jesus from the dead.

Spirit-filled has become a term that overwhelms some believers with fear and apprehension. Yet it is a biblical description of our position and power in Christ. We must reclaim it, believe it, receive it, and start walking out this privileged position in our daily lives. It is our inheritance, a necessary part of God's gift to us.

A part of God's Plan A was to saturate us in his Holy Spirit—to live in us, to fill us, and flow out of us on a continual basis. Like a hand that fits snuggly in a glove, so too the Holy Spirit should fill and saturate each of us.

The enemy fears nothing more than a person saturated in the presence and power of the Holy Spirit, for he knows he cannot withstand that person no matter what temptation or trial he hurls. The Holy Spirit was the power source for Jesus, the author and finisher of our faith, and he must be ours as well. He is, according to Peter who stood on the Day of Pentecost and explained the marvelous gift he had just received, for every believer. "For the promise [i.e., the gift of the Holy Spirit] is for you and your children, and for all who are far off, as many as the Lord our God shall call to Himself" (Acts 2:39).

So, the question remains: Are you sealed, Spirit-filled, and saturated with the Holy Spirit?

> *Abba Father, you have given me all that I need to be all that you desire. I confess I have attempted to walk out my destiny and my purpose in my flesh, through my own strength and will power, and I have failed miserably. I thank you for indwelling me with your Spirit and sealing me until the day of redemption. I confess in faith that I am an authentic son/daughter because of your Spirit's presence in my life. I choose to rest in Christ's finished work and trust your Witness who lives within me as a guarantee that I am eternally secure. I ask you to baptize/fill me with the power of your Holy Spirit. I confess I cannot do anything to please you apart from the power of your Spirit. O God, I cry out for the power that was present and active in the early church. I yearn to do the works Jesus did and even greater ones so that I might cast them as crowns of thanksgiving at your feet—tangible tokens of my love for you. I humble myself before you and cry out for a fresh baptism of/filling by your Spirit that I might fully reclaim the identity and inheritance you declare is already mine. Come, Holy Spirit! Come, O holy Catalyst! You be the hand that guides me and I will be your willing vessel. In Jesus's name, amen.*

Chapter 12
A Victor, Not a Victim

> Today we do not fight for victory;
> We fight from victory.
> ~ Watchman Nee

The Christian life is a militant lifestyle lived out on a deadly battlefield. We face a real enemy who has been defeated by Jesus Christ but not yet destroyed. He has been stripped of his authority but not of his power. He has been mortally wounded, but that wounding makes him extremely dangerous. A defeated foe is a deadly foe when he has nothing else to lose. Therefore, he has set his sights on you.

Satan is a gambler who bets the odds. He is playing a high stakes game, wagering that we have little, if any, clue concerning our identity or our inheritance in Christ. And the chances are pretty good he is right. Most of the Church is unaware of his purpose and blind to his game. Ignorance or uncertainty in this area makes us a viable target because we pose little or no threat to him.

Many in the body of Christ have ingested the bogus propaganda he has been putting out for hundreds of years. Powerful—yes! But he is a created being that was defeated at the cross, decimated by the resurrection, and is doomed to the lake of fire by God's judgment.

He is not God's equal, meaning his opposing counterpart. God has no equal. There is no battle between God (the forces of good) and Satan (the forces of evil). That is dualism, the belief that there are two opposite and equal forces struggling for an ultimate outcome still in question. On the devil's best day, he can't even register a tremor on God's power scale. One single word from God and he would cease to exist. A creature in rebellion has no response to omnipotence, much less omniscience and omnipresence.

Yet Satan has convinced many Christians that we are less than who and what God says we are, and thus we feel inferior to other believers. With Christ's sword still sticking in his black heart, Satan has lied to us, telling us we cannot defeat him. He has convinced many that we are victims rather than victors.

You may be thinking, "I don't believe that! I believe Jesus defeated the devil and we can live the victorious life through Christ (or at least that's what I've heard)." That's a great belief, but unless you are living it out as a daily reality, it's not a personal belief—it's only a mental hypothesis you learned in Sunday school. A hypothesis is an untested theory that may or may not be true. What we truly believe, we live. What we think, in effect, is who we are. Just because we say something does not mean we actually believe it. Talk is cheap. Actions speak far louder than words.

The truth is, regardless of what the devil says, as a son or daughter of God, born from above by the power of the Holy Spirit through the grace of Jesus's sacrifice for our sin, we are victors—not victims. We have been placed in Christ. That is our position as a believer, meaning we are already seated with Jesus Christ on the winning side. Due to the enemy's defeat, we fight our daily battles *from* the position of victory rather than *for* victory. In other words, each day we have the privilege of enforcing the victory of the cross in every situation and circumstance we face.

If this is not what you are presently experiencing, God is offering you an opportunity to reclaim all of your inheritance and identity in Christ. You are a victor, not a victim. The time has come to recoup your losses and access the riches of Christ's blessing. God is unfolding his Plan A, and you are an integral component in it.

The Victim Mindset

Far too many Christians live defeated lives, harassed by the devil but self-induced by our own amnesia of who or whose we are. It starts with our thought processes—our thinking. This is the battlefield on which our wounded nemesis is so agile and experienced. Here he does his most effective and fouling work.

In Chapter 4, I referred to this mindset as a slave mentality. This stinking thinking pollutes our ability to reason biblically and cripples our desire to experience God on a personal basis. It fills us with shame and unworthiness, telling us we are not good enough, humble enough, or holy enough. The false guilt it creates causes us to abandon that prized position of being seated with Christ in the heavenlies and drives us down once again deep into those same dense bushes that Adam struggled to hide in. Here in this seemingly hopeless place the devil helps us craft a new mindset that enables us to get by—to slide through life—to survive. This mindset renders us ineffective on the battlefield and for all practical purposes incarcerates us in our very own self-imposed prison cell of persistent fear and perpetual failure. I call it a victim mentality.

This victim mentality is a mindset forged in survival, not dominion. God's plan is that we thrive, not simply survive. He gave us dominion, which is rulership as his stewards over this planet. Adam fumbled it, the devil stole it, but Jesus restored it—and we must reclaim it.

Most Christians feel powerless and, due to this, are unable or unwilling to take appropriate action to resolve situations that affect their well-being. In other words, they refuse to take a stand against evil, resist the devil, or even live out what they claim they believe. They assume the position of a victim rather than a victor. They are experiencing domination rather than exercising dominion. They live defeated lives because they harbor defeated thoughts and attitudes. It is a learned helplessness; it has no biblical basis.

It is also a chronic choice of self-condemnation. Please allow me to explain with a simple illustration. The enemy condemns all of us, every day. He is our slanderous adversary continually accusing us before God. His plan is to beat us with the stick of condemnation long enough that we will eventually believe the lies. At the moment we began to believe his lie, he hands off his rod of condemnation, takes a seat, and watches us flagellate ourselves senseless and without mercy. In a real sense, we beat ourselves to death. This is the sad picture of a Christian with a victim mindset.

This learned helplessness blames others rather than accepting responsibility. They have convinced themselves this is just the way it is, that they are not "good" Christians. Therefore, they don't deserve any better. When push comes to shove, they can argue fairly convincingly as to how they ended up in this situation and why there is no help for them. They may listen to someone show them the fallacy of what they believe, but they consistently reject biblical solutions and constructive criticism. In their mind, they are the *one* person God is unable to help. They are the perennial hearers of the Word but refuse to be doers.

Their number is legion and their solution is to hunker down in a foxhole on the battlefield and pray—pray—pray that Jesus will return soon and rescue them. They would rather give up than get up. They would rather roll over than stand firm. They would rather surrender than resist. And the sad thing is this is the fastest growing brand of Christianity on the market today.

This victim mindset permeates the Church. We sing songs, preach sermons, and teach lessons about hanging on till Christ returns and rescues us. Christ rescued us the first time he came and left us in charge of the mop-up operation with the responsibility of destroying the works of the devil until he returns again. We were supposed to kick down the gates of hell and set the captives free, rather than trembling in fear and shame caused by accusations of condemnation from a dying, defeated enemy.

This victim mentality is saturated with excuses as to why these things are not happening. "I can't...." Surely God does not expect me to do something I am not able to do. "I must...." I really didn't have a choice; therefore God will certainly excuse my inability. "I don't know...." I don't know the how; therefore it's not my fault. This mindset is not inherent, it is learned. Thus we must trade the cowering cringe of a victim for the swagger of a victor. We need a change of attitude if we ever expect to exceed our current altitude.

A New Attitude

God has gifted each of us with the ability to choose, to use the gift of the will he gave us. Our decisions ultimately determine whether we experience all that God has for us. He has set the banquet table, placed all the delicacies of citizenship and blessing before us, positioned us in a prominent seat, and filled our plate with lavish grace. But we must pick up the fork and put it in our mouth. His Plan A is, after all, a partnership of commitment and trust. Thus we need a new attitude.

To enjoy the fullness of Christ's victory, we must understand his demand and obey his command. Remember we fight from a position of victory, not for victory. But we still must fight. Warfare is nothing more than resistance. If we go along to get along, we are not resisting, and thus we are not engaged in warfare. We have an enemy who must be resisted.

The disciples who followed Jesus understood this. They lived a militant spirituality on a daily basis. Listen to their instructions to other believers. Peter, the acknowledged leader of the early church, said, "Be of sober spirit, be on the alert. Your adversary, the devil, prowls about like a roaring lion, seeking someone to devour. But resist him" (1 Peter 5:8-9).

James, the half brother of Jesus, wrote, "Submit therefore to God. Resist the devil and he will flee from you" (James 4:7).

Ultimately the apostle Paul, who wrote much of the New Testament, exclaimed:

> *Finally, be strong in the Lord, and the power of His might. Put on the full armor of God that you may be able to stand firm against the schemes of the devil. For our struggle is not against flesh and blood, but against rulers, against powers, against the world forces of this darkness, against the spiritual forces of wickedness in the heavenly places. Therefore, take up the full armor of God that you may be able to resist in the evil day, and have done everything to stand firm* (Ephesians 6:10-13).

The tactic all three of these seasoned warriors agree on is that for us to be victorious we must have an attitude of resistance. That is, we must stand firm on the ground Christ has given us and hold it.

"Stand firm" is the last command a Roman centurion would give his squad of soldiers before they went into battle. These warriors were expected to hold the ground they stood upon—the space between their feet. They were to plant their feet firmly and withstand—that is, resist the enemy's best shot. No matter what transpired during the battle, they were not to retreat or allow the enemy to overwhelm them. They were to hold their position at all costs. They were to stand firm!

As each centurion gave this command, he also told them it would be better for them to die in honor on the battlefield than to break ranks and run in fear. Roman soldiers who did this were stoned to death at the hands of their own squad whom they had abandoned in the heat of battle.

The main difference between a victor and a victim is the simple choice to resist or stand firm. That means when we are confronted by the devil and his schemes, we don't blink or back up. We don't panic, break ranks, or run. We stare him down and stand firm, dressed in Christ, which is part of our unique position of inheritance.

Sadly, the enemy has convinced many of us that he is far more powerful than he really is. We have come to believe his lie that he can do anything anytime he wants. We act as though everything that goes wrong in our life is an attack by the devil. In believing these lies we have actually attributed far more power to him than he actually has. He is impotent in your life—powerless, unless you choose to partner with him. He can do nothing without God's permission and your partnership. He is limited—by God and by you!

Instead of resisting in faith, we cower in fear, unwilling to stand up and push back. We allow the devil to bully us, and we accept the way things are and remain prisoners (you and I make this decision) in a cage that we (not he) have constructed. We believe the lie that we are powerless, that God's Word works for others but not us, that what Jesus did is not enough for whatever we've done, that our past is too much, that our sin is too black, or that our situation is too far gone.

When we believe any of these lies, we transform ourselves into victims rather than victors who are confident of their position in Christ. It is our choice, not the enemy's power or God's will. It is all about our attitude.

Eagles are majestic birds that were made to soar and ride the upper currents of the wind high above the earth. They were not created to live in cages. Just imagine that an eagle landed in unfamiliar terrain, was captured, and imprisoned in a small, cramped cage for a long period of time. In this constricted prison, the eagle is unable to fly or even unfurl his great wings. He is restrained by the bars of the cage and restricted from doing what comes naturally to every eagle. One day the unlatched door swings open and the sky beckons the great bird to freedom. Instead of flying, the eagle steps out of the cage and screams, "I wish I could fly, but I can't," and steps back into the tiny cage. That helplessness has been learned. That is the same victim mindset that infects much of the body of Christ.

Eagles were not created to live in cages, and neither were the sons and daughters of God. We were created to soar on the wings of the Spirit, to ride the currents of grace. Jesus opened the door on our cage and he is inviting us to soar with him once again. This is our heritage. This is our identity in Christ. But—this must become our attitude if we hope to change our current altitude.

Fresh Ammunition

Most of us need some fresh ammunition. The old stuff we have been firing at the devil is obviously not having the desired effect. It has become wet and worthless. Perhaps we have believed some lies rather than the truth. Perhaps if we knew the truth, the truth really would set us free. What would happen if we really started to believe we are who God says we are instead of who the devil says we are? What we believe is who we become.

Are you a victim or a victor? The only thing that will defeat the power of the lies we have believed is truth. And God wants to equip us with truth, with fresh ammunition.

The apostle John wrote these parting words in a letter to a group of believers just like us: "We know that no one who is born of God sins; but He who was born of God keeps him and the evil one does not touch him. We know that we are of God, and the whole world lies in the power of the evil one. And we know that the Son of God has come, and has given us understanding in order than we might know Him who is true, and we are in Him who is true, in His Son Jesus Christ. This is the true God and eternal life. Little children, guard yourselves from idols" (1 John 5:18-21).

This is a powerful passage of Scripture, and if we understand it, believe it, and apply it, it will set us free to be victors rather than victims. These are bullets that we can use no matter the battle we face.

A genuine believer does not live a life marked by continuous sin. That is what John means when he says, "We know that no one who is born of God sins." This verse does not teach sinless perfection, meaning once we come to Christ we no longer sin. We all sin. Yet, as Christians, we are not sinners saved by grace (we discussed this at length in Chapter 9), but rather through God's grace we are now saints who sin occasionally. A lifestyle dominated by sin is not the mark of one who has been born of God, but rather of one who still lives in darkness. The issue is lifestyle. Our lifestyle dictates whether we really know Christ. Lifestyles don't lie.

When we are born again, Jesus takes responsibility for our eternal security and our day-to-day protection. The Holy Spirit places each of us in Christ. We are in Christ and Christ is in us. The devil does not have carte blanche access to our lives. If he did, he would most certainly kill all of us immediately. He only has one purpose, and his calling card reads "to kill, steal, and destroy" (John 10:10).

We are not at the enemy's mercy. Instead, we are protected by God. Jesus put it this way: "My sheep hear my voice, and I know them, and they follow Me; and I give eternal life to them, and they shall never perish; and no one shall snatch them out of My hand. My Father who has given them to Me, is greater than all; and no one is able to snatch them out of the Father's hand. I and the Father are one" (John 10:27-30). This promise should cause our spiritual backbone to straighten, stiffen up, and cause us to stand a little taller. It should put a little swagger in the way we walk. It should cause us to lift up our head, throw out our chest, and plant our feet a little firmer on the battlefield.

Why? Because our position in Christ (our identity and our eternal destiny) cannot change. The devil cannot alter this truth, so he feeds us a lie in hopes we will believe him rather than God. Victims believe lies, but victors stand firm in the truth.

If this were not enough, John tells us in 1 John 5:18 that "the evil one does not touch [the word is *seize*] him." Because we are protected by God, covered with the blood of Jesus, and sealed by the Holy Spirit, the enemy cannot grasp us, seize us, or hold us with his fist for the purpose of inflicting eternal harm on us. He cannot destroy us. We are not powerless before him and vulnerable to his every desire. He wants us to believe this, but God will not allow it because we belong to God.

There are many reasons we undergo trials, testing, and temptations. The devil would like us to believe he is responsible for all of it because it makes him seem more powerful, but he's not. Some of what we want to call the attack of the enemy is really the result of our own stupid decisions and sin. Some are the result of someone else's wrong choices. There is a spiritual law of reciprocity at work in creation. Whatever a person sows they will eventually reap. Our ability to choose has responsibility, therefore we must choose prayerfully and carefully.

Some of what he might like us to think are his attacks are nothing more than the results of living in a sin-cursed world. Some, though they might seem like an attack, are really God systematically exterminating our old sinful behavior, thought patterns, and desires—what the Bible calls our flesh. And some really are the attacks of the devil and his demons. It is very important in every situation to discern the ultimate source of the trial, testing, or temptation.

Dealing with Dangerous Idols

It is rather interesting that John, as he writes to this group of believers, closes out this passage in chapter 5 with these words, "Little children, guard yourselves from idols" (1 John 5:21). Why would he bring up idols? Idols are false gods, aren't they?

Yes they are, but they can also be unsurrendered places in our life. An idol is anything that we give preeminence to other than God. It can be a hobby, a relationship, or job. It can be a vain attempt to worship God in the way "we want to." It can be a wound or hurt that we refuse to let go of because we have allowed it to define us and give our life its meaning. It can be a fear or failure that keeps us from stepping out in faith. It can be a pet sin we keep hidden and bring out from time to time to caress and nurture. It can even be the solace we receive by telling everyone how tough things are and the relentless attack we live under from the enemy. It can be playing the victim.

The greatest threat of idolatry we face is our own selfishness of wanting what we want when we want it. And let's be transparent and honest here—we all want what we want, when we want it, the way we want it, because we are all selfish.

This is not the life of a victor, but rather the secret dream of a victim. This is not the life God presently promises us or the environment in which we live. This is idolatry.

And the devil loves to brush against us and find those dark little compartments of idolatry. When (not if) he does, he will manipulate, orchestrate, and devastate if he finds you or me to be a willing partner by our choice to harbor idols. And when he finds a partner, he will wreak havoc in every area of that person's life.

Far more mayhem is caused by our selfish idolatry than is caused by the devil. If he finds nothing in us, he cannot touch us. If he can make no connection, those superficial probes become nothing more than brushing up against or bumping into someone in a crowded room. There is no harm and certainly no foul.

Jesus put it this way: "I will not speak much more with you, for the ruler of the world is coming, and he has nothing in Me" (John 14:30). Literally, the Greek text reads, "And in Me—no—he has nothing." Satan could not touch Jesus. He had no idol with which to work. There was no issue he could forge into a partnership. Jesus was a victor, not a victim.

Satan did not kill Jesus. He did not take Christ's life. He is not that powerful. Jesus died at the hands of God, who sacrificed his Son so that we might have the kind of life that allows us to soar with the eagles, not haplessly flap our wings against a victim's cage of our own construction. Jesus gave up his life willingly.

If we are in Christ, the enemy must have a legitimate claim to gain anything in us. We must let the idols go. Perhaps you are flapping your wings in a cage, beating yourself to death over a past decision. Let it go! Perhaps you are calling your idol God, but the god you are worshipping is really yourself. Cast it down! Perhaps you have made the things of God such as worship, church, or teaching your god. Pull those idols down! Perhaps you find great pleasure in being pitiful, helpless, and defeated because it gives you the attention you hunger for, and you would rather be a victim than deal with the real idol you stare at every morning in the mirror. Repent and ask God to forgive you! You must deal with your idols if you really want to walk as a victor.

Enforcing Victory

We are soldiers on a mission with a specific purpose. We are to enforce the victory Jesus Christ won at the cross. To enforce something, one must have authority and power. A policeman carries a gun. That gives him power. But the badge he wears that bears the name of the city, county, or state gives him the authority to use that power. God has given us both and the mandate to replicate the works he did. "The Son of God appeared for this purpose that He might destroy the works of the devil" (1 John 3:8).

As enforcers of Christ's victory we must imitate Christ. Jesus proclaimed the gospel of the kingdom, and he demonstrated it. God's Word was presented in both word and deed, and power and authority were present with both the declaration and the demonstration. First Corinthians 4:20 describes it this way: "For the kingdom of God is not just a lot of talk; it is living by God's power" (NLT).

We live in a church culture where there is lots of talk with little walk. Plenty of Christian words but little or no demonstration of Christ's power. We have been taught a gospel of declaration without ever learning how to demonstrate it; and many are entering the battlefield woefully underprepared. They don't have the foggiest idea how they are to enforce Christ's victory. A punch here, a sword slash there, a few enemy arrows stuck in their chest, and most fall prey to the victim's mindset without any idea of what they should do next. They surrender, throw up their hands, and hope Jesus will return soon and rescue them from the devil's gilded cage they call the normal Christian life.

Our problem is that we attended the initial class and heard the lecture but missed the lab. Jesus taught his disciples—his storm troopers and siege warriors—to declare the truth, demonstrate the truth, and demolish the gates of hell. He exercised his authority and his power in the power of the Holy Spirit, and the works of the devil were consistently destroyed.

Paul exemplified that when he went to Corinth. "And when I came to you, brethren, I did not come with superiority of speech or wisdom, proclaiming to you the testimony of God. For I determined to know nothing among you except Jesus Christ, and Him crucified. And I was with you in weakness and in fear and in much trembling. And my message and my preaching were not in persuasive words of wisdom, but in the demonstration of the Spirit and of power, that your faith should not rest on the wisdom of men, but on the power of God" (1 Corinthians 2:1-5).

God's plan was that we exercise dominion on this planet. Therefore to enforce Christ's victory is to exercise Christ's dominion. Jesus taught those first disciples how to do this as they walked with him each day. They learned through demonstration, explanation, and then application. They watched him do it. He would often explain it and then allow them to try it. When they made a mistake or failed, he corrected them and encouraged them. Very soon, they were doing the exact things he did. That's why his message turned the world upside down in less than three hundred years. With every proclamation of Christ's truth, there is to be a demonstration of Christ's power. This is the evidence that the kingdom of God is at hand.

Perhaps an example from the life and ministry of Jesus will clarify this point. After his baptism in the Jordan River, Jesus marched straight from the wilderness of temptation to the northern end of the Sea of Galilee, to a city called Capernaum. Here in this little town much of his ministry would take place. He planted the flag of the kingdom smack-dab in the city center at the Jewish synagogue. Here was Jesus the Victor at work.

> *And they [Jesus, Peter, Andrew, James, and John] went into Capernaum; and immediately on the Sabbath He entered the synagogue and began to teach. And they were amazed at His teaching; for He was teaching them as one having authority, and not as the scribes. And just then there was in their synagogue a man with an unclean spirit; and he cried out, saying, "What do we have to do with You, Jesus of Nazareth? Have You come to destroy us? I know who You are—the Holy One of God!" And Jesus rebuked him, saying, "Be quiet, and come out of him!" And throwing him into convulsions, the unclean spirit cried out with a loud voice, and came out of him. And they were all amazed, so that they debated among themselves saying, "What is this? A new teaching with authority! He commands even the unclean spirits, and they obey Him." And immediately the news about Him went out everywhere into all the surrounding district of Galilee* (Mark 1:21-28).

I'll bet the news of this service spread like wildfire. If it had happened in one of our churches today, someone would have posted it on YouTube and it would have gone viral. Proclamation and demonstration like this capture people's undivided attention.

Jesus exercised his authority and his power, the very same ones he has given each of us. He was not preaching dos and don'ts—rules and regulations. He was giving them a banquet plate filled with life from God's Word. They were astonished—that is, fear, wonder, and even joy overwhelmed them as they listened to his teaching. The difference between this sermon and most of the ones we preach or hear was not his command of the nuances of the language, or how many verses he could quote from memory, or three alliterated points, a poem, and a prayer, but rather it was authority of his message. Jesus had kingdom authority.

Authority is the power or right to act in a specified way, having been delegated to do so by another. In this case, Jesus was using kingdom authority, which is the power or right to act for God. He was acting without fear or hesitation. He was proclaiming God's good news to those who were in bondage. His message—freedom, deliverance, salvation is here!

God has given each of us the very same authority. It's part of the package and an intricate part of Plan A. We have kingdom authority as citizens of his kingdom. Are we utilizing what he has given us?

We have the right and the power to speak the Word of God into every situation and life we make contact with. We bring the kingdom of God close every time we encounter another person. The kingdom of God resides within us. God dwells in us. We are the King's domain. And wherever we go we take the kingdom of God with us. Are we using it? God has given us the victor's weapons to enforce the victory of the kingdom. It has the capacity to decimate and destroy the kingdom of darkness all around us, but we must draw our weapon and pull the trigger.

The victim's excuse of "I don't know how" or "I don't know what to do" is not a viable excuse. It is an admission of defeat and a testimony of unbelief. The body of Christ, of which you and I are a part, has been given the authority and the power to drive out the demons that are destroying our churches, our government, our society, our families, friends, and neighbors. But we are sitting idly by, praying and begging God to do something he has already given us the power and authority to do. It is called enforcing the victory of Calvary. God will never do for us what he has given us permission, authority, and power to do for ourselves. That's a fact!

Let's go back to the synagogue for a moment. The devil had to do something. His nice comfortable Sabbath service filled with all the wrappings of powerless religion was unraveling. The praise and worship service was threatening to go ballistic in the Holy Spirit. The preaching was getting too close for comfort and was beginning to step on toes. So he sent an emissary, one of his demons, to shift the focus of the service off who God is and onto a person, even if that person happened to be Jesus. At this point, no one knew who Jesus really was—at least not yet! The people in that service had not repented and returned to God, how could they embrace Jesus as the Messiah? This spirit hoped it could create a little chaos, and thus with this interruption create a little disruption.

But Jesus acted immediately. That's what victors do when they enforce the victory. He had already proclaimed the Word of God, now he demonstrated it by acting with the very same power and authority. He used command authority to remove anything that was an enemy of the kingdom or a stumbling block to his mission. He confronted the spirit head-on rather than crumpling up in the corner in a fetal position and crying out to God, "I told you they wouldn't listen."

Jesus planted his feet and stood firm. He did not even blink. He spoke—with authority, two simple words in the original Greek. I'll paraphrase. "Shut up! Get out!" Jesus did not ask. He made no request. He commanded the demonic spirit to be muzzled and cast out. He did not mess around. It was command authority, the same authority we have been given in Christ.

Perhaps you are struggling a bit with believing we have this same authority and power. Listen to the instructions Jesus gave and the words he used: "And He [Jesus] called the twelve together, and gave them power and authority over all the demons, and to heal diseases. And He sent them out to proclaim the kingdom of God, and to perform healing" (Luke 9:1-2). Perhaps you're thinking, "I'm not an apostle."

"Now after this the Lord appointed seventy others, and sent them out two by two ahead of him to every city and place where He Himself was going to come.... And he said to them, 'I was watching Satan fall from heaven like lightning. Behold, I have given you authority to tread on serpents and scorpions, and over all the power of the enemy, and nothing shall injure you'" (Luke 10:1; 18-19). Perhaps you are still thinking, "I wasn't there. I'm not one of the seventy!"

This next passage contains some of the last words Jesus spoke to all of his followers before he ascended into heaven and sat down at the Father's right hand. We call them the Great Commission, but sadly we have made them the Great Omission because we have not obeyed them fully: "All authority has been given to Me in heaven and earth. Go therefore and make disciples of all nations, baptizing them in the name of the Father and the Son and the Holy Spirit, teaching them to observe [to guard and do] all that I commanded you" (Matthew 28:18-20).

This verse is for all of us, and everything Jesus did and taught he expected his disciples, his followers, to do. We have the authority and power of Jesus so we can enforce the victory of Jesus. We are victors, not victims.

The devil will always challenge our proclamation if we are not prepared to follow with a demonstration of the Spirit's power. God has given us the authority and the ability, but we must exercise it.

Back at the Bird Cage Door

Remember the cage with the eagle that refused to fly, a victim of its own chosen circumstances? The cage door is still open. It can't be shut for you ever again. Jesus Christ knocked it off its hinges. No believer has to live in a state of *less than*. You can fly. You can soar.

Perhaps you have played the victim card and gotten a lot of sympathy and attention with it, but all of a sudden you realize you are still in a cage. Perhaps things are not going well for you. Your life's a mess. Or your marriage is a mess. Or your kids are a mess. Or your finances are a mess. Perhaps the mess extends as far as you can see.

Then stand up! Straighten up! And clear your throat! Decide right now, right here that you will no longer be a victim, but rather you will be the victor Christ says you are. Open your mouth and with authority and power tell the enemy to shut up and get out in Jesus's name. Don't argue with him. Don't listen to his worn-out lies. Use the command authority Jesus has given you, the kingdom authority that comes with your citizenship and your calling to enforce the victory Christ has already won. The gun is loaded with devil-killing bullets. For heaven's sake, pull the trigger!

Once you've done this, shake those eagle feathers back into place and walk over to the door of the cage. Take a deep breath and stop listening to the voice of the enemy and the voice of your own selfish soul and step out and flap your wings. You will not fall and go splat on the concrete. It cannot happen. Instead, you will catch a little current of the Spirit's breath and you will begin to rise upward. Open your eyes and look at the world around you from this vantage point. It looks far different up here than it did down there.

Stop flapping, relax, rest on the wind, and soar steadily upward, upward until you reach that place where you are once again seated with Christ as a victor in the heavenlies!

> *Abba Father, I confess I have listened to the lies of the enemy and believed them for far too long. I repent and make the choice to believe the truth of your word. I cast down the lies that have imprisoned me for so long in this cage. I declare in Jesus's name that I am a victor and not a victim. I receive and believe you have given me both your authority and power so that I might proclaim and demonstrate the victorious message of Jesus Christ. I reclaim the promise that you give strength to the weary and increase the power of him who lacks might. Though youths grow weary and tired, and rigorous young men stumble badly, yet those who wait for the Lord will gain new strength; I will mount up with wings like eagles. I will run, and not get tired, I will walk and not grow weary. With your help and through your grace from this day forward, I will fight not for victory, but from my position of victory in Christ. In Jesus's name, amen.*

Chapter 13
Total Access with Full Confidence

> Few delights can equal the presence
> of one whom we trust utterly.
> ~ George MacDonald

There are moments in the life of every family when a vacation is not just desirable, it is necessary. For Thomas and Mary that moment had finally arrived. Their business was booming and their company was growing, but they needed a break, so they planned a family vacation to a secluded cabin on a hidden lake. No hustle, no bustle, just some quiet, quality time to spend with one another and the kids.

The three-hour trip seemed much shorter, and they soon arrived at their dream destination. Over the next few days, the constant stress of months spent dealing with emergencies and deadlines began to melt away as they relaxed and reconnected with one another. Early mornings were spent sipping coffee and watching the fog slowly rise from the glimmering surface of the lake as the kids slept in. Their days were filled with hiking back country trails, fishing, and swimming in the cool water of the lake. It seemed like paradise.

Their three children, Mollie, age twelve, Mark, seven, and little Mikee, four, settled quickly into the lazy cycle of life on the lake. Though busy entrepreneurs, Thomas and Mary had poured themselves and their values into their kids, and their investment was paying off as they watched their children play and care for one another.

Upon arriving at the lake, Thomas had given the children two rules that were non-negotiable. The first was no one goes near the lake or pier without an adult. The second, you must wear a life-jacket while playing in the water or on the pier. As the week unfolded, Mollie and Mark took more and more responsibility for little Mikee, allowing Mom and Dad some much needed time alone.

On Thursday afternoon after a lunch of peanut butter and grape jelly sandwiches washed down with cold glasses of milk, Thomas sat back in the faded blue Adirondack chair on the deck, propped his feet up, and closed his eyes. *It doesn't get any better than this*, he thought. His three beautiful children were playing hide-and-go-seek as his eyes slowly shut and visions of catching that elusive ten-pound largemouth bass danced through his mind and soon overwhelmed him.

Just as he was about the land the lunker of his dreams in his dream, a blood-curdling scream shook Thomas wide awake from his nap. Mollie and Mark were yelling, crying, and pointing toward the little pier that jutted out into the lake. It seemed little Mikee had slipped away to hide on the dock and had fallen into the lake. His precious little boy could not swim, and his life jacket was still hanging on the handrail, drying in the sun.

Thomas raced down the hill and onto the pier, desperately looking for any sign of his son in the spot where Mollie and Mark were pointing. He dove into the lake and went all the way to the bottom, frantically feeling around in the opaque green water for his little boy. Finally, he ran out of air, pushed back up to the surface, sucked in another huge gulp of air, and anxiously went down again hunting for Mikee.

On his way down the third time, Thomas felt his little boy's hip brush against his own back. He turned and found his four-year-old with his arms and legs wrapped tightly around one of the pier pilings, about three feet below the surface of the water. Quickly, Thomas pried Mikee loose, lifted him out of the water, and carried him onto the lawn, where the whole family collapsed in a heap of tears, hugs, kisses, and long deep breaths.

Thirty or so minutes later, as the family regained their composure and calmness returned, Thomas took Mikee up in his arms and asked him this question: "Son, what were you doing down there, hanging on to that piling?"

Without any hesitation, Mikee looked up with his big blue eyes and replied, "I was waiting on you! I knew you would come and get me!"

This story captures my attention. I love the confidence of this little boy's reply. He had a full assurance that his dad would come for him. He knew this because over the last four years of his short life his dad had always been there for him. When Mikee entered his father's presence, whether working in the office or relaxing in the La-Z-Boy, his dad had immediately stopped what he was doing, put down the paper, or told the person on the other end of the phone to wait, or turned off his laptop, or hit mute on the television, and had given his full and undivided attention to his son. This little boy had grown up with full access to his father.

So when Mikee stumbled and fell off the boat dock and into the water, it wasn't a hope so, but rather it was "I know so! Dad is coming for me. I can count on my dad!"

Mikee's faith in the present was founded on facts proven by countless encounters over the past four years with his dad. This little boy had a confident expectation and hope anchored in the proof of personal experience.

Wouldn't it be awesome if each of us had this same kind of confidence in our heavenly Father? Take a moment and think about your own personal relationship with God. What is it really like? If you found yourself in a situation similar to Mikee's, how would you sum up your expectation? *I hope so!* or *I know so!*

The Issue

Most Christians are extremely passive in their faith relationship with God. For many, the image of a man or woman aggressively pursuing an intimate relationship—a deep, abiding, and loving connection with God—seems out of place, as well as out of reach. Salvation certainly keeps us out of hell but provides far more than that. One of its greatest benefits is that it gives us total access to God, the same God who spoke and the stars assembled themselves in galaxies and constellations. "The eyes of the Lord are upon the righteous, and His ears attend to their prayer" (1 Peter 3:12). God is never too busy!

One of the most glorious aspects of God's Plan A is that God created human beings to experience an intimate heart and spirit bonding with him. That relationship is to be experiential, that is, our connection with God provides us with a real capacity to know him in every aspect of our spirit, soul, and body.

It is also a mutual relationship. God desires to know us even as we come to know him. God is omniscient—he knows everything. There is nothing he does not already know about us. But the desire of God's heart is for us to open ourselves up willingly and be transparent. Not because we have to, but simply because we want him to have access to all of us.

True friendship, true intimacy, allows each participant to look fully into the heart of the other. Nothing is held back. All is exposed. I know I am treading in an area that seems unachievable because we are talking about God who is infinite, and we are not.

Perhaps it's the mystic in me, but my heart longs to know God at a deeper level. Psalm 42:1-2 expresses this yearning in words I wish I had written: "As the deer pants for the water brooks, so my soul pants for You, O God. My soul thirsts for God, for the living God: when shall I come and appear [literally 'see the face of God'] before God?" Each time I get a glimpse of him, I see something totally new. I cannot get enough. This thirst should drive each of us into his presence, but this is not always the case.

Fear and shame brought on by feelings of inadequacy or failure often send us running in search of a hiding place rather than into God's presence where we can bare our failures and find love, support, and healing. The false sense that we are unworthy or the lie that God is somehow too busy to be concerned with our petty needs in comparison to the needs of refugees fleeing civil war in Syria or the persecution of Christians in the Sudan leaves us filled with guilt. Together, this fear, shame, and guilt rob us of our confidence.

This lack of confidence causes us to avoid things. We get quiet. We stop stepping out in faith. We start to hide who we truly are and what we really believe. We begin to fret and worry. And if this were not enough, we reach down and pick up the devil's stick once again and beat ourselves up because we know deep in our heart we should be bolder and more confident.

Confidence comes from experience and faith. Experience comes from observing, encountering, or undergoing something. We gain experience through repeated experimentation. We try things, and the things that work become a part of our life and the things that don't—don't. It is that simple.

Faith, on the other hand, is a gift from God that grows as we gain experience. Faith, according to Scripture, "comes from listening to this message of good news—the Good News about Christ" (Romans 10:17, NLT). As we listen to the good news Jesus came to declare, faith begins to germinate and grow, ultimately producing fruit. The *Good News* of this verse is *all* that Jesus did, *all* that Jesus taught, and *all* that Jesus gained through his obedience in life and death.

We express little faith because we have little experience. And nowhere is this more obvious than in our understanding of our personal access to God. The issue is we have no confidence because we have little relationship. As our relationship expands, our faith will deepen. The depth of our faith will then determine the capacity of our experience, which is the fertile soil of confidence.

Gaining Confidence

Confidence is "knowing" that we know something. It is "know so," not "hope so." It is a sense of absolute certainty. We have talked about God's choosing us, labeling us as a saint, providing full salvation for us, saturating us with the Holy Spirit, and making sure we are a victor, not a victim. Understanding these facts should give us a certain amount of confidence, and perhaps a bit more holy boldness if we really believe these things in our heart (faith in Christ and what he has done) and not just in our head.

This confidence I'm talking about is not a confidence in ourselves, although there is absolutely nothing wrong with self-confidence as long as it is does not translate itself into arrogance and cockiness. I'm talking about becoming confident of who we are in Christ. If we understand who we are and what that means, we will live it out, and one of the byproducts will be that our self-confidence will soar and boldness will replace timidity and hesitation.

It is time to get rid of the milk-toast brand of Christianity that the twenty-first century church has settled for. This powerless expression would have us keep our faith a secret and stay out of sight. It is the same mentality that says, "Dig your foxhole a little deeper and hold on. Jesus is coming soon, and one of these days he will save us from all this." We have forgotten that as the Church we are not a pathetic, ill-equipped group of soldiers under siege. We are the victorious invading army of the Lord Jesus Christ, standing at the gates of hell, lacing up our butt-kicking boots to knock the gates off their hinges! Or—at least that's who we are supposed to be according to Matthew 16:18: "Upon this rock I will build My church; and the gates of Hell shall not overpower it." This kind of confidence only comes when you know that you know that you have full and total access to God twenty-four hours a day, seven days a week, fifty-two weeks a year.

Perhaps you are shocked by the brand of boots I am advocating. Perhaps you find this hard to swallow because your confidence level is on empty. Perhaps you have tried and it didn't work out. Real relationship is, after all, hard work.

Perhaps you have done like many others and accepted the next best thing—religion. The only problem with this is Jesus did not start a religion, he reinstated relationship. If you are willing to settle for less, the devil will serve up all you want every day. Today is about stepping into more and laying your hands and your heart on the best and refusing to take less than what God is offering all of us in Christ.

We must reclaim our confidence in Christ. To do that we must fully understand what total access to God means and experience what full confidence in God looks like.

Restricted

God is love. That is, the essence of God is love. Everything he does, he does out of love to demonstrate his love, because that is his nature.

Nothing can separate you from God's love. In Romans 8:29-30, the apostle Paul makes a statement with profound meaning: "For God knew his people in advance, and he chose them to become like his Son, so that his Son would be the firstborn, with many brothers and sisters. And having chosen them, he called them to come to him. And he gave them the right standing with himself, and he promised them his glory" (NLT). Other translations would use terms such as *predestine, called, justified,* and *glorified*. His point is that God has opened the door for us to come into his presence. God enables it and God empowers it, and he does all of this through his great love.

He is the parent willing to lay aside anything to take us up in his arms and hold us close to his heart. He is the lover who tenaciously pursues the object of his love. He is the shepherd willing to leave the ninety-nine to find that single lamb wandering lost in the desert. God loves us.

As Paul finishes what may be the grandest, most encouraging chapter of the entire Bible, he asks a simple, yet profound question: "Who shall separate us from the love of Christ?" (Romans 8:35). And then he displays the kind of confidence God wants all of us to possess with this answer: "For I am convinced that neither death, nor life, nor angels, nor principalities, nor things to come, nor powers, nor height, nor depth, nor any other created thing, shall be able to separate us from the love of God, which is Christ Jesus our Lord" (Romans 8:38-39).

To separate is to split, divorce, disconnect, undo, divide, or shut out. In other words, Paul is declaring that nothing can block us or stop us from entering into the presence of God. He used Jesus as the key and opened the door. "Therefore having been justified by faith, we have peace with God through our Lord Jesus Christ, through who also we have obtained our introduction [our access] by faith into this grace in which we stand; and we exult in hope of the glory of God" (Romans 5:1-2).

Perhaps you are a parent. If so, this illustration will clarify what I'm trying to say. Do you remember the moment when the doctor finally handed you that little bundle of joy—that baby boy or girl—you had waited on for nine long months? What did the doctor say? "Here is your new son. Here is your new daughter." That is exactly what the preceding verse means. Through natural birth, babies gain full access to their parents, and through the second birth believers gain full access to the presence and grace of their heavenly Father.

Jesus, who is the embodiment of God's love, made the introduction (opened the door) through his sacrificial death. "For through Him [Jesus Christ] we both [Jews and Gentiles] have our access in one Spirit to the Father. So then you are no longer strangers and aliens, but you are fellow citizens with the saints and are of God's household" (Ephesians 2:18-19). You have a permanent passport to access God rather than a temporary visa just to visit.

What does access really mean? It is the unhindered approach to God's presence. It is a freedom or right to enter at any time without invitation.

We have been given an introduction by Jesus so that we might be received by God rather than rejected and tossed out. An introduction was needed in the ancient world if you wanted to see the king. The king or emperor sat on a throne, and opportunity to gain an audience with the king came by invitation only. If you were not granted an audience, you did not get in.

It was your responsibility to travel to wherever the king was. You had to enter his castle or palace through a gate guarded by soldiers who were armed to the teeth and ordered to kill any unauthorized person who approached. You were then escorted by these soldiers through a maze of hallways that were guarded by more soldiers. You were stopped at the door to the throne room, searched, and made to wait. You were allowed in only if the king at that moment invited you in, and then you were only allowed to get within a certain distance of the king. To gain an audience with the king was almost impossible for the common person.

Do you remember the Old Testament story of Esther? Even though she was the queen of Persia and the wife of King Ahasuerus, according to law she could not barge into the presence of the king. This is why Esther was afraid to go and plead against Haman's plan to exterminate the Jewish people—her people. To enter the king's presence without him first extending his scepter was against the law and subject to immediate execution. Esther paused at the curtains that separated her from the king's presence and waited patiently. Ahasuerus saw her and extended his scepter of invitation. She had her introduction.

Let me paint another picture that begins in the early pages of the Old Testament and reaches to the last pages of the Gospels in the New. When God's presence rested over the Mercy Seat of the Ark of the Covenant in the Tabernacle, and later in the Temple, man's entrance into the Holy of Holies was highly restricted. Only the high priest could enter that place and he could only do it once a year on the Day of Atonement. Sin separated man from God, and this separation was symbolized in the way the Tabernacle/Temple was set up and where you went in those places.

If you were lame, cripple, or diseased, you could never enter or even get close—ever. If you were non-Jewish, a Gentile, you were stopped in an area known as the Court of the Gentiles on the outer limits of the property and forbidden on penalty of death to proceed any closer. If you were a Jewish woman, you could go a few feet closer into the Court of the Women, but no farther. If you were a Jewish man, you could enter the Tabernacle/Temple area proper where the altar was located, but you could go no closer. If you were a priest, you could enter the Holy Place only when you were chosen to serve there for a specific period of time. And if you were a member of the priestly family of Aaron—a direct descendant—and the High Priest (who was chosen for life), you could enter the Holy of Holies, where the presence of God dwelled, once a year to offer sacrifice on the Day of Atonement.

Do you grasp how restricted access was to God's literal presence? Sin had separated all humanity from God. It began with Adam, yet we are all born separated by sin from God. We could not find God; therefore, he came looking for us.

God sent his Son to open that doorway and blaze a new pathway back to the presence of God, a pathway every human being has the potential of traveling.

When Christ died on the cross, the great veil that separated man from God was torn, even as his own body was torn and his blood spilled in payment for our sins. Matthew 27:51 records the literal ripping of this temple veil with these words: "And behold [stop, look, and pay attention to this], the veil of the temple was torn in two from top to bottom."

Early Jewish tradition claims that this curtain was as thick as a man's hand, likely about four inches. It was sixty feet high and thirty feet wide. It was claimed that horses tied to either side could not have ripped this massive veil apart. Yet it is a historical fact that this curtain was ripped in half—and not from the floor up, but rather from the top down to the bottom.

God's scepter (Jesus Christ) was extended to his children (those who would be born from above—born again), and now we have total access to the personal presence of God the Father at any time and for any need. As a child of God, we have complete and total access to God just like Adam and Eve enjoyed before the Fall. A vital piece of God's Plan A is now restored and available.

Relationship Brings Access

The only reason any of us can enter the presence of God is due to our position in Christ. Location is everything. We don't enter due to our accomplishments, position, or prominence. Money cannot unlock the door, and hard work won't budge it either. Only our relationship with God through Christ brings us access. We are the King's kids, and the door to his offices has been blown off its hinges.

Are you starting to grasp the meaning of this? God, who is Creator and Sustainer of the universe, who is now our Father, has given you and me complete, unrestricted access to his presence at all times. We don't have to go through anyone—not a priest, a preacher, or a pastor. We all enter on equal footing; there is no clergy or laity distinction here, only sons and daughters.

And here's the key: Do you want to? It is all about desire. Do you desire to have a passionate, intimate relationship with God? One where you become more than a servant or a slave, but rather a child, friend, and yes—his bride! That scares most people to death. Yet deep within all of us is a hunger that longs for this kind of relationship.

The first step is to use the access you have been given. Take a step out of your religious comfort zone, open your heart and your mouth, and talk with God. Have a conversation with your heavenly Father. I'm not talking about you sharing your wish or grocery list, but admit your fears and your failures, while sharing your deepest dreams and desires. I am purposely not using the word *pray* here. Prayer makes religious people do stupid things. Talk with God like you would talk with someone you love.

Quiet yourself and listen for his reply. Yes, God still speaks, especially when we seek him with all our heart and listen closely. You may hear his voice within you in the theater of your spirit. You may hear him speak out of the pages of Scripture. His voice may come to you in the words of a song or poem. God even speaks from car tags and billboards. God is not limited in how he speaks or what he says. The only limit that exists is whether or not we are listening.

You may fear this kind of intimacy because your father figure was not a good example. God is not like that person, so don't compare them. He is not out to get something. He is there to give something.

Perhaps you have endured some tough times or experienced a traumatic event and blamed God. God does not cause everything. Perhaps the hesitation comes because God is not a person with skin you can see face-to-face, and yet you still have an unsatisfied yearning within you. That something is the unconditional love your heart aches so desperately to embrace. Push past the fear with which the devil has infected that emotional wounding you carry and step into the unrestricted access you have. Ask God to touch that wound and heal it. Pour out your pain in his presence. Whisper your failures and shortcomings in his ear.

God has made himself available to you in Jesus Christ. You have his undivided attention for as long as you want it.

Nothing irritates me more than to be talking with someone, and their cell phone rings and they answer it. Or they receive a text, read it, and then reply—right in the middle of our conversation. That sends a clear message to me that our conversation or relationship is not as important as the person who interrupted us. I clam up, and the meeting is essentially over. God will never do that. He will not put you on hold or ignore you.

You have access, and that access is not based on anything you've done, so you cannot lose it by anything you might do in the future. It is guaranteed by the payment of Christ. You can't lose it, misplace it, or forfeit its benefits.

Go ahead and step into his presence. Better yet, press in and get as close as your passionate pursuit can handle. How far you go and how long you stay is up to you. God is eternal. He has no appointment to keep or schedule that would force him to leave you waiting with a receptionist. Look deep into his heart and experience the peace and fulfillment only he can give. You have his undivided attention—if you want it!

Access Breeds Confidence

Confidence is a natural resource that thrives in an environment of faith. As we press into God's presence in faith, the peace that Christ has purchased for us is uncovered and experienced. Shame and fear melt away. Doubt and unbelief flee. Every time we step into his presence,

God sees his beloved Son Jesus as he looks at us. Jesus is always with us (we are in Christ); therefore the access is always open.

That should cause confidence to soar. This kind of confidence is holy boldness, a willingness to push further and rise higher than our present location. It is not impudence or presumption—far from it. It is a holy hunger that consumes someone who has been in the presence of God and has tasted his goodness.

Moses was not satisfied with just hearing God's voice on Mount Sinai or seeing God's power displayed in Egypt and the wilderness. He wanted more! And in a moment of holy boldness Moses cried out, "Please let me see your glorious presence" (Exodus 33:18 NLT). God responded by allowing Moses to visibly see his glorious presence as his goodness passed by. Moses's request was not presumptuous or impudent, or God would not have honored it. Its source was faith, a confident expectation in Moses that God was who he said he was and that he would do what he had promised. And without faith it is impossible to please God according to Hebrews 11:6. The level of God's response indicated the level of his pleasure in this audacious request.

The Holy Spirit invites us to come with boldness. "Let us therefore draw near with confidence to the throne of grace, that we may receive mercy and may find grace to help in time of need" (Hebrews 4:16). He tells us to draw near or press in with confident expectation.

This kind of confidence is the freedom to speak without holding anything back. It is openness to say what's in our heart without any fear. It is total freedom, a divine endowment of free speech. We don't have to choose our words. This is no place for memorized or ritualistic prayers. This is not the place where we get someone else to pray for us. This is where we are free to say those things hidden deep within the caverns of our soul.

In this place we have an audience with the King. We have his undivided attention, and we don't speak as condemned prisoners headed for execution. We speak as his beloved sons and daughters. We speak confidently because we are family who share his riches and inheritance, not beggars crying for a scrap of food to get by.

Here in this place, miracles happen. So stop praying, "God, *if* this is your will!" That is not a prayer of faith, although it sounds rather righteous. *If* is a word indicating doubt and uncertainty, and the presence of God is no place for either.

Begin to cry out, "God, show me your will! Speak to me! Show me how to pray! Teach me to ask for what you want to give me! Show me what you are doing in this situation or circumstance!" Now is the time for faith to arise.

A child who spends enough time with his father knows the heart of his father and what his father wants. That child does not wonder; he knows what pleases his father. Intimacy reveals the heart of the Father. The reason we don't know the will of our heavenly Father is that we have not spent enough time with Him. We don't know his heart. When we find the heart of God in any situation, we will find his will.

When we spend enough time with God we will become very bold—not arrogant, boastful, or cocky. We will find out what God wants and learn how to accomplish things his way. This kind of confidence will set us apart from the teeming crowd that calls themselves Christians.

Unfortunately, most of God's kids are insecure, fearful, painfully silent, and religious. That is, until they catch a glimpse of one who has spent time in the Father's presence. The glow of God's glory, the residue of accessing and spending intimate time with the Father, usually causes them to react in a negative way. Don't be surprised if they talk about you, call you names, or lump you in the fanatic file. Be encouraged—religion opposed Jesus as well, and eventually it stood and shouted, "Crucify him! Crucify him!" Hopefully, that will not be the case for you, but this kind of intimacy with God brings out the jealousy, envy, and persecution of those who are unwilling to access the same joy and grace.

Listen to the warning the writer of Hebrews issued to those who were going through conflict and suffering due to the boldness produced by a confident faith built through a constant access into God's presence: "Therefore, do not throw away your confidence, which has great reward. For you have need of endurance, so that when you have done the will of God, you may receive what was promised. For yet in a very little while, He who is coming will come, and will not delay. But My righteous one shall live by faith; and if he shrinks back, My soul has no pleasure in him. But we are not of those who shrink back to destruction, but of those who have faith to the persevering of the soul" (Hebrews 10:35-39).

The writer of this epistle tells us that relationship brings access and access produces confidence. Faith is nothing more than the visible demonstration of confidence in what we have accessed while spending time in God's presence. Confidence increases as we exercise our faith and carry out God's will.

Confidence Inspires Action

Hudson Taylor spent fifty-one years as a missionary to China. He founded the China Inland Mission, now known as OMF International. He was a man of great faith that revealed itself in supreme confidence in God, no matter what situation he faced. It was said of Taylor by historian Ruth Tucker in her book *From Jerusalem to Irian Jaya: A Biographical History of Christian Missions* (Zondervan, 1983), that no other missionary in the nineteen centuries since the apostle Paul has had a wider vision and has carried out a more systematized plan of evangelizing a broad geographical area than Hudson Taylor.

When he initially went to China in 1853, he made the voyage aboard a sailing vessel. As the ship neared the channel between the southern Malay Peninsula and the island of Sumatra, the young missionary heard an urgent pounding on his stateroom door. He opened it, and there stood the captain of the ship.

"Mr. Taylor," he said, "we have no wind. We are drifting toward an island where the people are pagan, and I fear they are cannibals."

"What can I do?" Taylor asked.

"I understand that you believe in God. I want you to pray for wind."

"All right, Captain, I will, but you must set the sail."

"Why, that's ridiculous! There's not even the slightest breeze. Besides, my sailors will think I'm crazy."

But finally, because of Taylor's insistence, the captain agreed. Forty-five minutes later he returned and found the missionary still on his knees. "You can stop praying now," the captain said. "We've got more wind than we know what to do with!"

Confidence in God inspires action. Confidence lays hold of the promises of God and brings them into our possession. Confidence is faith in action. Hudson Taylor understood God's promises, and he had spent time in God's presence. He used the access he knew he had, acted in faith, and God answered.

God loves audacious prayers, the ones that are so big that only he can answer them. If you or I can somehow answer our own prayers, they are far too small. Yet most of us are afraid to pray those kinds of prayers because our confidence in God has not yet grown to arouse this level of action. This changes when we use the access we have been given and really get to know God through intimate relationship.

Do you remember Mikee, the little boy with his arms wrapped around the pier piling, three feet below the surface of the lake? He had no doubt in the relationship he had with his father. His unrestricted access to his father had built confidence within him that caused him to act in faith. He wrapped his little arms around that piling and held on with all his might, although he could not breathe under water. He held on because he knew his father was sufficient for his every need.

What about you? Do you really believe God is sufficient and that you have instant and unlimited access to him at all times? Have you accessed this remarkable relationship that is available to you? Are you enjoying intimacy with God that births supernatural confidence?

The time has come to reclaim a faith that inspires actions that only God can empower. That has always been the desire of God's heart and a part of his plan for all of his children. He longs to empower his people to accomplish extraordinary feats of faith. These exploits bring God glory and capture the attention of those who have not yet received a proper introduction to his love and grace. These deeds of faith demonstrate in a visible way the proclamation of the gospel. These acts become living illustrations of God's love, and they have their genesis in those quiet moments when we go confidently into his presence and spend time in his heart.

The book of Acts illustrates what can happen when God's children access his presence. Holy boldness (confidence gained through relationship with God) spurs incredible action. In Acts 4:13, the Sanhedrin, the Jewish counsel that had condemned Jesus to death, saw and heard the holy boldness of Peter and John. These scholars and lawyers knew the disciples were not educated or trained in the Scriptures, yet this council marveled at their preaching and teaching. They recognized clearly that they had spent time in the presence of Jesus.

Later God poured out his power on his kids because they entered his presence and accessed his mercy and grace which had been made available to them in their time of need. "And when they had prayed, the place where they had gathered together was shaken, and they were all filled with the Holy Spirit, and began to speak the word of God with boldness" (Acts 4:31). These disciples refused to cave in to the threats. Instead, their confidence responded with action and their preaching became even bolder.

Throughout Acts, bold actions empowered by the Holy Spirit characterized the followers of Jesus. Ultimately Acts 28:31 ends with Paul in Rome "preaching the kingdom of God, and teaching concerning the Lord Jesus Christ with all openness, unhindered." But the book of Acts is yet being lived out by the followers of Jesus and will continue until he returns. We live in what many have called the Acts 29 era, the continuation of the bold actions of believers filled with the Spirit, redeemed by the Son, while enjoying an intimate relationship with the Father.

This openness that Paul experienced was boldness or confidence. Why? Because he, like every other believer who has spent time in the Father's presence, soon realized he was a son of the King, and that access made him bold. These believers are the ones who turned the world upside down, toppled kingdoms without ever firing a shot, and transformed their culture from the inside out. They knew who they were in Christ and walked out this identity with full confidence. They reclaimed the access Christ had recovered, the same one God offers to each of us.

God is still seeking men and women who will walk with him in the cool of the day in the garden. He is seeking you.

What will you do? No one can push or force you into the throne room of God. You must step into his presence of your own volition. There are no doors to push open or guards to deal with. The access is open.

Will you be that bold?

> *Abba Father, thank you for removing the veil of sin that has separated me from you through Jesus Christ. I confess I have allowed fear and ignorance of what*

you have done to keep me from accessing all that you desire to share with me. I confess I have depended on my own goodness rather than Christ's righteousness. I confess I have often entered your presence to get things I thought I needed, rather than to simply spend time with you, O Lover of my soul. Please forgive me for wasting those opportunities. Father, in the name of Jesus, I reclaim what Adam forfeited, Satan seized, but Jesus Christ recovered! Precious Father, my spirit, soul, and body hunger for more of you. Satisfy that hunger, O God, and may greater confidence arise. May holy boldness seize me in such a way that, inspired by your love, I will be willing to obey you immediately and absolutely—no matter what I may face. Thank you for the revelation of who you are and all I can be in Christ. In Jesus's name, amen.

Chapter 14
Fearless

> A Christian is fearless.
> ~ Tertullian

Fearless is a word I like. Fear-less! It reminds me of famous figures from history I have studied or scenes in movies I have seen. I love the way the word sounds and the images and emotions it conjures up within me. It is a powerful word that few can suitably wear.

When I dream of what this word means, I can see William Wallace of *Braveheart* fame, standing motionless with his Claymore held high on the battlefield of Sterling Bridge as the superior English cavalry charge toward his ill-equipped Scottish brothers. The ground is shaking as these horsemen bear down on these seemingly vulnerable foot soldiers. And then at the precise moment his great sword drops—and with one word, "Now!"—the Scottish lances come up. In a blink of the eye that mighty cavalry is decimated, and the king's undefeatable army is routed and driven from the field. One word, for me, describes the stand made by the seemingly hopeless army of Scotland—fearless!

Perhaps you remember that memorable scene in *Gladiator* where Maximus and his successful squad of gladiators are marched out into the coliseum, thinking they will face another group of similarly armed warriors to fight for the pleasure of the Emperor. Once on the stadium floor they face a terrifying attack by a far superior enemy of charioteers. Undaunted, Maximus takes command and orders his hapless band to come into a formation where they lock their shields in what a legionnaire would call the *testudo* or tortoise. From that position, they wait for their moment. The chariots sweep in again and again, looking for an opportunity to break their ranks by picking the gladiators off one by one. But the *testudo* holds until Maximus gives the command—"Now!" And in a few moments, the scattered charioteers lay dead in the dirt of the coliseum floor. In that "now" moment they spring to victory because they have remained fearless.

In my office hangs a picture painted by Jean-Léon Gérôme called the *Martyr's Last Prayer*. It is a haunting scene from the floor of the Roman Coliseum during the terrible persecutions carried out against Christians by Emperor Diocletian.

There are twenty or so believers, ranging in age from a very young girl, who is perhaps six years old, up to an old bearded man who is standing in their huddled midst, leading them in prayer. The day is ending and darkness is falling, and their plight is illuminated by other Christians who have been dipped in pitch, crucified, and are now being set ablaze.

The stadium is filled to capacity with the crowd screaming for the release of the great cats that will execute this little group by ripping them limb from limb. To me this frozen moment portrays a scene of abject horror and yet a sense of absolute serenity at the same time. The terror is evident based on the fate that awaits them. But the serenity comes from the peace this group of believers is presently experiencing in a "now" moment. This peace makes them fearless. It grips me and speaks to a place deep within me.

In my dreams this is how I want to face every situation, circumstance, or enemy I come in contact with. I want to be fearless, and so should you.

Those "now" moments come into my life on a fairly consistent basis. It's not a question of "if" but "when."

What about in your life?

How do you respond? Do you have peace that prevents you from panicking? Are you so confident in your Leader that you will stand unblinking and stare down an enemy that is terrifying? Are you confident enough in who God says you are to stand firm in who you are and the training you've received through the life lessons you've encountered up to this moment?

Are you fearless or fear-filled?

Taught to Fear

I love to watch little kids. They are fearless. My granddaughter

Audrey just celebrated her sixth birthday with a party at a gymnastics school. During the party, the kids could jump off the balance beam, vault, or tower and into a pit filled with large pieces of foam. There was one little boy named Brandon who climbed to the highest point at every station and jumped—over and over. He charged up every piece of equipment without hesitating. Nothing seemed to bother him or shake his confidence. He was in his own little world, and he was the courageous king conquering every obstacle that appeared in his path. He was fearless!

Children believe they are untouchable. Confidence builds as they grow. At an early age, most of them will try anything. They want to explore, to climb higher, to swing farther, or to go faster. They are on an intrepid quest to find out the answers to the *why* and *how* questions their inquisitive minds uncover as they begin life's journey. Over time, they pick up the fears of their parents and others they are around, and those fears become their fears. By the time most children become adults, they will no longer push the existing boundaries or try new things because self-preservation has become their number one pursuit.

Each generation passes their fears to the next. I can remember the atomic bomb drills we did in elementary school in the sixties. Each child crawled up under their desk and promptly tucked their head in between their knees, following the teacher's instruction when the bell sounded. Honestly, what kind of protection is that against a nuclear attack? All that position ensured was that when our bodies were discovered (that is, if we were not instantly incinerated), our remains would only take up half the space. This training offered no real protection at all against the explosion of an atomic bomb. We were doing drills because the generation before us was terrified that a nuclear attack was imminent and we had to do something, even if it was a waste of time. They taught us their fears, and we passed them on to the next generation, and so it goes.

Eventually, we all grow older and lose that childhood sense of fearlessness. Most of us stop taking chances, acting on dares, or stepping out into the unknown to see what's there. Instead, we become fearful. In other words, fear fills us rather than the curiosity, wonder, amazement, and awe that filled us as kids. And those "now" moments seem to come and go on a regular basis without us ever doing anything with them.

That fearless spirit we once had as children dries out from lack of use and shrivels into complacency, hesitancy, and timidity. Life's voyage of discovery turns quickly into a shipwreck on the shores of survival. The questions of *how* and *why* soon become *what if* rather than *what is*.

Civil War

Fear was never a part of God's plan because there was nothing to be anxious or apprehensive about. The garden was a paradise, not a threatening jungle. There was no reason to worry. Everything the first man and woman needed, God had provided. They fumbled this with disobedience, but Jesus re-instated it through his complete obedience, which resulted in his sacrificial death as the full payment for the sin of disobedience.

When we were born again, we were given a fearless spirit, not a fear-filled spirit. It is a spirit that is unafraid of any created thing, a spirit that knows who he or she is and who their heavenly Father is. Somewhere deep within every believer that spirit resides, but like little kids in the natural, we quickly pick up all kinds of garbage. Or worse, we are taught all kinds of garbage, and over time this misinformation or lack of information spiritually imprisons our fearless spirit. Instead of being spiritually fearless, we become fear-filled, anxious, and so cautious that it smothers out our deepest desire to discover more of God. We become afraid and hesitant in those *now* moments God sends us on a consistent basis, and thus we miss our opportunity to unearth, encounter, and experience that deeper relationship he has in mind.

We claim to be faithful, which means *filled with faith*. We allege that we are Spirit-filled, which means *full of the Holy Spirit*. How is it, then, that there is any room in us to be fearful, which means *filled with fear*? How can we be fearful over everything—our past, our present, our future, the economy, our children, our marriage, our health? You name it and it creates fear. We cannot be full of faith and full of the Holy Spirit and still be filled with fear all at the same time. It is not possible. We are full of something all right, but it's not faith or the Holy Spirit!

As sons and daughters of God, he has given us his Spirit, who then gives our spirit the ability to be fearless. This should be the one word that describes every believer. It should be our name, but it's not. A question then arises: If not, then why not?

The answer is that most believers are unbelievers when it comes to the reality of God's unconditional love for us. We really don't believe God loves us, and thus we find it hard (almost impossible) to trust him explicitly. Trust means to put our confidence in someone and rely on them—biblically speaking—to exhibit faith. Fear is the absence of faith.

If we visited a hundred churches and asked the crowds gathered there on Sunday morning whether they believe God loves them, most would give a rousing yes. We would hear cheers and hearty, "Amens!" Heads would nod up and down in the affirmative, and some would even clap or lift their hands. Sadly, many would confess this, but most have never possessed it. They have read it in the Bible and heard their pastors preach and teach it, but they have never really embraced it or experienced it. It is a concept in their head—the Bible says so, therefore it must be so. But it is not a reality in their heart. It is hope so—not know so (an experience of faith)! The uncertainty is the breeding ground of fear.

This unbelief has created a spirit of fear. According to 2 Timothy 1:7, this spirit of fear or timidity, which is a spirit of cowardice, does not come from God. It was not part of God's original intent. Biblical fear in relation to God means *a reverent awe*, not a terrified, timid heart afraid to approach. Awe and terror are opposite extremes. Both take your breath away, but awe compels you to pursue, while timidity freezes you in your steps.

Since God has not given us a spirit of fear, it must have another source. I believe it is a demonic infection that we allow to take hold. It is a foothold, a small advantage the enemy takes in our life when there's tragedy, emotional wounding, an out-of-control situation (and most are), a catastrophic event, disappointment, failure, sin, or moments when God doesn't seem to come through as we thought he would or should.

This infection can also be caught from our parents. Our spiritual insecurities are often the result of what we have seen modeled before us. Our relational experiences with our parents are often the initial basis for our relationship with God. This can be good or bad. It has the capability of enhancing or crippling this bond. Fear is taught more often than it is caught.

In those moments of distress, uncertainty, fear, or disappointment, the devil digs a little foxhole in our soul and settles in, awaiting the next *now* moment God sends our way. When that moment comes and we are faced with a decision or an action that must be taken, an argument erupts within us. A war breaks out, not between us and the devil, but rather between us (our soul) and us (our spirit). Our spirit—which is fearless and guided by the Holy Spirit—says one thing, and our soul—guided by our mind, will, emotions, and the reservoir of our personal experiences—says something totally different. Our spirit seeks to embrace God in a deeper experience, while our soul hesitates at the uncertainty of the unknown and frantically seeks the security of certainty or retreats into the safety of past experiences.

A civil war ensues. We start fighting ourselves rather than our enemy, and guess who wins *all* the time—our enemy. Jesus said, "A kingdom at war with itself will collapse. A home divided against itself is doomed" (Mark 3:24-25 NLT). The enemy ducks back down in the foxhole to watch us destroy ourselves.

God ordains our decisions, actions, and attitudes to follow the guidance of our spirit, not our soul. Our spirit is the dwelling place of the Holy Spirit. Our spirit has the capacity to clearly hear God's voice and then translate it into a language the soul can understand. Apart from the leadership of our spirit, our soul will only listen to the voice of itself, which is often locked in survivor mode.

Most believers live with this reality because their fearless spirit is neither large nor in charge. It is weak and weary because we don't nurture or exercise it. Thus we have a fearless spirit imprisoned by a fear-filled soul that hobbles through this life in a fear-riddled body. In other words, we cannot experience a *now* moment with God, because we have never embraced an intimate relationship with God. Fear, not faith, drives us; and without faith it is impossible to please God.

The Contrast

God's answer for our dilemma is his unconditional love. God is love in both essence and character. Most theologians, teachers, and preachers would call this kind of love *agape* love. Most of us have heard a sermon on *agape* love. We have all heard it defined as God's kind of love. That's a great phrase, veiled in a syrupy heavenly mystique. It sounds really spiritual, but to the average believer it means absolutely nothing. If it has no comprehensible meaning to someone in their head, how can that person ever hope to experience it in their heart? You know the answer. Most won't and don't.

Therefore, we need a good definition for unconditional love—one that describes what it is. Thankfully, we don't have to search far to find the one authored by God and, true to his nature, a definition he wants us to fully experience rather than rationally squeeze into systematic expression. As you read this definition, allow your spirit to drink from its cool depths and feed on the significance of its meaning.

"Love is patient and kind. Love is not jealous or boastful or proud or rude. Love does not demand its own way. Love is not irritable, and it keeps no record of when it has been wronged. It is never glad about injustice but rejoices whenever the truth wins out. Love never gives up, never loses faith, is always hopeful, and endures through every circumstance. Love will last forever" (1 Corinthians 13:4-8 NLT). This is unconditional love—God's kind of love.

A fearless spirit is energized and empowered by this kind of love. A fearful soul is paralyzed by it and refuses to believe it. The fact remains, God's love is unconditional, no matter what you or I think.

Fear screams, "Don't believe that! If you mess up—and you will— God will get you. He will punish you. There's no way a holy God will accept you. Anything less than perfect won't cut it. And you know the best you can hope for is not good enough. This is a trap!"

And fear always invites other members of its family to move in when he takes charge of our life. Suspicion and dread unpack their bags as well. A fear-filled life leads to a life of suspicion about God's promises (they may be for everyone else, but they're not for me) and a dread of God's presence (due to a feeling of condemnation and false belief that I am worthy of nothing but God's punishment). Listen to me! Fear is a liar! It was spawned by the prince of liars, and as long as you believe this lie you will never be fearless.

John was known as the apostle of love. Of the disciples, he seems to have enjoyed the most intimate relationship with Jesus. John refers to himself as the *disciple whom Jesus loved* (John 13:23; 19:26). John writes a great deal about *agape* love. He categorically states "there is no fear in love; but perfect love casts out fear, because fear involves punishment, and the one who fears is not perfected [has no maturity] in love" (1 John 4:18).

Fear and unconditional love cannot co-exist in the same place. One casts the other out. The one you default to—or give first place to—matures, and then it casts out the other one. If fear wins, you get suspicion, dread, anxiety, worry, depression, discouragement, and hopelessness as the fruit. If God's love matures, fear is cast out. It is driven out of your soul, and that fearless spirit given to you at the moment of your second birth is set free to embrace God and experience all that he has for you. No person can serve two masters—not even a believer.

The Solution

As you read the new few paragraphs, listen intently to the voice of the Holy Spirit and tell every other voice to shut up, even if that other voice is the arguments of your rational mind, the cries of your wounded, broken soul, or the distracting voice of the enemy. God wants to speak to your spirit, but you must pay careful attention if you hope to fully reclaim all your inheritance and step completely into your identity.

Jesus said, "If you abide [pitch your tent and put down your roots] in My word, then you are truly disciples of Mine; and you shall know [experience with your spirit, soul, and body] the truth, and the truth shall make you free" (John 8:31-32).

Freedom is a prerequisite of being fearless. If you are truly free, you will be fearless. But you can only be free if you put down deep spiritual roots in the promises of God's Word. God does not lie! He cannot lie!

We were inwardly fashioned for faith, not fear. Adam knew no fear before the Fall. He lived by faith because he had no other experience to draw from except freedom. Jesus knew no fear although he knew what he must freely experience. His impending death on a Roman cross could not stop him. Nor could the knowledge deter him that he would not only pay for our sin but would become our sin. He acted in faith, and it freed him to accomplish all that God had planned in eternity past.

Faith is the currency of heaven, and our bank account has been stuffed full of faith by Jesus. In fact, all we could ever need is already on deposit and available for withdrawal when needed. It requires us to take up the pen of freedom and write the check and present it to be cashed.

Perhaps what you need is a deep breath of spiritual freedom to fill your spiritual lungs. If so, allow your spirit to grab hold of this promise from God. Breathe it in. "There is therefore now no condemnation for those who are in Christ Jesus. For the law of the Spirit of life in Christ Jesus has set you free from the law of sin and death" (Romans 8:1-2).

Paul's admonition declares that since we are believers, meaning we have been born from above, we are "in Christ." God has given each of us a new identity. Because of this new identity and position "in Christ," God no longer condemns us for our sin.

"Whoa! You don't know what I've done! You don't know the real me!"

You are correct, I don't. But God does, and he chose you, saved you, sanctified you, and glorified you (all in the past tense), and he says, "I don't condemn you!"

Condemnation is a legal term that dictates the appropriate sentence for a particular crime. It is the sentence of punishment one deserves for the crime that has been committed. The law demands a penalty of payment each time it is broken. All of us have broken God's law—right? Without Jesus we are all condemned. Our sins condemn us, and this condemnation cries for one penalty—"the soul that sins shall die" (Ezekiel 18:4).

But (I am so thankful for this little conjunction) Romans 8:1 says there is no longer any penalty for the sins we have committed or will commit. God blotted them out with the blood of Jesus. He erased them with the cross. Our sin no longer has a penalty because Jesus swallowed it up in his body.

Therefore, the fear of God punishing us for our sins is only the smoke and mirrors of the devil's lie. We no longer have to live in dread that we will get what we really deserve, think we deserve, or what the devil has been whispering we deserve. Bad things are not happening to you or your family because God is angry with you.

Bad things happen to all of us—no one is exempt. They occur because we live in a sin-cursed world and because we have a mortal enemy who is roaming to and fro, seeking someone he can devour. We experience bad things as the result of our wrong decisions and countless other wrong decisions made over the millennia since the original bad decision. Bad things happen because Satan is doing his best to thwart what God is doing in our life by destroying us along with everything that has meaning to us.

But here is the good news—God is no longer angry at us! Jesus embraced the wrath of God—the very same wrath that we deserved. Because of this, there is no longer a penalty (condemnation) for the sins of those who are "in Christ." That debt has been paid in full and applied to our account. The old bill of debt has been torn up and our receipt is Jesus Christ.

Therefore God is free to love us unconditionally. Yes, in spite of you and all those things you think should somehow diminish his love for you. That lie has struck fear in your heart for too long. The enemy has used it like a wet blanket to smother the fire of your fearless spirit and kept you chained with the shackles of fear. You are not the first to be snared in this trap. It is as old as humanity.

The question is, will you believe what God has declared—the plan he has revealed? If we don't believe, we will not experience it even if it's true. To experience it we must first hear it with our spirit and believe it. "So faith comes from hearing, and hearing by the word of Christ" (Romans 10:17). Faith displaces fear one word at a time.

God has declared his love for us over and over. Yet we often take his declarations and make this fodder for discussion and debate. We reason through them but never allow them to move from our head to our heart. Faith comes from hearing God's Word, and fearlessness is the result of faith. Perhaps the time has arrived for us to listen with our spirit, soul, and body to God's absolute word on the subject of his love for us.

"What then shall we say to these things? If God is for us, who is against us? He who did not spare His own Son, but delivered Him up for us all, how will He not also with Him freely give us all things? Who will bring a charge against God's elect? God is the one who justifies; who is the one who condemns? Christ Jesus is He who died, yes, rather who was raised, who is at the right hand of God, who also intercedes for us" (Romans 8:31-34).

Listen with your heart to the questions Paul is answering. He is responding to the accusations of the enemy. These are the same ones he places in our head—those thoughts of unworthiness, guilt, and shame.

But Paul is building an airtight case, and his questions are rhetorical. He doesn't expect any answer based on the facts and evidence he has presented. Who is against you? Who will bring a charge against you? Who will call for the debt to be paid again? Who condemns you? Who? Who? Who?

It is certainly not God! And if it's not God, why are you worried? Since God is the chief justice of the highest court of final appeal, then why are you fearful? Let faith arise! God has set you free. He has justified you. Jesus intercedes for you. He pleads your case and defends you. Take courage, he is undefeated. You can't lose!

Oh but there's so much more. Listen to the next sentence if you have any argument left. "Who shall separate us from the love of Christ? Shall tribulation, or distress, or persecution, or famine, or nakedness, or peril, or sword?" (Romans 8:35).

Let's break that down so it really soaks in:

"Who shall separate *[divide/tear apart]* us *[insert your name here]* from the love of Christ? Shall tribulation *[the world's pressure coupled with tough circumstances]*, or distress *[when difficulty forces you into a tight place with no apparent way out]*, or persecution *[torment and harassment]*, or famine *[hunger/starvation without a solution]*, or nakedness *[utter poverty]*, or peril *[dangerous situations that come out of nowhere]*, or sword *[war or violent death]*?"

Paul leaves nothing to argue. He covers the full span or extent of things that could possibly separate us from God. He names seven things. Seven is the number of God, the number of completion or perfection. It is a definitive way of proclaiming that this list covers anything and everything you can think, imagine, or argue.

In grand style Paul has nailed the coffin lid shut on fear and the lie that God's love does not apply to you. But he has one nail left, and it is a doozy. Listen carefully and allow even more faith to arise! "But in all these things we overwhelmingly conquer though Him [Christ] who loved us" (Romans 8:37).

How can any of these things separate us from the love of Christ? If their power has already been defeated by Jesus and we are in Jesus, how can they defeat us? How can they tear us away from his love? The answer—they can't, because we are super-victors (the meaning of *overwhelmingly conquer*). Let me put it in the literal context of its first-century usage. We have rubbed their noses in the dust and placed our feet on their necks as a symbol of victory. They are done. Stick a fork in them—utterly defeated!

How? Through the finished work of Christ accomplished completely as the ultimate expression of God's love. So you see, he really does love us.

A "Now" Moment

You are about to embrace a *now* moment. If you will force your spirit, soul, and body to drink deeply one final time. Faith will arise and fear must flee. Allow these words, the very Word of God spoken through the Holy Spirit, to gently speak to the deep places within you: "For I am convinced that neither death, nor life, nor angels, nor principalities, nor things present, nor things to come, nor height, nor depth, nor any other created thing, shall be able to separate us from the love of God, which is in Christ Jesus our Lord" (Romans 8:38-39).

Again, let's break this down for clarity:

"For I am convinced *[fixed without doubt like a secure anchor]* that neither death *[the cessation of life]*, nor life *[the fullness of living]*, nor angels *[the holy ones]*, nor principalities *[the unholy ones including Satan and his demons]*, nor things present, nor things to come *[this present age or the one to come]*, nor height, nor depth *[astrological terms—many believed that the stars had power/influence over their destiny]*, nor any other created thing *[no thing created—not you or even something that may appear from another world or spiritual realm]*, shall be able to separate us from the love of God, which is in Christ Jesus our Lord."

Nothing can separate you from the love of God. No thing created, and that's everything except the Triune Godhead of Father, Son, and Holy Spirit. And God has already declared his everlasting love for you through Jesus. Your supply of God's love is unlimited!

You can do nothing to make God love you less, nor can you do anything to make him love you more. He loves you. At this very moment all his love is available to you. It will be there despite what anyone has told you or what the enemy is screaming in your ears. God loves you whether you believe it or not. That simple fact is fixed for eternity. It cannot change.

Allow this to sink in. Read Romans 8:31-39 over and over again out loud. Let faith arise! Allow God's perfect love to cast out all the fear hidden within. Speak with command authority to your soul and tell that spirit of fear to leave. You belong to Jesus; it has no place in your life.

Relax and let the love of God flood your spirit, soul, and body. Fix your eyes on Jesus and allow his perfect love to embrace you, erase all doubt, and then eliminate all fear.

This is a *now* moment for you, so that you might reclaim all the elements of God's Plan A for you. He has no Plan B. At this very moment you may even hear the thunderous voice of God explode deep within you as he calls out, *"Now!"* Allow his Spirit to cleanse those wounded and fear-filled places. He will bring healing, but you must receive it now! Let God tear down the walls you've constructed to protect your wounded heart from being hurt again. Ask God to shatter them—now! Don't leave one stone of fear resting on another. Drive the enemy out of the stronghold of fear and reclaim the fearless mantle God gave you at the moment you were born again.

We must cry out to God and ask him to come in power and grace, with healing in his wings. "Arise O Lord, and let your enemies be scattered! Let them flee before you!" (Numbers 10:35 NLT).

A Fearless Postscript

As I began writing this chapter, I had an experience in the natural that I believe has a spiritual significance for me, and perhaps for you. Hopefully, it will illustrate the message of the chapter and this book.

It was late afternoon, and I had just finished mowing my yard. The sun had set, and the temperature was cooling a bit. I bounded up a step into my carport and crossed to the backdoor with two things on my mind: air conditioning and a cold Diet Mountain Dew. For no apparent reason, as I was about to go in the house I looked back from the direction I had just come. And at the top of that step on the other side of the carport (the exact pathway I had just taken) lay a snake approximately five feet in length.

I hate snakes—all snakes! To me, there is no such thing as a good snake and bad snake. In my opinion the only good snake is a dead snake with its head separated from its body. Did I mention I really, really hate snakes?

I fear snakes. They terrify me! I do not want to be around them. I have no desire to pick up or handle a serpent. A snake causes some kind of primordial fear to arise within me, and I typically scream like a baby when I initially see it. Then once I've regained my composure, I find a hoe or shovel and kill it.

This snake was between me and everything else. I had nothing to kill it with except a one-gallon aluminum water bucket, so I picked it up and did my best, but the snake would not cooperate. It wiggled, coiled, reversed direction, and headed at full crawl back where it had come from. In a second or two, if something radical did not occur, that snake would slip safely off my carport, through the lattice, and under my deck.

It was a *now* moment! Without a hoe or a stick, I knew I would not be able to stop Mr. No Neck from getting away and terrifying me again at another moment of its own choosing. All of a sudden anger rose up from deep within me. And strange boldness came over me. I grabbed that snake by the tail in my right hand, and with one motion like popping a bullwhip, I brought it over my head and smashed its head on the concrete floor. One swift action in the blink of an eye, and the snake was dead.

Fearless describes the rush of emotions that swept over me as I stood holding the tail of this ancient, now lifeless foe. I felt undefeatable—heroic! daring! intrepid! confident!—like I could take on anything and win. Fear no longer suffocated me with it constrictive coils. In that *now* moment I had overcome life-long fear by responding with action rather than being paralyzed in terror.

Spiritually speaking, God gave Adam a fearless spirit empowered by his unconditional love, so that when he faced an enemy he would respond in confidence because he knew he could not lose. Adam failed, and the serpent took his identity and his inheritance as the spoils of war. A fearless Jesus crushed the serpent's head and took back the inheritance and identity, bequeathing them once again to each of his followers as tokens of his unconditional love. We now stand secure in this love, ready to crush the head of the serpent every time he reappears.

I am often asked why God has allowed Satan to do the things he has done. Why didn't God just destroy him? It was God's eternal plan that Satan and his strategy be humbled, humiliated, and utterly defeated at the hands of those who walk out God's original plan in full obedience and total dependence on the Holy Spirit. That is God's Plan A—his only plan for you!

Therefore we must all rest in the assurance of God's unconditional love, reclaim our full inheritance, and re-assert our true identity. We must leave the bushes of fear and stand firm in who we are in Christ.

Fearless is our name!

> *Abba Father, your love is like no other. You have demonstrated it by giving your Son as the price of my redemption. I confess I have not understood the extent of your love or the depth of your desire for me. I have pulled back in fear from your touch, believing your promises were too good to be true. I confess I have believed the bitter lies of the serpent and not the sweet truths of the Savior. I have often desired your incredible blessings apart from an intimate relationship with you. I renounce all those lies, and because of your lovingkindness I rest in faith that I am loved by you with an everlasting love. Expose every vestige of fear that remains within me and release my fearless spirit once again. I reclaim my inheritance and my identity in Christ. Teach me to love you and others with the same fearless love with which you love me. In Jesus's name, amen.*

Chapter 15
A Final Word

> In literature and in life we ultimately
> pursue not conclusions but beginnings.
> ~ Sam Tanehaus

We have come to the end of this book, but this is certainly not the conclusion. It is only the beginning. Which plan are you pursuing? Plan A gives us a relationship with God, an identity from God, and a purpose in God. This is God's schematic masterpiece for the ages.

And Plan B? There is no Plan B!

Plan B is nothing more than a deceptive labyrinth of endless dead-ends filled with smoke and mirrors designed by Satan to keep us from embracing, exploring, and experiencing the relationship God has designed especially for us. Plan B does not exist for us—at least not in God's mind.

God's desire is that our knowledge of him be intimate, not informational, and through this passionate relationship discover our true identity in Christ—who God says we are. For too long the Church has taught and modeled a responsibility of impossibility built on serving, placating, and earning favor with an angry god rather than a relationship of intimacy with a loving God. God is not mad at us—he is not angry with you!

Jesus Christ is the last Adam. He is the fountainhead—the progenitor—of a new species of human beings. The old has passed away, behold all things have become new. As Christ-followers we are new creations—a part of this new species. The old us has passed away and with it should go all the vestiges of a mind cluttered with the dim diagrams, drawings, and directions from the devil's Plan B.

Jesus as the last Adam demonstrated how to effectively walk with God as a man filled with the presence and power of the Holy

Spirit. That perfectly executed plan was taken directly off the original blueprints of creation. Adam lost it, but everything Adam lost has been restored in Jesus Christ and given to us by virtue of our position in Christ. As a result, we have been given the authority and power to do all the things Jesus did and even greater ones. This position guarantees that we can live a victorious life and overcome through his power any enemy or opposition we may face. This position demonstrates our legitimacy as sons and daughters of God and validates his connection with us and our connection with him. It endorses our existence and solidifies our true identity.

Jesus has restored all of this to every believer, but as believers we must individually reclaim our identity in Christ and reach for the fullness of our inheritance from Christ. A true relationship with Jesus is marked by both a desire to give and receive. We are limited in our ability to give if we limit our willingness to receive. We must be willing to receive all that Christ has given us. This freedom to receive and thus reclaim will set our feet on the path of a new journey—a new beginning. The time has come to live out God's Plan A—to be doers of the Word not just hearers.

A journey always begins with the first step. Along the way we will encounter opposition, ridicule, and outright hostility. We will face those who are convinced there is a Plan B, or Plan C…or even a Plan X, Y, and Z. They will eagerly and vehemently argue with you that Plan A no longer exists—that it is impossible to live the kind of life we are pursuing.

When, not if, that happens remind yourself of these truths:

- God has chosen you. His choice is not based on your ability but rather on his unconditional love for you. He chose you for himself.

- God says you are a saint—a holy one—not a *sinner saved by grace*. It is God's declaration that you have been set apart by him, for him, and made holy in Christ.

- God says your salvation through Christ is complete. Forgiveness of sin, deliverance from torment, and healing of disease and sickness is a part of his gift to you. Access to all of it is yours through Jesus Christ. God has saved all of you; therefore use all of you to pursue him.

- God has given you the Holy Spirit. Through his indwelling, your authenticity in Christ is validated and sealed. Through the filling or baptism by Christ with/in/by the Holy Spirit, you have the capacity to demonstrate the power of Christ in every situation. A true intimate relationship with the Father is marked by a life saturated in the Holy Spirit.

- God says you are a victor. He has given you the authority to enforce the victory of the cross. Therefore he has enabled you to stand firm and resist whatever the enemy sends your way. You are an overcomer who is already victorious!

- God says you have full access to him. You may come at any time, with any need, and you will never need an invitation. Step in and experience his presence and your confidence and faith will grow.

- God says you are fearless. It is the name he has given you to bear. Fearlessness comes from knowing that you are loved unconditionally by God. The absence of fear produces fearless faith in Christ.

God's Plan A is spread before you. It holds the chart designed to guide the course of your destiny and the directions that will allow you to fulfill your purpose. It awaits you. This is not the conclusion but rather the beginning—so step into it!

Acknowledgments

My eternal gratitude goes first to the Lord Jesus Christ. Although I have tried frantically over the course of my life to walk out other plans, he graciously draws me back to his original plan for my life every time. I now see the futility of those and the simplicity of his alone.

To Cathy—thank you for being my partner in this journey through life. You insisted that I go to the river, get alone for a week, and do nothing but write. Your persistence jump-started this book and caused it to become a reality. There are no words to express my heart of love to you for being my wife, my friend, and my partner in discovering and walking out God's plan for us.

To Eagle's Wing Church—we are experiencing this plan day-by-day as we struggle to become a place of refuge, restoration, and relationship, where those who are hurting can be re-shaped by the loving hands of God and embrace a life-giving relationship with Jesus Christ through the power of the Holy Spirit.

To Dr. Frank Thielman, Beeson Divinity School—thank you for listening to me as I shared the ideas of this book with you and confirming that I was not a heretic. I will be forever in your debt for the things I learned as a student in your Greek Exegesis class.

To Sylvia Gunter—thank you for reading the original manuscript, correcting the grammatical issues, and suggesting options that would make the tough theological issues clearer and more succinct. You are a teacher, a mentor, and a true friend.

To the staff at WhiteFire Publishing—thank you Roseanna White for appreciating the potential of this message and allowing me the honor and privilege of being the first male writer to join the WhiteFire team. To Dina Sleiman—thank you for recognizing the potential of this message during a short but providential pitch and prayer at the Blue Ridge Mountains Writer's Conference. And to Wendy Chorot—thank you for your editing skills and suggestions that have transformed this message into a reality that now has the potential to revolutionize the lives of those who read it.

OTHER TITLES FROM WHITEFIRE PUBLISHING

Guard Your Heart:
Purity, Perseverance, His Presence, & the Power of Prayer
by Audrey Phillips Jose

Listening Prayer:
Learning to Hear the Shepherd's Voice
by Joanne Hillman

www.ingramcontent.com/pod-product-compliance
Lightning Source LLC
Chambersburg PA
CBHW011343090426
42743CB00019B/3425